TADG FARRINGTON

THE AVERAGE LIFE OF THE AVERAGE PERSON

HOW IT ALL ADDS UP

◼ SQUARE PEG

LONDON

Published by Square Peg
2 4 6 8 10 9 7 5 3 1

Copyright © Tadg Farrington 2009

Tadg Farrington has asserted his right under the Copyright, Designs
and Patents Act 1988 to be identified as the author of this work

This edition published in Great Britain in 2009 by
Square Peg
Random House, 20 Vauxhall Bridge Road,
London SW1V 2SA

www.rbooks.co.uk

Addresses for companies within The Random House Group Limited can be found at:
www.randomhouse.co.uk/offices.htm

The Random House Group Limited Reg. No. 954009

A CIP catalogue record for this book
is available from the British Library

ISBN 9780224086233

The Random House Group Limited makes every effort to ensure that the
papers used in its books are made from trees that have been legally sourced from
well-managed and credibly certified forests. Our paper procurement policy can be found at:
www.randomhouse.co.uk/paper.htm

Printed and bound in Italy by Graphicom, srl

This book is dedicated to Brian and Olivia Farrington.
Two of the wisest, most interesting and entertaining of all the
1,964 people I am ever likely to meet.

'In this work, when it shall be found that much is omitted, let it not be forgotten that much likewise is performed.'

DR SAMUEL JOHNSON,

from the Preface to *A Dictionary of the English Language* (1755)

CONTENTS

ACCIDENTS

Think of all the times in your life you might have died. Almost got run over, went too close to the edge, changed lanes without looking or changed a light bulb while standing in the bath … You've been dicing with death all your life and one day, your luck is going to run out.

Most accidents are not fatal. Taking an average amount of care, you can expect to visit hospital because of an accident every 22 years. That's between three and four times in your life.

There is a 61 per cent chance one of these visits will be the result of a fall. A 31 per cent chance you will have cut yourself and a 35 per cent chance you will have just stupidly walked into a wall or other immovable object.

These accidents will rarely be serious brushes with death. You are much more likely to die simply because your body lets you down, rather than because you peed on an electric fire while sleepwalking. But what if your body didn't let you down? You didn't get old and you didn't get sick? How long could you hope to dodge an accidental death?

The statistics for all forms of death are recorded using an internationally agreed system called the ICD-10 codes. There are 259 codes that relate to accidents, ranging from: V01 *Pedestrian injured in collision with pedal cycle* to X57 *Unspecified privation (including destitution)*. These would seem to cover every conceivable kind of misadventure, including: W58 *Bitten or struck by crocodile or alligator* and X52 *Prolonged stay in a weightless environment.* In spite of this, there is still a need for code X59 *Death by accidental exposure to unspecified factor.*

X59 contains all the accidents that don't fit in to any of the other 258 categories. Accidents that did not involve any type of land or water or airborne vehicle. The victims did not fall, trip or drown. They did not succumb to fire, smoke, poison or sharp or blunt instruments. They did not die as a result of a doctor's mistake, electricity, radiation, cave collapse or falling safes or pianos. In other words, category X59 contains the freak accidents. Bizarrely, around 3,500 people will die in freak accidents every year: the biggest cause of accidental death, higher than Falls (3,390), Transport (3,090), Poison (1,026), Fire (284) and Drowning (200).

This isn't surprising. An accident that someone can think up a category for is the sort of accident you can predict and avoid, which is something we have become good at. After all, over the last 3.8 billion years all our ancestors have avoided being bitten by rats (W53) or crashing their three-wheeled vehicles into railway carriages (V35) long enough to mate and pass on their genes.

So, if we were all imperishably young and immune to illness, 12,361 of us would still die every year. However, this means that you could still expect to live to the surprisingly ripe old age of 4,901 before the reaper caught up with you.

THE AVERAGE LIFE OF THE AVERAGE PERSON   3

ALCOHOL

We have been using alcohol for longer than any other drug. We just love the way it simultaneously increases our turnover of dopamine and reduces the excitability of our neurons.

In a year, you will drink 10.39 l of pure alcohol, or 666 l in a lifetime. Britain is twenty-second in the world for alcohol consumption between the two extremes of Saudi Arabia (0 l per year) and Uganda (19.47 l). In order to be too drunk to drive a car, the average person has to drink about 40 ml of pure alcohol. If you drank that much every day for a year you would consume 14.6 l of pure alcohol. The average pure-alcohol consumption of Luxembourg, the Czech Republic and Uganda is all well above this figure. Ireland, the fourth-drunkest nation, is just under at 14.45. In Britain, drinking your daily average in one swallow would not put you over the driving limit, but it would mildly intoxicate you.

Drunkenness is only part of the story. Getting clean water to drink is essential for staying alive. In the past, when waterborne diseases like cholera and typhoid were rife, fermenting the sugars from hops, grapes or honey in water to make beer, wine or mead was a way of making the water safe to drink. In Britain, thousands of years of this practice have given us an inherited tolerance to alcohol. This means we do not get drunk as quickly as people who come from cultures like China, where water has traditionally been purified by boiling it to make tea. Our inherited tolerance to alcohol is a sign that for a significant part of our history, drinking alcoholic beverages has been a factor in our ability to survive. If you did not drink alcohol you were more likely to die of dysentery before mating and passing on your genes.

And today, alcohol still plays an important role in mating and passing on your genes. By and large drinking is a social activity. You are going to spend 273 days of your life drinking round the clock in bars, clubs and pubs. Drinking alone is frowned upon almost as much as being the only person who is not drinking. This must make life hard for the 10 per cent of the population who do not drink any alcohol at all. However, they will have the compensation of being better off by £25,536, which is how much you will spend on alcohol in a lifetime.

APPLES

Apples came to us along the Silk Road from Kazakhstan and the Tien Shan mountains of north-west China. The ancestors of all the apples we eat today can still be found growing there on the slopes of the Ili Valley. It is likely that the apple was the first tree to be cultivated, more than 4,000 years ago. There are good reasons for this as not only is the fruit delicious, it keeps very well, longer than almost any other fruit. Traditionally, apples would have been kept in a cool, dry fruit cellar and you could expect to be

eating fruit that was picked in the autumn the following spring. There is nothing wrong at all with eating an apple that is four months old.

Unfortunately most of the apples you eat will be considerably older than this. In Britain, the last apples of the year are harvested around October, which means if you buy a British apple in July it is going to be a minimum of nine months old. In some cases you might actually be eating a birthday apple, which is the industry term for an apple that has celebrated its first birthday since it left the tree.

Just like our hairy primate ancestors, we choose fruit mainly with our eyes and apples can be kept looking delicious longer than any other fruit. The beauty parade begins before the apple is even grown. Commercial apple varieties have been developed to have colourful skins without russeting (the rough skin gives a more flavoursome but less attractive apple). They must store well, be robust and easy to transport, have a regular shape and a long stem that allows pesticides to penetrate the top of the fruit easily.

Once they are harvested, the apples are washed with soap and chlorine, then rinsed in hot water. This process removes the apple's natural waxy coating, which most producers replace using shellac. This compound is secreted on tree bark by insects and is also the main constituent of French polish. It takes around 300,000 insects to produce 1 kg of lac resin and during collection it is inevitable that many of these will be crushed, killed and mixed up with the shellac. Though the shellac is perfectly harmless this does raise the possibility that some apples may not be suitable for vegetarians.

After the freshly coated apples have been dried and buffed with brushes they are ready to be sorted. Most large-scale apple packers use computer imaging and analysing machines such as the Greefa intelligent Quality Sorter. These can be programmed with the buyers' exact requirements down to the gram, millimetre and the subtlest shades of bloom and blush.

First of all, the Greefa spins the fruit at high speed, taking up to 70 colour photographs of each apple. These are automatically analysed for size, blemishes and characteristics such as the proportions of red and green on each apple. Next is the intelligent Flavour Analyser, which shines a high-intensity halogen light through the apple, revealing the density, whether the apple is rotten and the Brix value – a measure of how much sugar the apple contains. Finally the intelligent Firmness Detector makes up to 20 measurements around the apple to give a clear indication of firmness, from which the degree of ripeness, best time for eating and storage life are determined.

Now, the apple is ready to be sold and while it waits for that happy day it will be kept in a computer-controlled environment. For long-term storage the temperature is lowered to 0 °C and the concentration of oxygen in the air is reduced to put the apples to sleep. They can stay this way for over a year.

You will eat 7,388 apples in your life. That's two for every star visible in a clear night sky.

One-fifth of these will come from Britain. The rest will each have travelled an average of 1,854 miles. Around 573 of them will have made the 12,000-mile trip from New Zealand. Your food miles from apples alone will total 1,397,352.

If you find any of this the least bit disturbing you should stick to organic British apples but this does mean you will only be able to eat them between August and January.

ATOMS

Our world will come to a quiet, modest end. Unlike high-mass stars, our small Sun will not become a supernova that illuminates the universe, inspiring riots and religions on distant worlds. Instead, 7 billion years from now, as the fuel runs out it will turn a dim red and swell to enormous size before collapsing in a cloud of gas.

The Earth and everything that's on it will be destroyed. However, the atoms we are made from will survive as they always have. After all, they were here long before the Earth was formed. So, on one measure, you are more than 4.6 billion years old. The atoms you are made of were once stardust, primordial ooze, the dinosaurs and Mozart.

One of the subtlest ways we interact with the past is the simple act of breathing. You take an average of 16 breaths a minute. That's 665,650,000 in a lifetime. As each is around about half a litre, you will breathe out over 332,820,000 l of air. Enough to blow up a balloon 265 m long and 40 m in diameter. If that were a bottle, it would be big enough to house the *Titanic*.

In his 35-year lifespan, Mozart did less than half this much breathing. Each litre of air contains 26,000,000,000,000,000,000,000 molecules. So in his lifetime Mozart breathed out a total of 3,944,500,000,000,000,000, 000,000,000,000 molecules. In terms of the Earth's atmosphere, one molecule in 27,030,000,000,000 was once exhaled by Mozart. The chances of you inhaling one of these would seem to be very small. However, as each breath you take contains 13,392,000,000,000,000,000,000 molecules, it is actually possible that up to 490,000,000 of them were once inside Mozart's lungs.

Even at this rate you would only accumulate enough Mozart in a lifetime to fill a balloon the size of a grain of sand. The actual figures are likely to be lower. Over time these molecules become incorporated into other living things, including you. In turn your atoms are ultimately going to be dispersed and recycled into new life. This is the closest thing to eternity that science has to offer.

Over the past 2,000 years there has been time for all the molecules that were breathed by or passed through Jesus to become thoroughly mixed through all the air, water, plants and animals on the planet. Transubstantiation aside, bread and wine already contain a tiny proportion of the blood and body of Christ. Of course, they also contain atoms that were once primordial ooze, the dinosaurs and Mozart. Ashes to ashes ... dust to dust ...

BACTERIA

You are never alone. There are more bacteria living on and in your body than you have cells. This means that in terms of numbers of cells, most of you isn't human. Bacteria are tiny in comparison to the cells that make up your body, which means that there is space for over 1,000 trillion bacteria, microbes and other organisms to consider you home. That's 153 thousand times the human population of the planet. After a good scratch there is the equivalent of the population of Europe under just one of your fingernails.

You are an ecosystem and like all ecosystems parts of you are more fertile than others. There are an average of 10 million bacteria living on each square centimetre of your skin. In the damp tufted areas of the body this can rise to as many as 100 million. These are essentially the rainforest areas of your body surface. A Brazilian bikini wax has more or less the same effect as felling the Brazilian rainforest when it comes to loss of biodiversity.

However, the numbers of bacteria only get really huge when you enter the long, warm, wet tube of your digestive tract. Your stomach and intestines contain about 1 kg of bacteria and they are multiplying all the time. In fact, 60 per cent of your faeces consists of bacteria that have bred inside you.

Becoming colonised with bacteria is an essential stage in development. Animals that are kept sterile will have to eat around 30 per cent more food to survive without the help of bacteria. Their immune systems will also not develop properly and they will be highly susceptible to disease and allergies.

In the womb, you are totally sterile. One of the things you inherit from your mother is a coating of her bacteria as you are born. These quickly colonise your digestive tract, though it will take around two years for you to develop a complete set. This process mirrors your move from milk to more diverse foods. At the same time, your developing bacteria are responsible for the change from relatively inoffensive baby poo to the more disgusting adult kind that makes toilet training such a priority.

The ecosystem of your body is self-regulating and very stable. Unless you suffer from a specific health problem there really should be no need to worry about the bacteria that make their home in your gut. We do worry, though. Every year British people spend over £1 billion on special probiotic foods – mostly yogurts and drinks. These contain either nutrients to sustain our existing bacteria or cultures of bacteria designed in laboratories to do the same job better. Over a lifetime you are going to spend over £1,300 on your gut bacteria. While this might make you feel better, there is no evidence that it actually improves your health if you were healthy in the first place. The amount we spend reflects the fact that many of us don't feel that healthy in the first place.

Your bacteria will outlive you, though the helpful ones will not outlive you for long. While you are alive they keep malign bacteria under control by competing more effectively for food and space. Once the food stops coming and conditions change, they quickly die off. New bacteria become dominant. Bacteria that want to eat you. Six feet under the ground, you will be the host, the venue and the buffet for the last party you will ever attend and there will be more than 1,000 trillion guests. Alternatively, you can be cremated and take the whole lot with you.

BAKED BEANS

Beans are eaten all around the world and practically every culture has some form of baked-bean recipe, from ful medames in Egypt, dhal in India, and any number of beans stews in the Far East to cassoulet in France, fabada in Spain and the pork and bean recipes of North America. If you take the pork out of the latter and cook them with sugary tomato sauce with plain sugar rather than molasses, you basically have the recipe for baked beans.

The first tin of baked beans went on sale in Fortnum & Mason in 1886. At the time they would have been something of an exotic luxury, combining the romance of being shipped in from the wild colonial outpost of Canada with the novelty of being in a tin. Presumably other countries were offered the baked bean but for some reason Britain is the only country where they really took off. British people now consume around 97 per cent of the world's total production of baked beans.

Even as a luxury item, in 1901 a tin of beans would only have cost you the equivalent of £1.50 at today's prices. Beans have always been cheap. The average cost of a 415 g tin is currently 45 p. Which means your lifetime's consumption of 1,094 tins – around about 454 kg – will only cost you £492.

Given our unique relationship with the baked bean, perhaps we should promote it more as a symbol of British identity. But then, would we want to be known as the most flatulent nation on Earth? Beans have this effect because they contain lots of soluble fibre and oligosaccharides that your small intestine cannot break down and absorb. When the bacteria in your large intestine go to work on them, large amounts of hydrogen, carbon dioxide and methane are produced.

You can buy products such as Beano that will temporarily equip you with the enzymes your small intestine needs to break down the oligosaccharides. It is also possible to ferment the beans slightly before preparation, which breaks down the soluble fibre. In theory, putting these two technologies together would result in a flatulence-free bean. It will be interesting to see how they market such a thing. Before buying a tin, you should probably consider that soluble fibre helps reduce cholesterol and prevent bowel cancer while oligosaccharides help stimulate your immune system and keep it healthy. A bit of flatulence is a small price to pay, though you won't always be the only one paying it.

BALLOONS

In a lifetime, you will buy 733 balloons at a total cost of £163. The majority of these will be helium balloons and if the figure seems ridiculously high that is because your average includes all the balloons that are released every year at school fetes, weddings, rock concerts and other events. We are living at the absolute peak of the helium-balloon bonanza. In the future we just won't be able to afford them.

Generally, the price of any resource like coal or oil or gold is related to how abundant it is. If gold were as abundant and as easy to get hold of as sand it would have no value. This means that in theory we can never completely run out of anything because as it becomes scarce, the price goes up so much that people can no longer afford it. When oil is as rare as gold it will be too expensive to run our cars and heat our homes. It will never run out completely because we will have to find an alternative or just do without.

Helium is the second most abundant element in the universe but here on Earth it is actually rather scarce. The problem is that helium is very light. Atoms of helium are produced very slowly by the decay of radioactive rock deep in the Earth's crust. These diffuse upwards into the atmosphere and away into space. All the helium we have comes from reservoirs formed by the same impermeable rock structures that trap natural gas. When the gas runs out, so will the helium. Despite the fact that it makes up 23 per cent of the mass of the universe, we are going to run out of helium within the next 50 years.

The thing about helium is that there are no alternatives. Its unique properties come from its atomic structure, which makes it the most chemically inert substance in the universe. It also means that helium is the only substance that remains liquid at absolute zero. These properties make it crucial in the production of computer chips, fibre-optic cables and also the supercooled magnets that are at the heart of every hospital's MRI scanner. In a world without helium, we will have to do without these things. As this is inconceivable we will probably start to extract helium from the atmosphere, but this will be very expensive. Weight for weight helium already costs more than gold. Extracting it from the atmosphere is likely to increase the price by more than 100 times.

Whatever the future holds, it is unlikely to contain helium party balloons. This means that we will be the last humans to sing to each other like Pinky and Perky till we are light-headed. The last humans ever to suffer the minor tragedy of accidentally letting go of a balloon and watching it float off into the same mental space as Amelia Earhart and Glenn Miller.

BANANAS

The banana is the most popular fruit in the world. In a lifetime, you will eat 13,674 of them. But unlike other fruit, the chances of you finding a seed in any of these bananas is very, very small. If you did, it might make you extremely wealthy.

The wild banana produces a fruit that is so packed with hard seeds it is impossible to eat. Around 10,000 years ago in South East Asia one of these plants produced a mutant banana with no seeds and we have been eating its seedless offspring ever since. With no seeds to plant, the only way to guarantee a future supply is to take cuttings. All the bananas we eat today are essentially Stone Age clones descended from those first cuttings.

But that is the problem for the banana. Banana plants haven't had sex in 10,000 years. This means they haven't been able to develop resistance to pests and diseases. In the 1950s the most popular variety, the Gros Michel, was wiped out by soil fungus. It was replaced by the Cavendish. There was quite a fuss at the time. People complained that it was tasteless and bland. One of the reasons banana flavouring is different from actual bananas is that it reflects the much stronger taste of the Gros Michel. Now it looks like things are all set to change again. A new soil fungus is threatening to wipe out the Cavendish. Banana crops are already the most heavily sprayed food crop in the world, but despite being sprayed with fungicide up to 40 times a year, growers are losing the battle.

Though there are many varieties of banana, only a handful are suitable for large-scale cultivation. Not being able to have sex means that cross-breeding to create new varieties that are is very difficult. Occasionally a genetic accident will result in an otherwise sterile banana producing a seed. In an attempt to provoke this sort of accident, banana breeders at the Honduran Foundation for Agricultural Research hand-pollinated 30,000 banana plants with pollen from wild bananas. Four hundred tonnes of fruit were peeled and carefully sieved for seeds. Fifteen seeds were found. Only four of these grew.

Estimate how much this process would cost, divide by four and that's how much you might be able to get for a banana seed. If you want to be a bit more entrepreneurial, you should backcross your freak banana plant with wild varieties that are resistant to fungi and name the new banana after yourself.

This is what the Honduran Foundation for Agricultural Research did with their four seeds. They named their banana the Goldfinger. It is a beautiful-looking banana. A little stouter perhaps than the Cavendish, but a marvellous golden yellow colour that unlike other bananas does not turn to brown when it is cut. The only problem is the flavour. Some people say the Goldfinger tastes like an apple.

BATTERIES

A battery contains a chemical reaction that produces electricity. The reaction can only happen if the electrons can flow through your phone or your torch to make it work. The battery will continue pumping electrons through your phone or torch until the reaction is complete, the electrons stop flowing and the battery is dead. Rechargeable batteries contain reactions that can be reversed by making the electrons flow the other way. Recharging a battery means you are returning the reaction to its original state. To make better batteries, you need to find reactions that happen more slowly, last longer, produce more electrons and can be run backwards more often and more quickly. Better batteries are one of the reasons we can have laptops, mobile phones and MP3 players and not have to carry around a suitcase filled with lead and sulphuric acid to make them work.

You will get through 861 batteries in your lifetime. As most rechargeable batteries can be reused up to 1,000 times this raises the possibility of getting through your entire life with just one rechargeable battery (or at least one of each size if you are being finicky). This would save you a lot of money as recharging a battery only costs 2 p whereas buying a new one costs around 80 p. This would leave you £671 better off. Unfortunately it would also mean that you would only be able to use devices that need more than one battery if you clubbed together with friends.

+ −

− +

BEARDS

From puberty onwards, men are faced with a daily choice about whether to fit in or not reduced to the simple question: should I shave today?

With facial hair growing at a rate of 0.44 mm a day, the pressure is relentless. Left unchecked, that could amount to a beard 9.8 m long getting in the way while you tried to blow out the 79 candles on your last birthday cake. With an average of 11,000 hairs in a beard, that's the equivalent of a single hair 107 km long. Keeping this under control will take around three minutes a day, which comes to 144 days standing in front of a mirror trying not to cut yourself.

Financially, a lifetime's shaving will cost you £676 in razors and £181 in shaving foam, gel or oil. These figures are quite modest – an average of around about £13.50 a year. The shaving industry knows this and is keen to bump these figures up. This explains the ever-increasing fanciness of razors and adverts that portray shaving as like driving an expensive sports car around your face. While they are competing with each other, they are also promoting the culture of shaving itself and the smooth-chinned route to success. The low figures also reflect the fact that there is a large section of the male population who are miserly when it comes to shaving. They use the cheapest possible equipment, may not even shave every day or perhaps, worst of all, wear a beard.

Beards cost the government money. If every man wore a beard then the Treasury would lose around £56 million a year just in VAT from shaving products. It could expect to recoup some of this from the sale of beard trimmers. From both the government's and the shaving industry's point of view, the best thing would be to encourage partial beard styles like the goatee. With a goatee most of the face still has to be shaved every day and in addition you need a beard trimmer for the bit in the middle.

Presumably in the time before razors you were simply either a man or a boy. The date of the first shave in the history of civilisation has gone unmarked. Since then, beards have waxed and waned on the chins of men according to the fashion of the time. If they had been Victorians, Superman, Batman, the Incredible Hulk and the rest would probably all have had beards. However, for most of the twentieth century beards have been out. There has never been a bearded Bond and in general romantic leads and sex symbols have been clean-shaven.

Though beads have a different significance for people who wear them for religious reasons, in general having a beard in twenty-first-century Britain is a rebellious act. The extent of the rebellion is in direct proportion to the extent of the beard. A measure of how far you are prepared to stand out from the herd. If you walk down the street with an extravagantly rebellious beard people will look at you and children may point. Occasionally people will shout witticisms like 'Gandalf!' or, if you are bald, 'Your head's on upside down.' There is a lot at stake when you decide whether to shave or not each morning.

BEER

Beer is often described as liquid bread, as if to include it in one of the virtuous food groups that can be consumed as part of a healthy, balanced diet. This doesn't work the other way round. No one calls bread solid beer. That just emphasises the fact that bread is not thirst-quenching, alcoholic or fun. Bread and beer are two of the oldest manufactured foods. They share many ingredients, have common origins and for most of human history have been important as food.

It is likely that bread came first and that somehow, about 8,000 years ago, a batch of dough went wrong or some leftover bread got wet, fermented and produced a rudimentary beer. All that had to happen next was for someone to drink the result, enjoy it and try to make some more. What is known about the earliest beers suggests that this is exactly what happened. The oldest known recipe for beer is preserved in a 4,000-year-old poem that describes how ancient Sumerians made beer by fermenting specially baked loaves of bread in water.

The first evidence of beer drinking in Britain dates from the Bronze Age with the Beaker people, named after their characteristically shaped clay beakers. The rapid spread of Beaker culture across Europe is often put down to the fact that although the beakers were used for refining metals, they were also used to make alcohol. While Beaker culture must have been partly about getting drunk for the first time in the history of Britain, brewing beer was also a good way of turning dirty water into a clean, nutritious, high-energy drink.

For most of the 4,500 years we have been drinking beer in Britain it has been an essential part of our diet. Although people of all ages would have drunk beer in preference to water, it was particularly important for people involved in hard physical work. In Das Kapital, Karl Marx said that the British worker's cost of production was beer, whereas in France it was wine. This was certainly true in the eighteenth century, when an agricultural labourer could expect to receive a gallon or 8 pints of beer a day. Workers in hot, strenuous trades such as foundrymen and blacksmiths could get through three times as much – up to 24 pints. Most of this beer was very weak by today's standards, as well as being flat and warm, but it was full of minerals and B vitamins. Like bread, it was one of the staples of daily life.

Beer's dominance as the workers' drink finally ended when tea became cheap enough for ordinary people during the eighteenth century. As well as being cheaper, it didn't have the stigma of being alcoholic and left you clear-eyed and alert enough to operate heavy machinery. Unfortunately, compared to beer, tea has almost no nutritional value at all. All those lost calories had to be made up somehow. In the period when tea was replacing beer as the worker's drink, Britain's imports of sugar went up even faster than those of tea. The modern cup of builder's tea – strong and heavily sweetened – is a legacy of the painful switch from beer to tea more than 200 years ago. Perhaps this is also why we talk about brewing up tea.

Beer remains the third most popular drink in the world after water and tea, but as drinking it is now purely a leisure activity we only get through a fraction of what we used to. An eighteenth-century agricultural worker might have got through 2,500 pints a year. You are only going to drink 168, or 13,342 pints in a lifetime, which still comes to a pint every two days.

In the ancient Sumerian epic of Gilgamesh, one of the characters, Enkidu, 'The Wild Man', drinks seven pitchers of beer, after which 'his heart grew light, his face glowed and he sang out with joy. . . 'Across a gulf of 4,000 years it seems that one aspect of beer drinking hasn't changed at all.

BIRTHDAYS

The path of the Sun across the sky is called the ecliptic. Since Babylonian times astrologers have divided the sky into 12 equal zones named after the constellations that lie across this line. The position of the Sun on the date of your birth determines your birth sign and can also influence your health, your personality, how lucky you are, whether you take risks and the kind of life you will lead. Patriotic, sentimental, home-loving Cancerians tend to be lucky. Spontaneous and risk-taking, Geminis are more likely to suffer from dyslexia. The happy-go-lucky Taurean is slightly more likely to commit suicide.

Saying that someone is a Taurean is simply another way of saying that they were born in the spring. Our seasons are caused by the tilt of the Earth combined with its orbit around the Sun. The effect becomes greater the further you move from the equator. Most of the tropics have only two seasons: wet and dry. In Britain we have four: a period of maximum sunlight in the summer and minimum sunlight in the winter separated by the transitional seasons of spring and autumn.

Studies of large groups of people who suffer from schizophrenia, anorexia, dyslexia and panic attacks have found that there is a significant relationship between the season you were born in and your risk of developing one of these problems. People born in February, March or April are between 5 and 10 per cent more likely to develop schizophrenia. April, May and June birthdays show a slightly greater risk for anorexia and suicide. Dyslexia is slightly more common for people born in May, June or July. You are more likely to suffer from panic attacks if you were born in the autumn or early winter.

Though the exact mechanism is not understood, it appears that the amount of solar radiation your mother experienced during pregnancy can influence your personality. It is thought that the most likely answer lies in the chemicals the body produces in response to sunlight, such as melatonin and vitamin D.

Your body's production of mood chemicals such as dopamine and serotonin also vary with the season of your birth. These chemicals affect your basic personality – whether you are cautious or a risk-taker, whether you seek out novelty or tend to get stuck in a rut. This may well explain why some people appear to be luckier than others. A survey of over 40,000 people who were asked whether they considered themselves to be lucky or not revealed that a significantly larger number of people born in the summer feel that they are. This corresponds to other research that found that summer people are more likely to take risks and seek out novelty. Perhaps lucky people are simply people who constantly put themselves in situations where they have the opportunity to be lucky. The luckiest month appears to be May, though this does come with a slightly higher risk of dyslexia, anorexia and suicide.

These effects diminish along with the seasons as you get closer to the equator and are reversed in the southern hemisphere. While there is good evidence that the star we are born under – the Sun – can have some effect on how we live our lives, it is negligible compared to the power of our own decisions.

Whichever month you are born in, you can expect to have 79 birthdays and receive 1,450 birthday cards at an average of 18 a year. This seems like a lot, but this figure has not been adjusted for all the celebrities who receive thousands of cards from people they have never met. Even the average person can count on a pretty fair crop up to the age of 21. The number will tend to decline as you get older, with the occasional bumper year as you cross the milestone of another decade on Earth.

The top-selling cards are for fortieth birthdays. The lowest volume of sales are for the sixtieth, seventieth and eightieth years. While this probably reflects the fact that fewer of your friends will be alive to send you a card, it also reflects the fact that birthdays are a much bigger deal when you are young. There seems to be a point where birthdays change from being a celebration of life to being a celebration of not being dead. Perhaps this is why there are practically no statistics relating to adult birthdays. This makes it impossible to work out how many presents you are going to receive, how many you will give and what they will cost.

Each birthday is a celebration of another trip around the Sun since you were born. The ancient Babylonians invented the zodiac as a way of mapping the stars and marking our passage through the year. There are actually

13 constellations that cross the ecliptic, but 13 is not an easy number to work with, so Opiuchus 'the Serpent Bearer' is omitted. If you were born between 29 November and 17 December you might want to adopt him as your star sign.

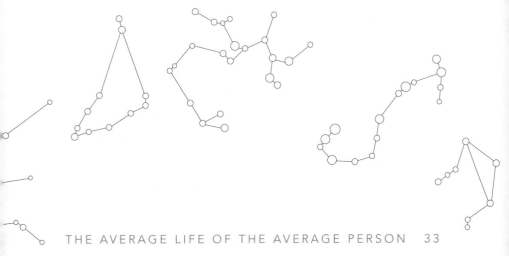

BISCUITS

TVA (Taxe sur la Valeur Ajoutée) was invented in 1954 by a French econo-
mist. In 1973 it was introduced in Britain as VAT. The sole function of
VAT is to raise money for the state. Traditionally you do not pay VAT on
things like food, medicines, cremation and other essential goods and services. In theory, therefore, the Revenue's list of things you do not pay VAT
on is a list of all the things that are essential to life. It is strange, then, that
while biscuits are on the list, women's sanitary towels are not.

A lifetime's supply of biscuits is about 1.5 tonnes and they will cost you a
mostly VAT-free £2,036. Biscuits are a strange food category as far as VAT
is concerned. You can fill them with jam, cream and chocolate chips, coat
them with sugar, dust them with desiccated coconut and silver balls and
they will remain an essential food staple. But, the moment you cover them
with chocolate (or 'product similar in taste and appearance'), they become
a luxury item and you must pay VAT. The extra you pay for chocolate di-

gestives is mostly VAT. Having the chocolate-covered Jaffa Cake classed as a cake was therefore a major coup for its manufacturers. The crucial point was that biscuits go soft when exposed to air while cakes go hard.

Though cakes are undoubtedly a luxury item, you don't pay VAT on them, no matter what they are covered with. This is largely down to the difficulty of defining a cake in a way that wouldn't include bread, which definitely is an essential food. Coming up with a definition of a cake that doesn't run into this problem is the Fermat's last theorem of the VAT world. Solving it would make you very unpopular with the general public. There would be no lecture tours, no honorary degrees, just a celebratory tea down at the Treasury perhaps with a VAT inspector bursting out of a giant cake with a packet of Jaffa Cakes in his hand.

BLOOD

Your heart is surprisingly small – usually a little bit smaller than your own clenched fist. It will start beating 21 days after conception, so by the time you are born it will have already beaten around 38,808,000 times. In the remaining 79.1 years, it is going to beat another 2,995,447,392 times. A total of just over 3 billion heartbeats in a lifetime.

The way your heart pumps blood around your body is one of the things you know without any memory of how you came to know it. It is just the way things are. It is hard to imagine that up until quite recently it was a fact that no one knew. Shakespeare might have listened politely as you explained your crazy theory about how blood is endlessly pumped around the body, but he would probably have just been annoyed with you for wasting his time.

Understanding the circulation of the blood is difficult because the problem is booby-trapped with misleading information. First of all, the plumbing associated with blood looks very different when it stops working. For instance, when you die your arteries empty into your veins. So, for a long time the arteries were thought to carry air around the body. Then there is the fact that parts of the system are just too small to be seen with the naked eye. This means that if you follow the large arteries and veins away from the heart, they appear to be like two separate river systems branching into smaller and smaller tributaries that eventually peter out at your extremities, without any visible connection between them. Finally, blood conceals its nature. Your veins look blue, as if they might contain a different kind of blood, but when you cut them, the blood that comes out is always red.

Three hundred years before Shakespeare, a 29-year-old Arab Muslim scientist called Ibn al-Nafis working in Cairo published a treatise on anatomy. In it, he became the first person to describe how the right side of the heart pumps blood through the lungs and into the left side of the heart. The left side of the heart then pumps the oxygenated blood along the arteries to all parts of the body before being returned to the heart via the veins so that the whole cycle can begin again. As well as being the first person to describe the circulation of the blood accurately, Ibn al-Nafis was a considerable polymath. Alongside all his medical discoveries and more than 80 books covering diverse subjects such as law, linguistics and logic, he is also credited with writing the first science-fiction novel.

Unfortunately for Western thought, this was at the height of the Crusades and most of his work remained undiscovered until 1924.

Meanwhile, in Europe, our ideas about blood were mainly derived from the work of the Greek physician Galen, who died in AD 199. His idea was that your liver and heart turned food into blood. The blood did not circulate, it simply made a one-way journey to different parts of your body, where it was consumed. This theory persisted for over 1,400 years, despite the fact that your heart and liver would have to produce 244 kg of new blood every day to explain the quantity flowing in your veins. In 1598, when he wrote Shylock's line 'If you prick us, do we not bleed?', Shakespeare could have had no conception of why we bleed, where blood comes from, what it does, or even have had the most rudimentary understanding of what blood actually is.

It wasn't until 400 years after the death of Ibn al-Nafis that the British scientist William Harvey was able to overturn the theories of Galen and bring an accurate description of how blood flows around the body. Neither Harvey nor Ibn al-Nafis were able to explain how blood got from the arteries to the veins, however. This final piece of the jigsaw had to wait until the invention of the microscope in the 1650s. In 1661, four years after the death of Harvey, an Italian called Marcello Malpighi studied a bat's wing under a microscope and described for the first time the tiny blood vessels that connect the arteries to the veins. He called them capillaries after the Latin for 'hair'.

The arteries bring the oxygen- and nutrient-rich blood to different parts of your body. The capillaries branch off the arteries and thread their way between your cells. Oxygen and nutrients in the blood pass into them through the thin walls of the capillaries. The blood leaving your capillaries and entering your veins carries away waste products to be removed by your kidneys and carbon dioxide, which you will breathe out. The lack of oxygen in your venous blood turns it a dark blue colour. You will never see this colour because the instant you cut yourself, the oxygen in the air turns the blood red again.

Your bone marrow is constantly producing new blood cells. They will last around 120 days before being broken up in your spleen. In a lifetime you will completely change all your blood 241 times. In terms of volume, that's 1,348 l or about ten baths full. Enough to make a 2.5-tonne black pudding.

Every minute your heart will pump your complete volume of blood round your body: 5.6 litres for each of the 41,603,436 minutes of your life. This comes to 232,979,241 l. If you were plumbed into an Olympic-sized swimming pool that would be enough to fill it to within 16 cm of the regulation depth of 2 m.

Every year in Britain 1,125,000 l of blood are donated. Sadly this comes from just 5 per cent of the population. If you are in that 5 per cent, you will donate a total of 17.8 l or just under 40 units of blood. Each unit can save up to three lives.

BREAD

You decide that what you need is a slice of hot buttered toast. As there isn't any bread in the house you go to the shops. This is where your problems begin. The instant you close the front door, the street, the town, the whole country disappears. Your house is still there, but the rest of civilisation isn't. All there is, as far as the eye can see, is an endless vista of grass, sky and occasionally a tree. You try lots of things: going back in and coming out again. Peering out through the letter box. You try to phone for help, but your house is like a theatre set, everything looks right, but nothing is connected up, nothing works. You try having a bit of a lie-down. From the upstairs windows you can see that the grass isn't quite endless, there appear to be mountains in the distance. Eventually, resigned to the new turn your life has taken, you walk out into the landscape. There, by one of the occasional trees, waist-deep in the whispering grasses some miles from your house, you become fixated on the idea that if you could only make yourself that slice of toast, then everything might go back to normal.

If this ever happens to you, the next step is to find some grasses with seeds big enough to make harvesting and grinding them worthwhile. Normally, cereals produce small seeds that scatter themselves in the wind. Occasionally, a lucky cross-breeding between wild grasses produces fat seeds that will not disperse themselves but can be made into flour. As the seeds cannot spread themselves, these new varieties will not do well unless someone cultivates them.

To cultivate them in any quantity, you will need to clear the land of other vegetation. It would be helpful to have tools for this, and they would make harvest easier too. The best option is to make one out of sharp stones and sticks lashed together with some kind of string, which you will also have to make. Obviously, something made out of metal would be much better, but unfortunately the skills necessary for finding metal ores and refining, smelting and forging them into edged tools are probably beyond you. So is the technology to make hand querns or millstones, let alone a water- or wind-powered mill. Without any of these things, making enough flour for a single loaf of bread using a couple of stones you found by a river will take at least a day, maybe more.

In order to make leavened bread you will need some kind of raising agent. As natural yeasts are abundant and the spores will settle and thrive on anything wet and starchy, nature will solve this problem for you. But nature is just as likely to turn your starter culture into a putrid mess of fungus and bacteria, so this may take a bit of time and luck. Then, with your dough risen, you need to build an oven and light a fire. Lighting the fire might take a couple of days, but once lit you can make an oven quite simply by creating a space in the middle of the fire with flat stones. You will probably set fire to your first few loaves.

Even the most fundamental building blocks of our civilisation rely on a huge amount of previous knowledge and technology. Making one loaf of bread totally from scratch might take you a couple of years if you were lucky and knew what you were doing. Setting up a system to provide you with a loaf of bread every day that you can just buy from a shop without any notion of how it got there or how it was made has taken thousands of years.

Our ancestors were probably forced into agriculture about 13,000 years ago by a period of cold and drought that lasted about 1,000 years. The change in the climate made food scarce and people were forced to start cultivating some of the foods they used to gather from the wild. The earliest wheat dates from this time, but it did not have a high enough gluten content to make bread. The first wheat suitable for bread-making appeared around 10,000 years ago, but it was another 4,000 years before the trick of leaving dough to rise was discovered and leavened bread started to be made.

Finally, after years of effort, you will carry your loaf of bread into the house. Before you close the door, you take one last look at the grasslands that now include a wheat field and a giant charred kitchen area. In the kitchen you use your stone knife for the last time to cut a slice of bread. Almost regretfully, you drop it into the toaster. You close your eyes and push down the lever. There is a click as the toaster comes on. There is a hum as everything electrical in your house comes back to life. You open your eyes. Outside the kitchen window, next door's dog is digging up your roses again and all you can do is laugh, helpless with relief. The memory

of the last few years drops away and by the time your toast pops back up all crisp and golden you have forgotten all about them. Perhaps this is why you don't hesitate when you discover you don't have any butter. You grab your keys and head for the shops. It isn't until the front door slams shut behind you and you feel the long grass whipping about your knees that you remember …

Every year you are going to eat 27.5 loaves of bread. In a lifetime that comes to 2,175 loaves or enough for over 50,000 slices of toast. These will go well with the 765 kg of butter you are going to get through. That's two 382.5 kg lumps of butter, each one the size of a fridge.

CARBON

In the 1960s, the British scientist James Lovelock got a job at NASA. They wanted him to help design the instruments that would be carried by the Viking probes to look for life on Mars. The possibility of life on Mars is exactly the sort of romantic notion that funds space programmes. No doubt there was a lot of other useful stuff to be discovered. But for the scientists, the politicians who approved the colossal budgets, the people who voted for them and the whole of the rest of the world who didn't, the main thing they were interested in was: is there life on Mars?

Obviously, what NASA wanted was a sort of clever box of tricks that would activate itself when it reached the surface, carry out experiments and send back its results. But how do you design an instrument that detects life? For that matter, what is life? Lovelock started to think about life on Earth and how it affects the planet. On Earth, the series of chemical reactions that support life are constantly pumping unstable elements and compounds such as methane, oxygen and hydrogen into the atmosphere. In fact there is no life on Earth that doesn't interact with the atmosphere. He reasoned that if Mars had life, it should also have an unstable atmosphere in an ongoing dynamic relationship with whatever was living there.

The thing is, they didn't have to go to Mars to find out about the atmosphere. That had already been done by telescope. In the 1890s. The Martian atmosphere was totally stable and inert: 95 per cent carbon dioxide. Lovelock suggested they were wasting their time landing on Mars to look for life. If they were going to find it the place to look was the atmosphere, and the chances weren't all that good.

Until quite recently, protecting the environment was about saving the whale and the crested newt, protesting against nuclear dumping and by-passes, defending hedgerows and stopping wild landscapes being turned into Surrey. It was also easy to convince yourself that it wasn't your fault. Now the environment is about how everything everyone does is wrong and trying to stop Surrey from turning into Mars.

No matter how hard we try we are not going to be able to kill off all life and give the Earth a Martian atmosphere, but it does look like we are giving it a go. Tunnelling miles under the ground, drilling far out to sea, removing entire mountains to mine carbon from the past so that it can be turned into CO_2 and returned to the atmosphere. Millions of stove pipes, flues, chimneys and smoke stacks reaching up into the sky. Then there is all the driving about and the occasional treat where we club together with other people to charter a plane and inject CO_2 high up in the stratosphere where it can do the most harm.

Carbon footprint is not a particularly good term as a footprint is always smaller than the person who makes it. There is a history of ill-chosen terms in the environmental debate that are either evidence of a certain lack of imagination and marketing skills on the part of environmentalists, or a case of very clever and subtle manipulation by the people with a vested interest in reassuring us that there really isn't anything to worry about. The threat of global warming – when the most polluting countries are in northern latitudes where people are constantly complaining about the cold – was a gift to the carbon companies. Climate change is more accurate but rather bland, and change is often something we are encouraged to embrace. Anything that spins the debate to make it easier for us to do nothing is a bad thing, which is why it might be better if we talked about carbon shadows. Shadows have a more sinister pedigree than footprints and are usually much bigger than the person casting them.

The term carbon footprint is a development from the idea of the ecological footprint, which is a measure of the amount of biologically productive land and water your lifestyle requires and is measured in global hectares (gha). The UK's average ecological footprint is 5.45 gha. This is much much bigger than the 2.1 gha we would have if all the biologically productive land and water in the world was shared out equally. Our ecological footprint is about our use of resources. We use more than twice our share. Our carbon footprint is about the damage we do – more than nine times our share. You will be responsible for putting about 9.6 tonnes of carbon back into the atmosphere every year, when a sustainable amount for the planet might be 1 tonne.

In the 1960s Shell asked a series of experts to make predictions for the impossibly distant and exotic year 2000 AD. Among the usual forecasts of family hovercrafts, flying cars and fridges that ran on nuclear fusion, one expert predicted that in the year 2000 atmospheric pollution would have got so bad that it would be affecting Shell's core business of selling carbon to the masses. Like NASA before it, Shell must have felt that James Lovelock was not joining in with the spirit of the thing.

James Lovelock now believes that we have passed the point of no return for the climate. There is nothing we can do to escape the consequences of what we have done to the atmosphere. Things are going to get very bad indeed. War, famine, pestilence, mega-death, gigadeath, mass migrations ... This is depressing when you consider how right he has been about this stuff in the past. For some people, this is a reason to do nothing. But, whether you are preparing for the coming disaster or trying to avert it, you will have to learn how to do more with less.

The search for life on Mars continues. In the last 30 years, the focus has shifted from looking for life to looking for evidence that there used to be life. Recently, however, there has been a lot of excitement over the discovery of methane on Mars. As James Lovelock predicted, this was found in the atmosphere using observations from Earth. A probe will now have to be sent to sample the atmosphere and determine whether the tiny quantities of methane that have been observed are being produced by something that is alive. The best we can hope for is likely to be some sort of thin film of slime under the surface. While this is very exciting if you are a xenobiologist, it is unlikely to fire the enthusiasm of the general public, who are slowly turning to the next romantic possibility: a manned mission to Mars. Some people see this as the next step towards ensuring the survival of the species, moving some of us off-world as the odds of a catastrophe down here get ever shorter.

CARS

If you fell from a height of 4 m, you would be travelling at 20 miles an hour when you hit the ground. Imagine launching yourself into a belly flop from the top of a stationary double-decker bus and you have some idea of what being hit by a car going at 20 miles an hour would feel like. If the traffic is travelling at 30 mph, being hit would be the same as falling 10 m or diving off the roof of the average house. The kerb is a cliff. If the traffic is travelling at 40 mph, the cliff is 16 m high – the same as swallow-diving off the highest board into an empty swimming pool. At 70 mph the impact would be like jumping on to the granite slabs of Trafalgar Square from the top of Nelson's Column. To get the full 50m fall required, you would have to be standing right on top of Nelson's cocked hat and be careful to miss the stepped base of the column and the lions.

If you are in a car, the physics are a bit more complicated as the weight of your vehicle and the immovability of what you crash into have to be taken into consideration. Travelling at 70 mph on the motorway feels perfectly safe, but just imagine how scared you would be if your car was balanced on top of Nelson's hat and you have some idea of the consequences of a momentary lack of attention sending you into a concrete bridge support. If you crash head-on into another car coming towards you at 70 mph you will have a closing speed of 140 mph. More or less the same as driving across an office on the forty-fifth floor of One Canada Square, Canary Wharf, through the plate-glass window and down four times the height of Nelson's Column, including Nelson and his hat.

All you have to do to make any of these things happen is move your hands a few inches in the wrong direction. At the same time, you are relying on all the other road users paying attention, staying awake and not swerving suddenly into the oncoming traffic to become the 200 m cliff that kills you.

You will drive 524,773 miles in a lifetime. Though around 3,000 people die every year in traffic accidents, the individual risk is surprisingly low. You could expect to live 255 lifetimes before being claimed by a fatal accident, 27 lifetimes before being seriously injured and 3.5 lifetimes before sustaining a mild injury.

The road is a cooperative enterprise with rules that we all agree on so it will work safely. As well as mastering the physical skill of driving, you also have to learn all these rules in order to pass the driving test. As a rule of thumb, doubling your age gives roughly the number of hours of lessons you will need before passing. The average person passes the test by the age of 21 after 45 hours of lessons. At an average of £24 a lesson, that's £1,080 plus £45 for the provisional licence and £28.50 for the theory test. Most people need to take two practical tests, which cost £48.50 each. Learning to drive will therefore cost you a grand total of £1,250.50.

Although you are now allowed out on to the road on your own it will take several years for you to gain enough experience to be able to predict the outcomes of the different situations you will find yourself in. This and a growing awareness of your own mortality means that insurance premiums get lower the longer you drive. Insuring your first car at the age of 18 may cost £1,250; by the time you are 40 it will have fallen to £400. If you are a woman, these figures will be lower, so the average woman will spend £27,334 on a lifetime's car insurance, compared to £31,402 for the average man. The minimum requirement is that you insure everyone and everything you might bump into. Third-party insurance is a legal requirement to minimise financial loss to others as a result of you incompetently or stupidly breaking the rules of the road.

Most of the Highway Code consists of informal rules that people obey by choice. However, some are legally enforceable and using the road is when people most frequently come into conflict with the law. Until 1930 the national speed limit was 20 mph, then it was abolished and unless your car contained more than seven passengers you could drive as fast as you liked. Speed limits were reintroduced at various times as safety measures in towns and on certain roads but there were no national speed limits until

1973. This was a temporary fuel-saving measure brought in during the war between Egypt and Israel. The speed limits we have today date from 1978, when these temporary measures were made permanent.

In a lifetime of driving you will get through 53,547 l of fuel at a total cost of £56,491. This would be considerably lower if you never drove above 50 mph, the speed at which it takes significantly more energy to overcome wind resistance and road friction. Vehicle tax used to be called road tax because it was originally introduced to fund building and maintaining the road network, with larger vehicles paying more because they do more damage. At an average of £156 a year, it will cost you £9,063 in a lifetime.

The total annual revenue from vehicle tax is £5.2 billion. The annual cost of building new roads and maintaining old ones is £7–8 billion. However, the annual income from fuel tax is over £23 billion, which leaves around £20 billion to spare. These figures are at the core of the fuel lobby's campaign to lower fuel tax. The government doesn't need the money to fund the road network so fuel tax can be lowered to stimulate the economy. Fuel tax is also a regressive tax in that for a rich person fuel tax is a smaller proportion of their total outgoings than it is for a poor person. While this is true, there is a resistance towards anything that encourages car use at a time when we need to be doing the exact opposite.

Since 2002, vehicle tax has been structured to reflect the amount of CO_2 a vehicle produces. This provides a small incentive to buy a less polluting car but it cannot take into account how that car will be driven once you have paid for it. This is a fairly simple problem to solve and systems such as the Lysanda Eco-Log are able to log every single gram of CO_2 as it is emitted. These are currently being marketed to commercial fleet managers as a way of reducing fuel costs by enabling them to monitor how efficiently their fleets of vans and cars are being driven. Expensive behaviour such as violent acceleration and speeding would cause alarming spikes on the log and bring reprimands down on the driver's head. Local authorities are likely to be next and from there it is but a short step to a nationwide monitoring system that charges you automatically for every gram of CO_2 you produce while driving. Though this is fairer than the current system, it isn't likely to be a very popular move.

For many people, driving is about freedom, which is why any attempt to put limits on car use is such a contentious issue. Speed cameras are particularly unpopular. Law-abiding citizens who approve of CCTV schemes in cities, where they have no proven effect on reducing crime, tend to be opposed to speed cameras, which do have a proven effect on reducing speeding and accidents. Speeding is probably the commonest criminal offence. At any one time, 18 per cent of all cars on the motorway are going more than 10 mph over the speed limit. On dual carriageways it is 12 per cent. On single carriageways 2 per cent of cars are over the limit, but where there is a 40 mph limit this rises to 10 per cent and in 30 mph limits is 19 per cent. Only a tiny proportion of people who speed are caught, so the average person will only get 3.5 speeding tickets in a lifetime, which will cost £210 in fixed-penalty fines.

The technology already exists to fit all of the 34 million vehicles in Britain with speed-monitoring devices. Using satellite navigation technology, these would compare your speed to the limit of whichever road you are on. You would be warned, then automatically fined if you continued to drive too fast. Any move towards this sort of system would provoke a massive reaction on the basis of civil liberties, practicality and cost. While these are all valid arguments, as with any opposition to the enforcement of speed limits they would also serve as rhetorical camouflage for the large numbers of people who object simply because they like driving fast.

Something similar is already available for parents. The RS-1000 teen tracking device can be fitted to a car so when your child gets home in the early hours of the morning you can review their driving behaviour on the family PC while sharing a cup of cocoa. Several studies have shown that children inherit their driving behaviour from their parents. Daughters drive like their mothers and sons drive like their fathers. It isn't surprising then that other studies have found that children of people with driving offences are in turn more likely to break the law when they are in a car. It is only a matter of time before someone follows this trail of evidence to look for links between parents who are killed or injured by their driving and whether their children go on to do the same. Driving safely and well when you have a child in the car has consequences far beyond simply surviving each individual journey.

When the cooperative enterprise of driving goes wrong the result is either an accident or road rage. There is an element of karma in road rage, as you are more likely to be a victim if you are also a perpetrator. In a survey in the US, 30 per cent of drivers found themselves regularly swearing under their breath about other drivers; 17 per cent shouted abuse; 3 per cent had either deliberately blocked in or aggressively driven after the person who had annoyed them; and 1–2 per cent had actually got out of their cars to argue with or attack other drivers.

Road rage has similarities to the problems experienced by some breeds of dog. Most dogs rarely let aggression get to the level of actually fighting, instead they have a series of signals – raised hackles, rigid tail, ears back, bared teeth – that allow them to work through things without having to tear each other's throats out. With short hair, docked tails, small, immobile ears and permanently bared teeth, dogs bred for fighting are constantly set in fight mode as far as other dogs are concerned and as a result are always getting into trouble. In a car, with just a set of lights and a horn, with our faces often obscured behind a reflective slant of glass, we are only able to communicate in a very limited way with other drivers. Though it might help, no car manufacturer has ever produced a car that has a tail, hackles and ears, though they do go to considerable trouble to give a car a face.

Road presence is one of the factors that influences your choice of car. You are unlikely to choose something that looks like a snarling panther to drive your kids to school. Sports cars are by far the most dangerous cars to drive. The chance of serious injury increases by 40 per cent in any crash involving a sports car. SUVs and 4 x 4s are the next most dangerous. Despite the illusion of security that comes with their bulk and height, you are just as likely to be injured or killed if you are driving one, though the additional height and weight do increase your chances of killing the people you run into.

The average person buys 14 cars in a lifetime at an average of £4,800 each – £67,200 for them all. Parking and tolls will cost you £9,446, servicing £14,641, spare parts £10,810 and tyres a further £5,405. The total of all these figures – from learning to drive to buying new tyres for your last car – comes to £203,902. In reality you will share some of these costs with a partner or spouse, bringing the actual figure down to £155,273. This may still seem like a lot, but over the last ten years the costs of owning and driving a car have actually gone down by 10 per cent while bus and train fares have gone up. At the same time, traffic levels have continued to increase by more than 10 per cent every decade.

For the last century, the solution to road congestion has always been to build more roads, the basic idea being that if we had more roads than we could all use at once, traffic problems would disappear. For decades, road construction has been led by the will-o'-the-wisp notion that this point was just another new road away ...

Allowing for the occasional ferry, the road outside your home enables you to drive to almost every other home in the world. You can seat yourself within an object more intricately constructed than a Fabergé egg and within a few seconds be going at speeds previously only achievable by hurling yourself off a cliff. As the thousands upon thousands of tarmacked miles unspool beneath your wheels, you will not be devoured by wild beasts, captured by pirates, murdered by brigands or succumb to some illness that is a mystery to medicine. As long as you don't jerk your hands a few inches to the left or right, you are more likely to arrive at your destination alive than at any point in the history of civilisation.

CATS

If you become infected with *Toxoplasma gondii* you may suffer headaches and a mild flu for a few weeks. Then again, you may not feel ill at all. In any case, the parasite will soon go into its latent phase, forming cysts on nerve and muscle tissue, and remain dormant for the rest of your life. You may already have it and not realise. Though toxo can infect any mammal, it can only breed in cats. One of the side effects of the global popularity of cats as pets has been to make toxo one of the most common human parasites in the world.

Cats started moving in to our houses around 10,000 years ago. The development of agriculture meant that grain had to be stored. It cannot have been too long before the first granaries were discovered by rodents. It would have been a golden time to be a rat or a mouse – vast, dehusked, ready-to-eat landscapes of grain to cavort about in. Then, the cats came …

Recent analysis of wild cat DNA suggests that all domestic cats are descended from just five individual wild cats in the Middle East around 10,000 years ago. This fits in with what we know about where and when agriculture began. For thousands of years wild cats avoided humans. In typical cat fashion they waited till we had settled in villages with nice warm houses and a steady supply of food before deciding to join us.

Cats are unique in that they effectively domesticated themselves. All we did was let them. This is why, unlike the animals we have more or less kidnapped from the wild, cats do not starve and die if they are neglected. They just leave.

Most cats are free to leave at any time. They only stay by choice. Why not, after all? You are a good hunter and provider. Your house is safer and much more comfortable than the wild. So, for the time being, the cat is happy to snooze on your windowsills, eat the food you provide and hang about for a bit of mutual stroking. If your cat thinks it will get a better deal at number 27, it will leave you. If you treat it badly, it will leave you. Occasionally, for no reason at all, it will just leave you. Cats return so easily to the wild it is debatable whether they have ever really left it.

Surprisingly, given the fact that cats only demand a Neolithic standard of living and all the mice they can eat, around 10 per cent of Britain's 9.6 million cats live in a semi-wild state with no human owners.

The average pet cat will cost £92 when bought as a kitten and will live for about 15 years at a cost of £330 a year or £4,950 in a lifetime. The majority of this money will go on food. Despite the impossibility of a pet cat or any of its ancestors being able to catch, much less kill, tuna, salmon, sardines, cows or sheep, this is what the majority of cat food is based on. Mysteriously, there are no brands of cat food made of mouse or rat.

As the prey of cats, rodents play an important role in the life cycle of *Toxoplasma gondii*. The most likely way for a cat to pick up the parasite is for it to eat a rat or a mouse that has been infected. The parasite breeds inside the cat, then releases eggs that are spread in cat faeces. Eating food or touching soil that has come into contact with cat faeces infects rats and mice. Now, in order to complete the cycle, the parasite has to somehow persuade the rat or the mouse it has infected to offer itself up to a cat.

This sounds like an impossibly tall order for a microscopic parasite. The curious thing is that once the parasite forms cysts on the rodent's nerves, brain and muscles, the rodent's behaviour starts to change. Tests have shown that rodents infected with toxo are more reckless, clumsier and have slower reaction times. If that wasn't enough, they also become irresistibly attracted to the smell of cat pee.

Humans are most likely to catch toxoplasmosis from coming into contact with cat faeces while gardening or dealing with cat litter, or from undercooked meat – chickens, sheep, cows and pigs commonly pick up the parasite from infected fodder and bedding.

Until recently, toxoplasmosis was thought to be dangerous only to unborn children who can catch it from their mothers, increasing the risk of miscarriage and other problems such as hydrocephalus and calcification of the brain. In the last few years, however, evidence has emerged that having a latent toxo infection has much the same effect on humans as it does on rodents. While there are no cats waiting to pounce on you as you scurry from your nest, if you have toxo, you are more likely to charge recklessly into the road, then react too slowly and jump clumsily in the wrong direction in front of a truck. In fact, if you are infected with toxo you are nearly three times as likely to have some kind of accident.

There is also some quite controversial evidence that toxo may cause subtle changes in personality that are different for men and women. Recent research by Professor Flegr of Charles University in Prague found that women with toxo were more sociable, more promiscuous, cared more about their appearance and were less trustworthy. Strangely, they were also likely to be more attractive to men. In contrast, toxo turned men into morose, scruffy loners who like to break the rules and start fights.

Fifteen per cent of British people are infected with latent toxoplasmosis.

CCTV

In 1897, while working on optical density, a scientist called Dr Jack Griffin discovered a substance that gave living tissue the same refractive index as air. His initial experiments on his neighbour's cat were so successful that it became completely invisible. Unfortunately his neighbour kicked up such a fuss about the missing cat that Griffin was forced to use the stuff on himself and go on the run. With no one able to see him, Griffin felt he was exempt from any moral codes. He could do whatever he wanted. So, he decided to embark on a reign of terror …

Things ended badly for the Invisible Man, but the idea that you can get away with anything if no one can see you is part of the rationale behind CCTV. The theory is that the feeling you are being watched is enough to make you better behaved.

Traditionally this has been one of the roles played by religion. In the place of high-resolution video-imaging equipment, there is an omnipotent entity watching your every move with the threat of judgement and eternal punishment waiting for you if you are bad. If you spent your life boosting car stereos, mugging people at cash machines and starting fights outside kebab shops, you would spend eternity in hell.

It is doubtful if the threat of hell has ever really worked. After all, people have tangible proof of the living hell of hangovers and lung cancer, yet still they drink and smoke. In the Middle Ages, when people truly believed in the burning fires of hell, you were 36 times more likely to be robbed or murdered. In general, crime rates have gone down as we have become less religious as a society. This suggests that the feeling of being watched, whether by an omnipotent being or a camera, has much less effect on people's behaviour than living standards, education and equality of opportunity.

Despite this, Britain has invested heavily in CCTV and we now supposedly have more cameras than any other country in the world. This statistic is based on a survey of two streets in Putney. By working out the number of people living in those streets per camera and extrapolating from this, the researchers came up with a figure for the whole of Britain of 4.2 million CCTV cameras, one for every 15 people. The truth is nobody has an accurate idea of how many CCTV cameras there are, but we all know it's a lot. This makes the other famous

One Nation, 4.2m Cameras

A CLOSED CIRCUIT PRODUCTION

CCTV

coming soon...

STARRING YOU

CCTV statistic – that you are caught on camera 300 times a day – more plausible. If each of these appearances lasts three seconds you will rack up a total of 7,223 hours of screentime over your life. Every five days you will star in a completely original, completely improvised feature-length movie. At 75 minutes, this is four minutes longer than the film of *The Invisible Man*.

No one is invisible in shopping centres, where you will find the highest concentrations of CCTV cameras. These feel like public spaces, but they are businesses with their own criteria of acceptable behaviour. Sitting in airless rooms, security guards exercise their omniscience using joystick-controlled cameras, banks of high-definition video screens and walkie-talkies. To be fair, if they saw you fall to the ground clutching your chest they would probably send help, but their main function is to look for unsuitable behaviour. While this does include all the stuff that is illegal outside the shopping centre, it also includes standing still. Standing still for long periods of time is a dead giveaway that you have nowhere better to go and no intention of spending any money. They do not want you cluttering up the place sheltering from the cold and the rain. If you stand there long enough someone will reach for a walkie-talkie and you will be made to leave.

CELLS

A small cut heals quickly and within a matter of days you will probably have forgotten you ever hurt yourself. More challenging cuts take longer and may leave a scar. If you do something drastic like sever a finger you will have gone beyond your body's ability to repair itself. Unfortunately, there is no central control telling your nerve, muscle, bone and skin cells to regrow a finger. The best you can hope for is that the skin will grow neatly over the stump. But why can't you regrow a finger? After all, you grew one in the first place.

When you were conceived, you were a single cell. After about 30 hours, this cell divided for the first time and you consisted of two identical cells, then four, then eight and then, somehow, just 500 hours later you were a complex organism with veins, arteries and a beating heart. Understanding the mechanisms that control the way your cells start out identical then differentiate themselves into all the parts of your body is one of the frontiers of biology. Solving this problem may allow us to regrow fingers, legs and spinal cords, or produce spare organs to order, or reverse degenerative conditions such as Parkinson's, Alzheimer's and perhaps even old age itself.

As an adult, you will consist of around 50,000,000,000,000 individual cells. Each of these is self-maintaining and self-regulating. Each one constantly repairs and renews itself from nutrients in your blood. At the same time, each cell has a set of specialised functions that are dependent on where it is in your body. It is these specialised functions acting together that enable each cell along with the 49,999,999,999,999 others to drink a cup of tea or read a book.

Your cells will continue to divide and replace themselves throughout your life. How long they live also depends on where they are. Cells on the front line, such as your skin, which have to rub up against the outside world, last only a handful of days. You replace your entire skin every two weeks. In a lifetime you get through 2,064 suits of skin.

Your liver deals with all the poisons you consume and must completely regenerate itself every 400 days to cope. This means you will get through 72 livers. Meanwhile, your skeleton is on a ten-year cycle of breakdown and renewal. When your bones are laid to rest, they will be the bones of your seventh skeleton. No matter how old you are or feel, your body is never much more than ten years old.

In fact, very little of you is original. The longest living cells in your body are in the lenses of your eyes, the muscles of your heart and in your brain. Exactly how your brain stores memories is still a mystery, but somewhere inside your head is the nexus of cells that contain your first memory. These are likely to be some of the oldest cells in your body. Over the years the various pieces of cellular machinery that keep these cells alive will have been renewed and replaced many times. Few of the original molecules will have survived. However, in the same way that your grandfather's axe is still your grandfather's axe even though your father replaced the handle a couple of times and you gave it a new blade, the cells that store your first memory are still the same cells and your memory is preserved. In fact your first memory may well be one of the oldest things about you.

Your body is a map of things that have happened to you. If you leave your body to science, the medical students that dissect you will know all about the alcohol you liked to drink, the cakes you liked to eat, the pain in your lower back, the trouble you had with ingrown toenails. As for the chipped tooth, the scar on your forehead and the missing finger, the memory of exactly how and when these accidents happened is still beyond their reach.

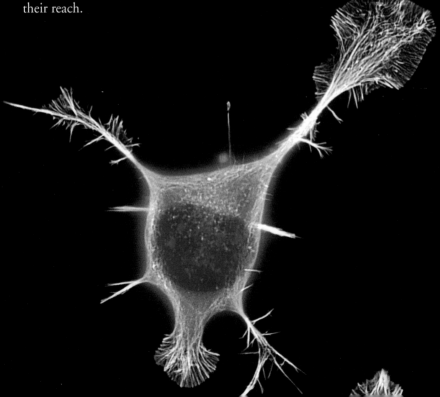

CHEESE

In 1940, the British Government banned the production of extravagant, luxury cheeses. All excess milk was now to be used in the production of the National Cheese. Anyone found wasting milk in the manufacture of treasonous fancy cheeses would be subject to the Emergency Powers (Defence) Act and imprisoned.

There have been two disasters in the history of British cheese. The first was the rinderpest epidemic of the 1860s, when thousands of cows were slaughtered. This created an acute cheese shortage that was quickly filled by American factory Cheddar and which paved the way for the industrialisation of British cheese-making. The second was the Second World War and Government Cheddar.

Forcing the British population to eat only official government cheese was a way of safeguarding the supply of liquid milk, which might otherwise leak away through the muslin bags and cheesecloths of traditional producers to be squandered with grapes, walnuts and fine port wine. In 1939 there were 1,500 farmhouse cheese-makers. By 1945, only 126 remained. By the time rationing was lifted in 1954 the average British person had learned to get by on 2 oz or 50 g of bland industrial cheese a week and there weren't any small producers left.

The direct result of this is that British people eat less cheese than any other European nation apart from Spain and Portugal. In Austria, Belgium, Finland, the Netherlands, Sweden, Denmark, Italy, Germany, Greece and France, people eat more than 16 kg of cheese per person every year. Britain is way below this with 10 kg. You will get through 791 kg of cheese in your life. Though the number of small cheese producers is rising – there are now around 60 more than at the end of the Second World War – nearly all the cheese you eat will be industrially produced Cheddar that is not all that different from the Government Cheddar of the 1940s.

Local cheese from your local dairy has bourgeois, pretentious, foodie associations. There is a theoretical past where free-range, organic chickens, dry-cured bacon, local cider, real ale, bread from the baker's oven, freshly laid eggs, hand-made butter and cheese were simply the sorts of things the average person ate every day without even thinking about it, but the average person never lived in this past.

The truth is that for the average person getting enough good food has always been a bit of a problem. Until 150 years ago just getting clean water was difficult, while most of the milk brought unrefrigerated and unpasteurised into towns would be diluted with water and on the turn. There would be a constant risk of botulism from tinned food; salmonella, E. coli and other murderous bugs from everything else. Meat was very expensive, so you ate offal or perhaps even bought other people's leftovers. Culinarily speaking, for the average person the past was not a great place to live.

Selling high-quality, sustainably produced food as a reinstatement of a traditional part of British life that somehow got lost during the Second World War does not reflect reality. Providing these things to the average person is actually as startling and modern an innovation as the Internet, genetics, artificial intelligence, nanotechnology or any of the other technologies with the potential to change our lives for the better.

CHILDREN

If children are the meaning of life, then the most meaningful life ever lived was that of Moulay Ismail Ibn Sharif, the Sultan of Morocco, who is said to have sired 888 children. He is unlikely to have known all their names or their charming little ways, organised 17 birthday parties a week, taught them to ride bicycles, waved them off to school, told them bedtime stories, taken them into his bed at night when they had bad dreams or ever really known them at all. He would, however, be assured that he had given his genes the greatest possible chance of surviving him and being spread around the world.

To achieve this level of breeding success you have be a ruthless and powerful individual. The more ruthless and powerful you are, the more successful you will be. In the late twelfth and early thirteenth centuries Genghis Khan raped and pillaged his way across Asia, founding the biggest land empire in history. If you have North African ancestors, there is a chance that you are related to Moulay Ismail 'The Bloodthirsty', but an estimated 1 in 200 of all the men alive today are directly related to Genghis Khan.

Even Genghis is outperformed by an unknown individual who lived perhaps 2,000 years before him. We are all related to this person, who probably lived out a quiet, average existence and may only have had one child. Our most recent common ancestor is not so much a person as an idea from population genetics, which takes what we understand about sexual reproduction and applies it to the size and mobility of the current population. Using statistical techniques you can then work out how far back you would have to go before everyone alive today would inevitably have one ancestor in common. There is some dispute about the influence of explorers in the sixteenth and seventeenth centuries who may or may not have brought genetic material to every remote tribe on Earth. You also have to make assumptions about the length of generations. So, the estimates of when our most recent common ancestor was alive vary between 1,000 and 8,000 years ago.

You can apply similar techniques to the mitochondria present in all animal cells. These tiny lozenge-shaped structures are how our cells turn nutrients into energy. They have their own DNA and you inherit them exclusively from your mother. Using what we know about how fast mitochondrial DNA evolves gives us the mathematical concept of a shared common female ancestor – Mitochondrial Eve. Arguments over how fast mitochondrial DNA evolves give widely varying estimates for how long it might take one woman's descendants to entirely populate the world. Sometime between 6,000 and 140,000 years. Tracing the Y chromosome, which is exclusive to the male line, gives us Y-chromosomal Adam, who is estimated to have lived between 60 and 90,000 years ago. A common misconception is that these individuals represent evolutionary bottlenecks, when a catastrophe reduced humanity to a few survivors we are all descended from. There is no evidence for this and no requirement for it either. Nor are these theoretical individuals fixed in time. As the date of now moves forward, so does the date when these individuals lived, which means one day it could be you.

If you are a man 60,000 years from now it is possible that you will be Y-chromosomal Adam. If you are a woman it might take up to 140,000 years to become Mitochondrial Eve. In a mere 3,000 years, either of you may be able to outperform Gengis Khan and claim to be the Great[100]-grandparent of everyone alive. All you have to do is have a child.

The average Briton will be involved in the creation of 1.6 children in his or her lifetime. Assuming you share the costs with the other parent, you will be liable for 0.8 of every figure that follows.

The Cost of a Child survey, which is carried out every year by the insurance and investment group Liverpool Victoria, currently puts the average cost of raising a child to the age of 21 at £194,000. Childcare will cost £53,818, though this assumes that your child will be in full-time day care from six months old until they start school (£35,854) and go on to use after-school and holiday clubs (£14,319). Education is the next biggest expense – £50,240 – but only if you pay university tuition fees, rent, bills and living expenses (£34,300). It isn't explained where the other £16,000 is spent.

There are unavoidable expenses that are closer to what you might actually spend: £17,205 on food, £13,281 on clothes, £11,920 on holidays, £10,313 on hobbies and toys, £2,366 on furniture, £7,415 on leisure and recreation, £1,037 on unexplained personal items and £4,144 on pocket money – an extravagant £6 a week from the age of five onwards.

The £194,000 also includes £11,207 to pay for birthday and Christmas presents, driving lessons and a car. You will also spend £10,826 on babysitting so that you can get away from this pampered little monster every once in a while.

In their defence it should be said that LV do introduce the survey by saying that parents *could* rather than *will* spend £194,000 raising a child to 21. All the same, it might be better named the annual Cost of Raising a Child if You Pander to Their Every Whim, Work Like a Slave and Hardly Ever See Them survey. Most people simply could not afford to raise a child if this is what it cost. Instead, childcare will require juggling between friends and relatives. University will involve student loans and part-time jobs if they go at all, and the average child doesn't. You are also unlikely to be giving your five-year-old six shiny pound coins every Saturday, and not all the clothes they wear will be new. The average parent will make considerable savings on all of these figures, taking the total to well below £100,000.

At the bare minimum, feeding and clothing a child to the age of 16 – when it becomes legal for your child to start creating their own children – will cost £24,307. Nearly 4 million British children live below this level. Being born into poverty has a profound effect on how your life will play out. At just two years old you are already likely to be showing a lower level of attainment than a child from a better-off family. By six, less able children from more affluent families will be overtaking you, and ten years later you are likely to do half as well in your exams before leaving school at the earliest opportunity. As an adult you are less likely to be able to find a job and more likely to have mental-health problems, suffer from chronic illnesses and die younger. You are also much more likely to be bringing up your own children in poverty, and so it goes ... This problem is getting worse. In 1979, 10 per cent of British children were living in poverty; today the proportion is 30 per cent.

Once children are properly clothed and fed, time is more important than money. No matter how much you spend on school trips, Christmas presents and cello lessons, the amount of time you spend with your children is likely to have a greater effect on their mental health, happiness and general satisfaction with life than anything else.

The Centre for Longitudinal Studies (CLS) is responsible for one of Britain's longest-running research projects on the effects of childhood and upbringing on later life. The initial group of children were born in 1958 and further groups were added in 1970 and 2000. The studies involve multiple surveys of thousands of individuals born in these years carried out at regular intervals throughout their lives. Over the course of 50 years a huge amount of information about education and employment, family and parenting, physical and mental health and social attitudes has been collected and analysed.

One of the discoveries has been a clear link between how involved parents are with their children up to the age of 16 and how well, happy and able to cope with the world the children are in later life. This holds true for all income groups and the effects of parenting will persist right through their lives. Unfortunately, the study has also revealed how we have got worse rather than better at spending time with our children.

It is usually working mothers who are made to feel guiltiest about the time they are away from their children, but the CLS studies haven't found any real difference between the parenting of working and non-working mothers. In fact, working mothers are significantly more likely to read to their children regularly, which suggests that they tend to compensate for the time they miss by making more of an effort when they are around. It is really working fathers who should feel guilty.

The general belief is that with the advent of the New Man, men are spending more time with their children and taking more responsibility for childcare. It is felt that this is something that we are now doing better. The reality is very different. In the 1960s, 60 per cent of fathers played an equal role in childcare, but by the late 1980s it had dropped to 46 per cent. In 2000 it was 39 per cent. There is a strong link between how well qualified and well paid fathers are and how involved they will be in their children's lives. Only 39 per cent of graduate fathers in professional or managerial jobs play an equal role in bringing up their children, compared with 60 per cent of fathers who work in semi-skilled and unskilled jobs.

The New Man is more likely to have been present at the birth of his child, but from then on will play less of a role than ever before in the 16 years that follow. This may not be good for the children, as the CLS research suggests that children with fathers who are actively involved in their lives tend to have higher IQs, be more socially mobile and are generally happier in later life. An effect that will outlive either of their parents by many years. While 70 per cent of women feel that they have plenty of time to spend with their children, only 22 per cent of men do. In fact, more than 50 per cent of fathers feel that they do not spend enough time with their children. Perhaps this is the real identity of the New Man: a father who wants to be more involved with his children but can't quite organise things to make it happen. The possibility of becoming Y-chromosomal Adam 60,000 years from now isn't much of a consolation.

CHIPS

The Queen hosts a state banquet for visiting leaders or monarchs every six months or so. Just laying the table takes two days, a process that is superintended by the Yeoman of the China and Glass Pantries, who folds all 170 napkins himself. The 32 flower arrangements take the Royal Florist and a team of flower arrangers 36 hours to prepare. One hundred footmen and pages wait on the guests, who will be guarded while they eat by the Queen's Bodyguard of the Yeoman of the Guard in full ceremonial uniforms complete with halberds. Curiously, the menu is always written in French, though there is usually an effort to have British produce. This is an important part of the general boasting about what a great place Britain is that goes along with these occasions. While the potato is one of Britain's most important crops and the chip is undoubtedly our favourite way of eating it, they are not served at state banquets. However delicious they may be, chips are not and never have been posh food.

Unlike other ubiquitous foods such as tea, coffee, chocolate, baked beans, ice cream, pineapples and bananas, the chip did not come to Britain and have a brief period as the most fashionable and exclusive thing you could eat before slowly spreading to the general population. No, the chip is on a different trajectory. It has always been a staple of the general population and is slowly working its way up.

The first mention of anything resembling a chip in Britain was in a low-budget cookery book of 1854 called *Shilling Cookery*, which contains a recipe for thin-cut potatoes cooked in oil. No one recorded the arrival of

The Chip in Britain, it certainly wasn't boasted about at fashionable parties, and by the time anyone noticed it, the chip had been around for years. The earliest mention of chips in the world comes from Belgium, where it is recorded that poor people in certain regions were in the habit of accompanying their meals with small fried fish. When the river was frozen, they would cut potatoes into long thin fish shapes and fry them instead.

In the early nineteenth century, chips were a northern working-class staple and were eaten on their own. In the south, particularly in London, fish fried in batter was very popular, but there were no chips. Battered fish is a Sephardi dish brought to Britain in the seventeenth century by Portuguese Jews. When the same dish was introduced in Japan by Spanish and Portuguese traders it became tempura. In Britain, of course, it eventually became deep-fried Mars Bars. Fish and chips finally joined forces in the 1860s with the first combined fish-and-chip shops appearing more or less simultaneously in Oldham and London.

In a lifetime, you will eat 333 portions of fish and chips bought from a chippy, costing you £1,566. You will also spend £1,401 on oven chips. In Britain, 1.25 million tonnes of chips are eaten every year. Your lifetime's share is 1.63 tonnes, which is enough to provide each of the 170 guests at a state banquet with a 9.5 kg portion. Served carefully, this would form a crisp golden cone that would easily cover the entire place setting – the six glasses, the ten pieces of cutlery and the exquisitely folded napkin.

CHOCOLATE

A particularly persistent urban myth is that you swallow spiders in your sleep. The next time you see a spider, blow on it. They do not like being blown on, which is why even if your bedroom was seething with spiders, the bit around your nose and mouth would be clear. It is therefore very unlikely that you will swallow any spiders while you are sleeping. You may swallow the occasional fly or other bug while you are talking or riding a bike, but this is insignificant compared to the number of flies, ants, spiders and other arthropods you are going to get through mixed up with your food.

You will eat up to 680 g of insect body parts a year – 54 kg of legs, 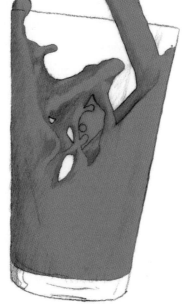 thoraxes, heads, wings and abdomens in a lifetime. This is an inevitable consequence of eating stuff that has been grown, transported, stored and manufactured in the real world. Insects aren't bad for you, but we are squeamish about them. This is a bit odd really, when you consider that most people are not squeamish about prawns, shrimps or lobsters, which are essentially insects that live under the sea. In many other countries land insects are eaten just as readily as marine ones. Witchety grubs, crickets, ants and maggots are all good sources of protein and vitamins. A big bowl of deep-fried grasshoppers makes an excellent snack with beer, apparently.

Insects get everywhere. As they do no harm, by and large there is no pressure to keep insects out of food completely, just an upper limit on how many are allowed. This is partly cosmetic – finding a grasshopper's leg in a sandwich is not a pleasant experience – and partly because high numbers of insects are a sign of careless manufacture, which can lead to more serious problems.

Cocoa beans come exclusively from the tropics where most of the world's 10,000,000,000, 000,000,000 insects live. It is

hardly surprising, then, that 100g of chocolate is allowed to contain up to 80 insect fragments before any action will be taken. In a lifetime, you will munch your way through 791 kg of chocolate and along with it up to 632,800 insect fragments.

If you buy fair trade then at least some of the £2,911 you are going to spend on a lifetime's chocolate will help to improve the lives of the people who grow and harvest the ingredients. On the other hand, non-fair-trade chocolate may rely on child slave labour and the exploitation of some of the poorest farmers in the world. The number of insects in either is the same.

CHRISTMAS

In theory only Christians celebrate Christmas, and the other five main religions in Britain have nothing to do with it. According to the 2001 Census, this would mean that nearly 30 per cent of people do not celebrate Christmas. This is clearly not the case. In fact, the festival we now call Christmas existed long before any of these religions reached our shores. Perhaps the real reason for the season is simply a deep-seated human need to hold a massive shindig at the start of the winter.

It is the most expensive day of the year. The majority of your money will go on gifts. In a lifetime, you will receive 954 Christmas presents. You can expect to give a similar number at a total cost of £21,725, wrapped up in 108 m^2 of wrapping paper.

Every year around 10 per cent of Christmas presents are either immediately thrown away or donated to charity shops. That means that in your life you are going to spend £2,172.50 on presents that people either do not like or do not want.

Christmas is a time of sharing. If we all spent Christmas alone eating under our personal Christmas tree, the following figures would all be 79, which is the number of Christmases you can expect to participate in. Celebrating those 79 shared Christmases will require: 45 Christmas trees, 39 turkeys and 33 Christmas puddings.

A lifetime's supply of Christmas decorations will cost you £823. You will also spend a ludicrous £658 on Christmas crackers. You will send a total of 2,212 cards. If you send these first class it will cost you £796.32. If you are a bit better organised you will save yourself £199.08 by sending them all second class.

These figures become even more outrageous when you consider that they represent what you will spend on just one day of your life. The bill for all 79 Christmases comes to £30,421. If you lived every day at this pitch of excess you would require £11,125,335, which more or less explains the lifestyle of Elton John.

CIDER

Cider has a shorter and slightly shadier history in Britain than beer. Druids are thought to have planted apple trees near sacred oak groves, but this is more likely to have been because mistletoe – a symbol of immortality – thrives on apple trees rather than because the trees were being cultivated for their small, sour fruit. Apples suitable for eating or making cider only came to Britain with the Romans.

In the past, cider has been less widespread than beer as grain can be grown almost anywhere in Britain and apples can't. Orchards also take more looking after than fields of grain and have to be nurtured for years before you get any return. This makes apples and cider more vulnerable to events. When the Romans left, apple-growing was more or less abandoned for 600 years until the Normans re-established it. Then the Black Death and the Wars of the Roses destroyed fruit production. Things got going again under Henry VIII, who began importing trees from France, and cider drinking increased continuously until the late seventeenth century. Then, the agricultural revolution meant that labour-intensive orchards were replaced with fields of grain or grazing for cattle.

Cider is also trickier to make than beer. It is acidic, which means that for centuries the use of lead and copper in cider presses poisoned and killed people, until the scientific expertise needed to prove this developed in the nineteenth century. Interrupted supply and bad PR meant that cider always lagged behind other alcoholic beverages until suddenly, about ten years ago, cider became fashionable. While this is partly down to clever marketing, it would not have been possible without the help of Her Majesty's Revenue & Customs.

All alcohol is subject to excise duty. This is not charged in a rational manner that relates to alcohol content but rather to the sort of drink the alcohol is in. The duty on 100 l of wine is £194, whereas on 100 l of beer it is £14.96 for every 1 per cent of strength, and on low-alcohol drinks it is £60 per 100 l. Spirits are £21.35 per 1 per cent strength. Cider, however, can be up to 7.5 per cent pure alcohol and only cost £28.90 in duty. An equivalent amount of alcohol from beer will cost you nearly four times as much (£112) in duty. Cider is simply the cheapest way to get drunk.

In the last 20 years British alcohol consumption has gone up by 31 per cent. Most of this growth has come from younger drinkers. They have less money to spend, and they are spending it on cider. In recent years, growth in cider sales has outstripped all other alcoholic drinks and Britain is now the biggest consumer of cider in the world – around about 3 million pints every day. Your lifetime share of this amounts to 1,385 pints.

CLOTHES

The people who study wildebeest, zebras and other herd animals on the plains of Africa have a problem. Sometimes it is necessary to capture one of these animals to take samples. Before being released, they are marked so that they can be recognised in the future. The problem is, your study animal is almost guaranteed to be the next one eaten by lions.

At first it was thought that the lingering effects of the tranquilliser might be to blame, but no matter how carefully they made sure the animal was fit to return to the herd, the same thing would happen. Over and over again. Finally, they realised that it was the marking that sealed the animal's fate. A lion faced with a herd of zebras can chase after one, then lose it, chase after another one, lose it and so on until the lion is too tired to chase any more. The zebras share the running away and don't get that tired. However, if the lion has a way of choosing just one zebra and chasing it relentlessly, it is much more likely to catch it. So, if you are a zebra, it is important to fit in. Your stripes are a uniform that camouflages your individuality so you can blend in with the herd and run laughing from the lions. Unless, of course, you have a patch of marking dye on your bottom.

You are unlikely to be chased and eaten by a lion no matter how you dress, but fitting in or not fitting in is something you have in common with the zebra, the wildebeest and all the other herd animals. Roll up one trouser leg, go to the shops and buy some milk. Put your coat on back to front

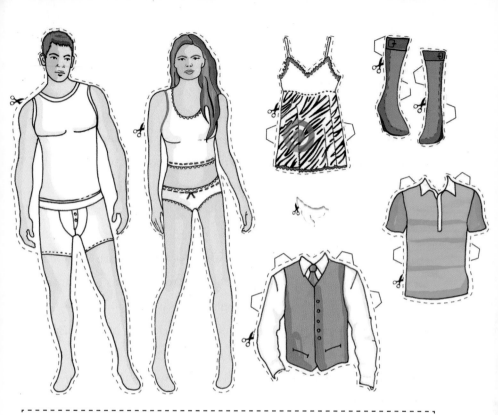

and get on a bus. Wear odd shoes for a day. If you are a man, put women's underwear on over your suit. If you are a woman, wear a large pair of Y-fronts like a shawl, with your head through one leg hole and an arm through the other. Do any of these things if you dare and see what kind of a day you have. Being chased and eaten by a lion might not seem so bad.

If clothing was just about warmth and modesty no one would pay any attention to what you wear. But we are all acutely conscious of the language of clothes. The best theory for fashion is put forward by Quentin Bell in his book *On Human Finery*. His idea is that the average person copies people

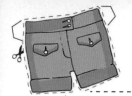

above them in status and the people at the top constantly have to change the way they dress to avoid looking like the people lower down. This creates the chaotic evolution and recycling of styles that we call fashion. Ironically, refusing to join in with fashion often creates new fashion, whether it is the lazy we-don't-care-what-we-look-like of grunge or the deliberately perverse bollocks-to-you-all! of punk.

Working with the cheapest possible prices, you can buy a complete change of clothing for every day of the week, two pairs of shoes and a jacket for under £100. That would satisfy the basic requirements of civilisation that you cover your nakedness and would also keep you warm and dry. The average person actually spends £504 a year on clothing. The additional £400 is pretty much the added cost of fashion. In a lifetime you will spend £39,866 on clothes, meaning that £31,600 of it will go on the desire to fit in or stand out.

Even if you don't care, you will be somewhat at the mercy of fashion. First of all, short of having clothes specially made, you can only buy what is in the shops – just try and get hold of a pair of half-mast burgundy Sta-Prest trousers on the high street these days. Secondly, people will come to conclusions about you based on what you are wearing. And, let's face it, you will do the same.

COLDS

There are more than 100 different cold viruses. We seem to have some sense of this because we usually talk about catching *a* cold rather than *the* cold, as if we are aware of just how many there are out there. These viruses have been with us for a long time. When you catch a cold you are the latest link in a chain of people coughing and sneezing in each other's faces that stretches back millions of years.

Under an electron microscope the rhino-virus that causes most colds looks like a tiny version of the death star. In order to infect you, just one of these malevolent spheres has to find a cell it can dock with. For cold viruses these are all inside your nose. Once the virus has landed and docked it forces its way into the cell and starts to replicate. At this stage, your body has no idea it is under attack. However, around 12 hours later the infected cell bursts, releasing a wave of invaders, and your body mobilises the troops in what can only be described as a massive overreaction.

All the symptoms of a cold are produced by a variety of substances called inflammatory mediators, which your body produces in response to the infection. These are what set off your sneeze and cough reflexes and the overproduction of mucus. If that wasn't enough, they also dilate the blood vessels in your nose, making it hard to breathe as well as stimulating nerve fibres, which causes you pain. All this adds up to a week of feeling dreadful. Bizarrely, none of it helps fight the virus. Around a quarter of the times you get infected, your inflammatory mediators will not come in to play, you will not have any symptoms, you will not feel ill and you will clear the virus from your body just as quickly.

While the inflammatory mediators are ruining your week with their pointless vandalism, your white blood cells are quietly eradicating the virus by destroying the infected cells before the infection can spread. At the same time, your body is developing a special force of white blood cells and antibodies that will give you some immunity to that virus in the future. In order to survive, the virus has to make it to another nose before this happens.

Though viruses remain infectious for a short amount of time on hands, doorknobs and tissues, they can only reproduce in people's noses. To survive, colds must constantly be moving from nose to nose. In closed, isolated communities like Antarctic research stations people do not get colds because the viruses run out of fresh noses and everyone is immune. But as soon as someone brings in a new virus from outside, everyone gets ill.

It usually takes your immune system about a week to kill off a cold. You can expect to get three colds a year, a total of 237 in your life. Three and a half years with dilated blood vessels, aching limbs and a constant oozing of snot.

Colds are an almost uniquely human ailment. They thrive because of our habit of living in giant colonies equipped with banisters, telephones, doorknobs, cutlery and lift buttons, with people who are constantly hugging, kissing, coughing, sneezing, shaking hands and picking their noses.

The good news is that as you deal with each virus you retain some immunity and are less likely to catch that particular cold again. The bad news is that there are more than 100 of them to collect and we live on a small, cold, damp island with 120 million British nostrils for them to hide in.

CONDOMS

Before it was called syphilis, syphilis had different names in different countries. These were often the name of the country your country caught it from. So the Dutch called it the Spanish disease, in Russia it was known as the Polish disease, the Turks called it the Christian disease and, depressingly, the island paradise of Tahiti called it the British disease.

In 1564, when the Italian doctor and anatomist Gabriello Fallopio's treatise on syphilis was published, it bore the title *De Morbo Gallico – On The French Disease*. His treatise contains the first written reference to the condom. Fallopio (after whom Fallopian tubes are named) studied men who were using condoms made from linen soaked in herbs and chemicals. 'I tried the experiment on eleven hundred men, and I call immortal God to witness that not one of them was infected,' he announced, and suggested that condoms be used to prevent the spread of syphilis.

The first part of the condom design problem is simple – bodily fluids must not be exchanged in either direction. In this it is similar to making a waterproof shoe, a wine glass or a barrel. The second part of the design problem is harder – it mustn't feel like you have a waterproof shoe, a wine glass or a barrel on the end of your penis. Though there are records of Japanese condoms made from

tortoise-shell and animal horns these are exceptions and condoms have generally been made from the thinnest suitable materials available at the time, such as oiled silk paper, thin leather and sheep intestines.

The caecum – the first part of the large intestine – of a sheep is very thin, very durable and easy to come by. The membrane would be washed, scraped and treated with lye – a caustic-soda solution – to stop it from going off, washed again, then sewn into a condom shape. It would have to be soaked to make it supple before use and tied firmly with a ribbon to keep it in place. In his memoirs, Casanova described this process as 'putting on my English riding coat before mounting'. Afterwards it would have to be carefully rinsed and hung up to dry. In the background of erotic prints of the late eighteenth and early nineteenth centuries you can sometimes see little wooden drying trees festooned with condoms. In the foreground, their owners, powdered wigs askew, are still cavorting with their companions of the night before. The comic possibilities of taking the wrong condom home from the brothel have been overlooked by the writers of the time, but it must have happened occasionally.

The first rubber condoms became available in the 1850s, after Charles Goodyear discovered the process of vulcanising rubber to make it flexible and elastic. Early rubber condoms were made by wrapping strips of raw rubber around wooden moulds. Chemical solutions were used to cure the rubber and weld it together, then the condom was trimmed and buffed by hand. The result resembled a bicycle inner tube and provided all the erotic potential of a wellington boot. The invention of liquid latex in the 1920s meant that condoms could be made by dipping glass penis moulds into liquid rubber and this is the way condoms are still made today. Early condoms were dipped four or five times, but higher quality materials mean that modern latex condoms need to be dipped twice only and are much thinner. In the last ten years the use of plastic or polyurethane has probably made condoms as thin as they are ever likely to get.

In a lifetime, you will get through 932 condoms, all of which are available free on the NHS. You may get through considerably more of these for non-sexual purposes. If you are in the army, your standard-issue condoms will keep muck out of the barrel of your weapon; if you are a soil scientist, they will keep your samples dry. In moist, humid environments they can be used to keep microphones, mobile phones and other sensitive equipment functioning, while in India sari-makers rub lubricated condoms on their spools of thread to make them run better.

Bringing the most sensitive parts of different bodies together without it feeling like there is something in between is very difficult. The ideal condom would feel like the inside of a woman for the man and the outside of a man for the woman. But no matter how thin you make them, polyurethane and latex do not feel like human tissue. Sheep's intestines have a real advantage over modern materials as they are actually made of skin. This is why you can still buy lambskin condoms. They are no longer hand-stitched by high-class glove-makers, but are mass-produced and sold presoaked in foil packages like normal condoms. They cost about £3 each, compared with around 70 p for the most advanced polyurethane models, while latex condoms are free on the NHS. As well as being expensive, lambskin is full of pores that may be too small for sperm to fit through but which are no barrier to bacteria and viruses. Fallopio would have got very different results if the men in his study could have afforded the best condoms available at the time.

The most successful diseases do not kill you, at least not immediately; they linger while you go about your life spreading the infection. Anything that increases the chances of it spreading makes a disease more successful. The most widespread human disease is the cold. It doesn't disable you and the infection provokes your body into doing things that help it spread – coughing, sneezing and dribbling snot. For a sexually transmitted disease, the best strategy would be to make your host sexually irresistible. Early syphilis did the exact opposite.

The first cases of syphilis appeared in Europe in the 1490s. It was a horrifying disease that quickly rendered you a sexual pariah, covered you head to foot in weeping pustules, ate through your soft tissues like acid, caused lumps of flesh to fall off and killed you within a few months. Bacteria can evolve very fast. In the right conditions, they can divide and reproduce themselves every 10–20 minutes. At this rate, bacteria can go through as many generations as there are between us and the chimpanzee in under nine years. By the 1550s the early, highly aggressive form of syphilis had moderated into the slow form we have now. This can take decades to run its course and has a long latent period where the disease is not visible, thereby greatly increasing opportunities for it to be passed on.

The first sign that you have syphilis is a chancre, or painless ulcer, that appears at the site of infection but will disappear of its own accord a few weeks later. A few months after that you might start getting rashes, fevers and headaches, but these will also clear up after a few weeks. The primary and secondary phases of syphilis usually take less than a year. Then the disease goes into hiding all over your body. The latent phase may last for years.

About 25 per cent of people make a complete recovery. The other 75 per cent may think they have made a complete recovery, but then tertiary syphilis sets in. Large tumour-like growths called granulomas appear randomly about the body, creating tennis-ball-sized bulges in the skin or deep inside constricting organs and throwing the whole body into an inflammatory crisis. At the same time there will be severe headaches, stomach pains and then, as the disease takes control, blindness, deafness, paralysis, insanity and death.

A game that biographers and historians often play at is diagnosing the ailments of long-dead celebrities. This is given an added spice in the case of syphilis because it is only ever sexually transmitted. Insanity, creativity and genius are also commonly linked. Napoleon, Beethoven, Van Gogh, Henry VIII, Keats, Nietzsche, Hitler, Ivan the Terrible, James Joyce, Abraham Lincoln and his wife, Sarah, and Lenin have all been posthumously diagnosed with syphilis. Some notable figures, such as Schubert, Toulouse-Lautrec, Karen Blixen, Al Capone, Gaugin and Schumann, were diagnosed during their lifetime. In the nineteenth and early twentieth centuries an

estimated 15 per cent of the adult population were infected. Given the link between fame and opportunities for having sex, it is likely that more than 15 per cent of all celebrities of the past had syphilis.

It has also been speculated that the first outbreak of syphilis occurred just after Columbus returned from the New World. This seems to be supported by studies of pre-Columbian bones on both sides of the Atlantic. Disease and travel have always been related. There is a particularly strong link between sexually transmitted disease and war, when very large numbers of fit young men are sent to foreign countries to kill people, confront their own mortality and miss their wives and girlfriends for years at a time. All of the European nations involved in the First World War understood this and condoms were standard issue along with the uniform, boots and steel helmet. At the time condoms were illegal in America and so were not issued to American troops. Despite entering the war late, it is estimated that 75 per cent of American soldiers returned with some form of sexually transmitted disease. The resultant epidemic helped to force through the legalisation of condoms for the control of disease. They did not become legal for birth control in the USA until 1936.

Unless you include abstinence, modern condoms are still the most effective protection against sexually transmitted diseases. After the Second World War, the triumph of antibiotics meant that there was a brief period when sexually transmitted diseases were less of a worry than ever before. Suddenly, in the 1980s, with the growing awareness of HIV/Aids, sexually transmitted diseases regained their power to terrify people. In the space of less than a year the condom went from the realms of taboo and murmured euphemism – 'Something for the weekend, sir?' – to being handed out free at shopping centres by people dressed up as enormous French letters, English riding coats, gentlemen's preservatives, rubber johnnies and love gloves.

Syphilis was finally given a name by an Italian and it is no longer known as the French disease in Italy or the Italian disease in France. In Britain, it was generally known as 'the pox', which has a genuine seventeenth-century feel to it. Syphilis also sounds like something only people in powdered wigs and velvet knee britches can get. Unfortunately, it is very much on the rise and, in common with other bacterial infections, it is evolving as fast as, if not faster than, our ability to develop antibiotics. One day it may once again become incurable. In 1998, 139 cases of syphilis were diagnosed at GUM clinics. In 2007 there were 2,680. A rise of 1,828 per cent. Perhaps a better name would be the Too Stupid to Use a Condom disease.

COWS

We take the domestication of animals for granted. It is impossible to imagine a world without them, but there must have been a time when no one had thought of it. Animals were wild and had to be tracked, stalked and then killed. The first person to have the idea that a wild animal might be captured, tamed and trained to stand about waiting patiently in a field until you were hungry changed the world.

Though there are around 150 large herbivores that might be suitable, we have only managed to domesticate a handful of them with any measure of success: pigs, goats, sheep, horses and cows. So why haven't we domesticated any of the fun animals, like zebras, giraffes, hippos, wildebeest or gazelles?

The truth is that only the most boring animals are suitable for domestication. Animals with violent personalities like the hippo, which will

attack you in a furious vegetarian rage whenever you approach, instantly rule themselves out. Zebras are also very bad-tempered and have resisted domestication. They remain truculent and aggressive and will attack humans and each other if they are kept in captivity. On the other hand, highly strung animals like the gazelle, which panic and flee from us, are also unsuitable. Although members of the deer family have been domesticated, they are tricky to keep happy. Farmed deer often need to be tranquillised so that they don't die from the sheer terror of being handled.

Entertainingly huge animals such as elephants can be trained to get along with people, but because they grow so slowly and consume so much vegetation in the process there is little point in keeping them for meat. There is also the problem of building an elephant-proof fence.

Another consideration is food. To keep animals in any quantities they have to be easy to feed. They must either be able to eat grass, which is found all over the world, or be very flexible and able to eat more or less any kind of

vegetation. Finally, they must be happy to breed in captivity. A surprising number of animals will not do this, either because they have complex court-ship rituals that need a particular environment or because they are painfully shy about it. Once all these criteria are taken into account, we are left with small herds of entertaining animals such as llamas, donkeys, water buffalo, camels, reindeer, yaks and alpacas. These animals have a value because they are suited to particular environments or tasks, but they are vastly outnum-bered by the more compliant and versatile pigs, goats, sheep, horses and cows that make up the majority of the world's domesticated animals.

The value of cows lies not just in the fact that they are prepared to stand about patiently waiting to be milked or eaten, but that they could also be used to pull a plough and produce copious amounts of fertiliser. The im-portance of the cow is tightly woven into our culture. The size of an acre is based on the ancient measurement of how much land one man could till in a day with the help of a cow. The letter 'A' is at least 4,000 years old and represents the skull of an ox, ∀. The cow is also inextricably linked to wealth. The words 'fee', 'feudal' and 'pecuniary' all come from ancient words for cattle. A favourable stock market – itself named after cattle trad-ing – is a bull market. A falling market is named after one of the least suit-able animals for farming – the bear.

There is one cow for every six people on Earth and in Britain we have precisely the average amount, with around 10 million cattle. Every year 2.6 million of these will be slaughtered. Of these, 450,000 are worn-out dairy cows and unwanted bull calves that will become pet food. The remaining 2.2 million will become Sunday dinners, steaks, burgers and other popular meat products. You can expect to get through 128 g of beef a week or 528 kg in a lifetime. As only 40 per cent of the cow is meat, this is equivalent to 1,320 kg of actual whole cow. We don't actually eat cows, of course: we eat heifers, steers and young bulls. The average weight of these at slaughter is 300 kg, which means you will get through 4.4 of them in a lifetime.

Domestication has been better for some animals than others. Dogs and cats are cherished pets and probably enjoy a much higher quality of life than they would do in the wild. While cows no longer have to run away from lions or wolves and have extended their range to almost every country on Earth, they do not get much else out of the bargain. In the wild, cows could expect to live for 25 years, whereas most beef cattle will be slaughtered before they are two. Dairy cows do a little better but generally they will be totally worn out by the age of five. Given the role they have played in the building of our civilisation, it is hardly surprising that there is something gently reproachful about the gaze of a cow.

CRISPS

Crisps were invented by George Crum on Wednesday 24 August 1853 at around 9 p.m. George was the chef at Moon's Lake House near Saratoga Springs. On that evening a customer sent back his chips complaining that they were too thick, too soggy and not salty enough. In a fit of pique, George shaved the potatoes ludicrously thin, then fried them till they were as brittle as glass and covered them in salt. Hopefully, if the customer wasn't injured by flying shards of potato shattering under his knife and fork, the salt would at least make him sick. Of course, the customer loved them, ordered more, told all his friends, who told all their friends and soon George Crum was the toast of Saratoga Springs with his own restaurant specialising in crisps …

With scientific discoveries the crucial thing is the date of first publication. The earliest reference to what we would describe as a crisp is in *The Virginian House Wife* by Mary Randolph, which was published in 1824. However, it is likely that people had been making crisps either deliberately or accidentally for centuries before anyone noticed or bothered to write about it. George Crum was not the first man to make a crisp any more than the Earl of Sandwich was the first man to put something between two slices of bread. To get the credit for cultural discoveries, it is more important to have the best story than it is to be actually first.

However, it is true that following that fateful night Saratoga chips became a local speciality featured on the menus of all the most expensive restaurants. It wasn't until the 1890s that someone had the idea of selling them in grocery shops. By the 1920s you could go into a grocer's anywhere in the USA and buy a scoopful of potato chips from a barrel. Meanwhile in London you could buy a greaseproof paper bag of crisps from the back of Frank Smith's pony and trap. At the time, the founder of Smith's Crisps was pretty much the only man in Britain making crisps. After the war he was joined by Henry Walker, and soon after that a Scottish baker founded Golden Wonder, which were the first crisps to be sold ready-salted.

Crisps remained either plain or salted for 101 years until Tayto crisps came along in 1954. At the time, Tayto crisps were being made more or less by hand in two small rooms in Dublin. Depressed by the blandness of ready-salted crisps, the owner of the company, Joe 'Spud' Murphy, ordered one of his eight employees to come up with a flavoured crisp. The employee, a man called Seamus Burke, working on nothing more sophisticated than a kitchen table, came up with cheese and onion flavour. It was an overnight success and crisp magnates from all over the world flew in to Dublin with suitcases full of money to buy the secret formula. Salt and vinegar flavour followed soon after and we now have the ridiculous situation where entire supermarket aisles are given over to crisps.

Of course a lot of the things we call crisps nowadays are not actually crisps. They can be deep-fried savoury foams of cornstarch or extruded and baked pastes of wheat flour, oil and whey. As long as they are salty, oleaginous and come in a small plastic bag puffed up with nitrogen to keep them fresh, we recognise them as crisps.

Just under 11 billion packets of crisps are consumed in Britain every year, more than all the other European countries put together, apart from Ireland. You will eat 175 packets every year of your life, or 13,842 packets in total. The most popular flavour is ready-salted, which has about 26 per cent of the market. If you wanted to buy an average lifetime's supply of crisps you would need 3,599 bags of ready-salted, 2,768 cheese and onion, 2,491 salt and vinegar, and 969 bags each of prawn cocktail and beef, which share fourth place. The remaining 3,046 bags could go on those experimental flavours that come and go – hedgehog, cajun squirrel, shark fin, chilli and chocolate, and (it's just a matter of time) cannibal feast. Gathered together, a lifetime's worth of crisps weighs 617 kg. As there is about 1.05 ml of cooking oil per gram of crisps, you will also incidentally drink down 648 l of cooking oil.

DATA

Though it is possible to find things out from statues and pictures, writing – whether pressed into clay tablets or scratched on to walrus tusks – is the only way to preserve complicated information. For a long time the problem of reproducing the written word meant that knowledge spread slowly.

There might be only one copy of even the most famous books. So, to be well read, you would also have to have been well travelled. If you wanted to read Aeschylus you would have needed to visit the great Library in Alexandria, which had the only complete copy of his plays. Unfortunately, having so few copies of everything made knowledge vulnerable. The Library in Alexandria burned on five different occasions, which is one of the reasons why only seven of Aeschylus' 80 plays have survived.

In the last 2,000 years, we have lost nearly all of the ancient Greek drama and most of the poetry. Lots of the Bible is missing, as is everything written by emperors Nero, Augustus, Caligula and Claudius (who wrote so many books they extended the library in Rome to accommodate them), and almost everything by Julius Caesar. All of Shakespeare's original manuscripts have gone too and some of the plays. All that is left of the most famous writer in the English language are six signatures. Occasionally, things resurface. The 4,000-year-old Sumerian epic of Gilgamesh turned up in 1850 on some clay tablets buried under the rubble of Nineveh.

Reproducing and storing knowledge is no longer a problem. Knowledge gets lost now not because it is destroyed but simply because it gets buried under other knowledge. You can gauge how much use has been made of a piece of scientific research by looking at how often it has been cited in subsequent papers. This information is collected by the Institute for Scientific Information, whose figures suggest that between 50 and 75 per cent of articles are not cited by anyone else in the five years after publication. One conclusion might be that a lot of worthless research is going on. Another is that there is now so much research going on that no one has time to read it, worthless or otherwise. In 1950 around 4,000 chemistry articles were published. In 2000 it was more than 70,000. There has been a similar increase in all other forms of information: TV channels, radio stations, newspapers, magazines and books – this book is just one of over 120,000 titles that will be published in Britain in 2009. However, all forms of media have been dwarfed by the Internet, which didn't even exist 20 years ago.

There are more than 100 million registered Internet domains, each of which has the potential to contain vast quantities of information. Wikipedia alone has over 10 million web pages in its domain. The Internet is so big no one actually knows how many web pages there are, but estimates range from 70 to 500 billion, which is between 1,200 and 9,000 web pages for each person in Britain. The biggest search engines cover about eight billion pages – just over one-tenth of the lowest estimate. Again, a lot of this may be worthless information, but how can we tell if we can't even find it?

In the   1970s Michael Land from the School of Biological Sciences in Brighton published a description of how a lobster's eyes use mirrors instead of lenses to focus light. While this is a beautiful thing, it is not obviously useful. In a totally unrelated field, the photographic process used to make microchips relies on light with short wavelengths. The shorter the wavelength, the smaller the components can be. The problem is that you can't focus very short wavelengths like X-rays with lenses. However, you can do it with reflection. X-ray lithography that uses bundles of lead glass tubes to focus X-rays in the same way as a lobster's eye is now cutting-edge technology in microchip manufacture. The thing about knowledge is that there is no way of telling whether it is going to be useful. Accumulating knowledge is a good thing, but as a civilisation we tend to be disorganised about storing it. That is why data mining is now one of the biggest business-es in the world. You do it every time you Google something or someone.

In the past, your data storage will have consisted of books, a diary, some photo albums, letters, bank statements and a system of shoeboxes. All told, perhaps one gigabyte of computer memory. You will undoubtedly still have all those things, only now you will also have a mobile phone, a computer, an MP3 player, a collection of CDs, DVDs and videos, a video/DVD recorder, a digital camera and memory cards. These represent around 2,100 gigabytes of data. Enough to store a library of 2,100,000 books, which is many, many more than there were in the whole world when the great Library in Alexandria went up in flames.

DEATH

The boundary between life and death is not clearly defined. It isn't a line you cross over or a doorway you pass through and it isn't always obvious when somebody is dead. In the past your relatives and friends would make this decision, and the practice of holding a wake or watching over your body for a few days before burying it was at least partly about making sure you weren't going to recover.

Now, when you are dying, your relatives and friends will bring you to a hospital where trained staff have the equipment to pronounce you dead. Up to the 1950s this was pretty much a case of looking for a heartbeat. That is what being clinically dead means. Your heart has stopped. The problem with clinical death as a definition is that it can occasionally be reversed. Most of the tissues of your body can survive without fresh blood and oxygen from the heart for at least 30 minutes before they start to deteriorate. Your brain is much less resilient. After only a few minutes without oxygen, brain cells will start to be affected and the longer they go without, the more extensive the damage. Once circulation is restored the damaged cells start to function again, but just long enough to die. Lowering the temperature of the brain while it is recovering greatly increases the ability of brain cells to start functioning and continue living. The ability to do this means that death can be used to save lives.

Some surgical procedures, such as repairing blood vessels close to the heart or in the brain, can only be carried out if clinical death is deliberately induced. This is done by lowering body temperature to below 20 °C, which stops the heart beating and protects the brain from damage. Blood is drained from the body. The repairs are carried out. The blood is poured back in, the heart is restarted, the body is brought slowly back to a normal temperature and the patient will go on to live a long and happy life despite having been dead for an hour one Wednesday afternoon. Occasionally people who have died in peculiar circumstances such as falling into very cold water have been brought back to life after being clinically dead for hours. Cases like these are why they have a saying in emergency medicine that nobody is dead until they are warm and dead.

For thousands of years, coming back from clinical death was a rare enough occurrence to count as a miracle. Nowadays, an unexpected clinical death is treated as a medical emergency and not an irreversible state of affairs. In the right circumstances several lifetimes' worth of medical training and experience will come together in a room with hundreds of thousands of pounds' worth of equipment and get a heart, a life, started again.

The introduction in the 1960s of defibrillators, ventilators and other machines that could bring people back from clinical death and keep them alive even though they may never actually live again meant that another definition of death was needed. This gave rise to the concept of brain death. This state, which is measurable only by sophisticated instruments operated by trained staff, is now the ultimate legal definition of death and enables organs to be harvested from clinically alive bodies. The problem with brain death is that the brain is the most mysterious and least understood organ in the body. Our ideas about how it works and our tools for studying it are developing all the time. The result is that the definition of death is constantly being revised and refined. As part of the ongoing debate, every four years the Definition of Death Network holds an international symposium in Havana. The next one is in May 2012.

For practical purposes, death is the point where there is nothing more to be done and there is no hope left. The increasingly complicated moral and philosophical issues surrounding death are the result of just how far this point has moved in the last 60 years.

Everyone you have ever met or known will die. Of the 1,964 people you have known:

354 will die of heart disease or a heart attack;

275 will succumb to cancer;

36 of the men will die of prostate cancer;

45 of the women will die of breast cancer;

205 by stroke;

106 of chronic lower respiratory diseases;

127 of influenza or pneumonia;

72 from dementia;

30 from heart failure;

25 from urinary diseases;

19 from aortic aneurysm;

40 will be killed in an accident.

DOCTORS

You will visit the doctor 316 times in your lifetime. At the start of each of these visits, no matter how ill you are, when the doctor asks, 'How are you?' you will instinctively reply, 'I'm fine thank you'.

But you will not be fine. You will have an unexplained swelling, a sore throat, vomiting and diarrhoea, a mild fever, intense itchiness, blurred vision, dizziness, throbbing extremities, tenderness, discharges of pus and a loss of appetite.

Using your medical history, the evidence you provide and their own observations, the doctor will fit your illness into one of hundreds of different categories of ailment. Then you will be sent away to get better with some tips on how to make things easier and a prescription. More rarely, you will be passed up to the next level of health care for specialised diagnosis and treatment. All in all, in the average visit, you will see the doctor for 11.7 minutes.

One of the criticisms of this process is that it treats the illness and not the person. Treating the illness by treating the person is one of the main characteristics of alternative medicine.

There is no such thing as alternative medicine. If it works, then it is simply medicine. However, the history of medicine is much more than a history of this filtering process. All the most significant advances in medicine have come from our growing understanding of Life. Having this knowledge enables you to make better guesses about what *might* work. It enables you to invent rather than just discover and when you find something that works, you have a way of building on that knowledge to find something that works better. As most alternative medicine is based on ideas that contradict what is known or can be proved, arguments about alternative medicine tend to be just about whether they work at all.

When subjected to careful scrutiny, the placebo effect is usually found to be the only effective part of the alternative treatment being tested. In a recent study on acupuncture, people getting real acupuncture for their back pain did no better than people getting fake acupuncture. However, both these groups did better than the people getting no acupuncture at all. The message for acupuncturists is that their treatment for back pain does not work. Something they are unlikely to take on board. The message for medicine is that the rituals surrounding treatment are very important and that it might be a good idea for doctors to spend more time with their patients. The NHS has no trouble accepting this rather obvious conclusion, there just isn't enough money to pay for it.

Like all the professions you will rely on, you pay your doctor's wages. The average doctor earns £110,000, which means that your family doctor will cost you around £70 a year or £5,537 in a lifetime. Your 316 visits of 11.7 minutes each will add up to two and a half days – the same as a long weekend.

DOGS

Every dog is a descendant of the wolves that scavenged on the fringes of our Neolithic society, attracted by our camp fires and the rubbish we left behind.

Bizarre as it might seem, friendliness to humans is hereditary. This is because the levels of hormones and neurotransmitters that determine behaviour are controlled by genes. These chemicals also play an important role in how an animal develops. In the early 1950s a Russian geneticist called Dmitry Belyaev started an experiment to selectively breed foxes for friendliness. By only letting the tamest foxes breed he was amazed to find that over a few generations he not only had friendly, playful foxes who answered to their names, he also had foxes that were all sorts of different colours, with floppy ears, shorter noses and more rounded skulls. Foxes that were, in fact, more like dogs.

It is likely that this is how wolves started to become dogs. The scavenging wolves that had the least fear of humans would get the most food and would be more likely to survive and breed. Over successive generations these wolves grew less and less afraid until at some point their own changing natures and the cajoling of their new human friends were too much to resist and they willingly crossed the line dividing the wild from civilisation.

The complicity of dogs is probably why they were the first animals to be domesticated. Our ancestors found them useful as guards at night and for hunting during the day. Later, they came to be used for herding and protecting stock, which means that dogs are the only animals that have been with us since we were hunter-gatherers.

Over the last 14,000 years selective breeding has given us hundreds of different kinds of dog, from the massive, silent dogs with powerful jaws used to hunt wild boar to the tiny, cuddlesome pillows of fur with a leg at each corner for keeping ladies warm in carriages. Despite these extra-ordinary variations, all dogs belong to the same subspecies of the wolf. In theory, there is nothing other than problems of size and a mutual desire to eat each other preventing any domestic dog and a wolf from having a family together.

We are able to get on so well with dogs because of the similarities between wolf and human societies. We are both pack animals with complex social structures. We also share a language: we look at each other with puppy-dog eyes, we snarl, we bark, growl, show our teeth and respond badly to being stared at. We also like the same things: we run after balls, we hunt

for its own sake, we eat too much and fall asleep in front of the fire. We find puppies cute and treat them like children. We are suspicious of strangers and do not like intruders. Dogs slot right in to the human family.

If you own one of the 7.3 million dogs living in Britain today you are expected to provide it with a scientifically balanced diet and a standard of health care that is still unavailable to most of the human world. Over the 12.8 years of its life, the average dog will cost you around £505 a year to feed, keep healthy and supply with squeaky chew toys. That's £6,746 lavished on an animal you do not need to guard your herd of cows or help you run down a wild boar.

Instead you will spend around 3,326 hours walking this dog in the tamed wilderness of the local park while you think about which ready meal to defrost and your dog plays at being a wolf in the ornamental shrubbery. Then there are the 15,308 turds to be dealt with. Either you can clear them up or risk having them posted through your letter box.

Between the ages of two and 16 weeks, a puppy (which will cost you £282) learns all of its social skills. For wolves this is the time when it learns the rules of the pack and how to hunt. Once the 16 weeks are up, a dog's social skills are more or less fixed for life. In this time, it must learn the rules of the human – dog relationship and come to view all humans as other dogs. The way we treat dogs as puppies means that they never fully grow up. They retain the infantile respect for authority and the childish need for affection that are such prized qualities in a pet. This is why stray dogs do not return to the wild. Instead, they act like delinquent teenagers, skulking about on patches of waste ground and at the fringes of our civilisation. Like their ancestors 150,000 years before, they are waiting to be invited to the fireside.

DOMESTIC APPLIANCES

In the 1950s, the science-fiction vision of the future was of automated homes serviced by robots. Your Silicone Valet would brush your clothes and get you dressed for dinner while the Gourmatic Food Compiler assembled a meal atom by atom. At the table, you would be served by your faithful Robo-butler. Afterwards, you'd jump into the gyrocopter and go to Mars for your holidays. We are now living in that future and science has largely failed to deliver on those promises. However, we do have robots of a sort to wash clothes, keep our food cold, heat up pies and do the washing-up.

In a lifetime you will buy 3.5 washing machines, 3.4 fridges, 3.2 microwaves and 2.8 dishwashers. These will cost you a total of £5,141. The theory is that these things will improve your life by saving you time and effort.

Before the invention of washing machines the average household's washing took one person about six hours once a week. In 1900, the average person changed clothes less often. Underwear was changed fairly frequently, but you would expect to wear shirts and dresses for days, if not weeks, between washes, only changing the collars and the cuffs. If we had managed to keep these habits after the washing machine was introduced, a week's washing might only take a few minutes.

If you divide those six hours a week by the average household size for 1900 (4.6), you get just over 78 minutes per person, per week spent washing clothes. The Office for National Statistics' Time Use survey for 2005 reveals that the average person now spends 11 minutes a day washing clothes. This doesn't include the time the machine is at work it is just the time you will spend retrieving the washing from the places it gathers round the house, sorting it, loading and unloading the machine and the dryer, then hanging up the clothes, before airing, ironing, folding and putting them away. In total 77 minutes per week. So, the washing machine saves you about a minute a week, which you might easily waste making futile attempts to open a door as impregnable as the porthole of a bathysphere until the machine decides it is safe for you to do so.

Of course, if the household of 1900 used the same quantities of food, cutlery, crockery, clothing and bedding as you, they would have had no time to do anything else. If you buy a dishwasher, the amount of time you spend doing the washing-up will go down for a while. But then you will start to use more plates because you think that the dishwasher is taking the strain. As a result, the amount of time you spend dealing with the washing-up will start to creep up again. The indications are that all labour-saving devices are prey to this effect.

A study of 4,500 households in Australia concluded that most domestic technologies made no difference to the amount of time spent on domestic work. It is very strange, almost as if

RAGE PERSON 123

the level of housework is somehow predetermined. The vacuum cleaners, super-mops, dishwashers, microwaves, juicers, smoothie-makers, tumble-dryers, steam irons, automatic self-cleaning ovens and induction hobs, all of which have the potential to save us time, simply encourage us to take on more work.

The average person will spend 41 minutes a day cooking and washing up, 31 minutes cleaning and tidying; 11 minutes on laundry and 17 minutes on repairs and gardening. A daily total of 100 minutes. In a lifetime, five years and six months of housework.

DUST

You shed skin at the rate of 1.5 million cells an hour. This might sound like an avalanche, but these cells are very light so they will only amount to around 4.5 g a week. That's just 18 kg in a lifetime.

The belief that most housework involves cleaning up our own shed skin and the dust mites that feed on it is a myth. If you want you can puff 5 g of talcum powder into your house to see what a trivial contribution this makes to the overall level of dustiness and clear up this myth for yourself.

You are most likely to do a thorough dusting before people come to stay. When you wave them goodbye from the doorstep it might feel like they have gone, but remember, until you have wiped them off the top of the picture frames and emptied the vacuum into the bin, your guests haven't really left.

EARS

You will gradually lose your hearing over the course of your life. The higher frequencies will be the first to go and as you get older, lower and lower frequency bands will be affected. When it reaches the frequencies of talk and music, hearing loss will start to be a problem. By the age of 60, over 50 per cent of people are affected.

Hearing loss is not, however, an inevitable consequence of getting old. People who live with low levels of noise lose very little of their hearing as they get older. The reason your hearing will get worse is because of the accumulated damage from getting older in a noisy world. Protecting your hearing is as simple as avoiding loud noises, but, unfortunately, avoiding loud noises may not be all that simple. Noise complaints to local government have increased fivefold in the last 20 years. The world gets noisier every day and consequently we are going deaf more quickly. The average 40-year-old now has the hearing of the average 60-year-old in quieter times.

We are programmed to respond to noise. In the distant past loud noises would almost universally have been a sign of danger and your body does not discriminate between the rumble of an avalanche, a truck driving past your house or the *EastEnders* theme tune turned up too loud. Your body simply reacts to the volume of sound and produces stress hormones to prepare you for the impending threat.

You might feel that you get used to noise. Though you can ignore it, even stop noticing it after a while, the part of your brain that responds to noise as a threat is still reacting. In a modern city you can live 24 hours a day in a state of constant alert. Over long periods of time, the raised levels of stress hormones can have a real effect on your health. The World Health Organisation estimates that 3 per cent of deaths from heart disease in Europe are caused by environmental noise. This figure is the tip of a noise-damage pyramid that includes tinnitus, stroke, high blood pressure, sleep disturbance and the unnecessary hearing loss that will ultimately affect us all much earlier than it used to.

There are 6.5 million people over the age of 60 who need hearing aids in Britain. As only 2 million have them, you will get through a modest three sets in a lifetime. Privately, these will cost you £6,000 for state-of-the-art digital ones in both ears. NHS hearing aids are free, but you only get one ear's worth.

EGGS

Adding value is a fundamental idea in economics. Industry works by adding value to cheap raw materials and selling them at a profit. Starbucks takes 10 p worth of coffee and sells it to you for £2. The car industry turns metal, plastic, rubber and glass into cars. Intensive livestock production is a way of adding value to cheap grain by turning it into meat. This process has found its most complete and nightmarish expression in the production of chickens.

Chickens are descended from the red jungle fowl of southern Asia and were one of the first animals to be domesticated. As long as you provided a safe place for them to roost at night, they would hang about, foraging for themselves, eating scraps and providing you with eggs every day. When a bird came to the end of its egg-laying life, you ate it. As meat was a by-product of egg production, chicken was an expensive, occasional treat. By and large, this is how chickens were kept from the Stone Age to just after the Second World War.

Since the war, American and European governments have subsidised the production of grains such as wheat and barley. Intensive meat production was developed to take advantage of these cheap subsidised grains. Although cows and pigs are intensively farmed, things have been taken much further with the chicken, which has several unique features that make it particularly well suited to industrialised farming.

First of all, chickens produce eggs. In the wild, eggs enable birds to have more young than they could if they had to fly about pregnant. This means wild chickens can have between 12 and 20 offspring a year, while bats have only one or two. In captivity, eggs can be taken away and ar-tificially incubated, prompting the hen to lay more. In this way, a broiler hen can produce 140 chicks in her ten-month lifespan.

Chickens are docile and highly sociable. Unlike pigs or cows, they can be kept crammed together in huge numbers – 30,000 to a shed. They grow fast, and perhaps most importantly of all, they can be grown to a standard size. It hasn't yet been possible to breed a standard-sized pig, sheep or cow, so much of the work in slaughterhouses has to be done by humans. Chickens can be bred to an almost exact size, which means that the only job a person has to do is hang them upside down on the line. This may be the only time the chicken needs to be touched while it is alive. Everything else, from the gathering of the egg to the breading of the nugget, can be automated and carried out by robots and machines.

Every year 791,600,000 chickens go through this process and you will eat 13 of them. In a lifetime, that's 1,033 chickens. The average age of these chickens is about six weeks. In the 1950s the chicken you ate, if you ate it at all, was between three and four years old and had spent those years as a free-range, egg-laying hen. Saying something tasted like chicken had a different meaning in the 1950s.

In 1946, 98 per cent of the eggs produced in Britain were free-range. By the 1980s this had dropped to 1 per cent. Things have improved since then and over one-third of Britain's 29 million laying hens are free-range. These 29 million hens lay 10.63 billion eggs a year and you will eat 175.4 of them. In a lifetime you will eat 13,878 eggs, 2,914 of them in restaurants and other catering outlets; 8,604 of them as whole eggs from the shops and the remaining 2,306 in processed foods. At an average of 22 p an egg, they will cost you £3,053.

The industrialisation of the chicken has meant that the broiler chickens we eat bear little resemblance to the ones that lay our eggs. Laying hens are small and brown. Broiler chickens are white, heavy and barely able to walk. The most popular breed is the Cobb 500, which replaced the Cobb 100 and is supposed to be five times better at putting on weight. Using completely different birds means that the chicken-meat industry is essentially separate from the egg industry. Over the last 60 years, this has made sense in terms of adding value as it is simply the most profitable way of producing eggs and meat. However, the cheap grains and fossil fuels that intensive agriculture relies upon are not as cheap as they used to be. Ironically, one of the things driving up the price of grain is the fact that there is now more potential for adding value by turning grain into biofuels than there is from turning it into chicken nuggets.

ELECTRICITY

In the early days of new technologies there is often competition between different ways of doing essentially the same thing. Usually both sides have invested heavily and they compete aggressively for our business till one of the brand-new, cutting-edge technologies is rendered obsolete by the fact that no one wants to buy it. The most recent victim was HD DVD; before that there was Betamax video, and long, long before that Edison's wax cylinder.

Edison was first to the market with his wax cylinders. You could buy recordings to listen to or blank cylinders to make your own. However, he soon found himself in competition with Emile Berliner and his shellac discs. Though they didn't sound as good and you couldn't record on them, they were cheaper to buy and easier to store.

This wasn't the only format war Edison was involved with at the time. He had pioneered the use of electricity and was responsible for inventing, or perhaps more importantly patenting, most of the technology used to produce and supply direct current electricity. On the other side were Niko-la Tesla and the entrepreneurial engineer George Westinghouse with their newfangled alternating current. Unlike direct current, AC electricity could be transmitted over large distances and easily changed to different voltages. In contrast, communities using Edison's electricity each had to have their own small power station supplying different voltages through different cables.

Unable to compete in terms of practicality, cost or common sense,

Edison set out to demonstrate that AC was inherently bad, dangerous and wrong. He organised public events where cats, dogs, cattle and horses were killed onstage by AC electricity. His 1903 film *Electrocuting an Elephant* features Topsy the circus elephant obediently stepping on to a copper plate and collapsing into the clouds of smoke produced by her burning feet when the power was switched on. Topsy had recently killed three men and her owners had decided to put her down. The original plan was to hang her, but then Edison suggested she should be electrocuted instead.

Edison had played an active role in the first human execution by electricity 13 years previously. At the height of his battle with Tesla and Westinghouse, Edison had secretly funded the design and construction of the first electric chair. Having successfully lobbied for AC electricity to be used, Edison then had the problem of getting a generator from Westinghouse, who naturally refused to sell him one. The simple ruse of pretending to be a South American university and having the generator shipped to New York via Brazil overcame that difficulty. On 6 August 1890, William Kemmler became the first person to die in the electric chair. It took eight minutes. The State of New York held a competition to decide on a name for the new form of execution. 'Electrocution' won, with 'electrocide' and 'electromort' the runners-up. Edison wanted to call it Westinghousing.

Edison hated to lose. Once he had lost the AC/DC war he sold all his interests in a fit of pique and concentrated on selling light bulbs. These worked with either system. His other format war turned out badly too, but it did at least give him some opportunity for revenge. After the public spurned his wax cylinders, Edison refused to allow any of his companies to produce records until 1910, when Berliner's patent ran out. That way, Berliner didn't receive any royalties.

Electricity will be carried to your home on the system Tesla and Westinghouse designed. The output from the power station will be stepped up to 50,000 volts and carried over the countryside on pylons. As it nears your house, it will be stepped down again in a series of local electricity substations to 240 volts. The first thing the electricity will power in your house is the meter. If Britain's entire electricity supply was routed through your meter it would rack up 340,043,000,000 units every year. Your share of this is 1,930 units a year, a total of 152,663 units in a lifetime or an electricity bill of £12,242. This only represents your domestic consumption. Your share of all the other electricity used in your lifetime in Britain for street lighting, trains, food production and industry would cost you another £23,300 if you paid for it at the average domestic rate of 8 p a unit.

Electricity is created when you move a wire through a magnetic field. The first person to do this was Michael Faraday in 1831. John Peel, the Chancellor of the Exchequer, is said to have remarked, 'Well this is all very interesting, Mr Faraday, but what good is it?' To which Faraday replied, 'What good is it? Why one day you will be able to tax it.'

Governments have been remarkably restrained about taxing electricity. VAT at a reduced rate of 5 per cent was added in 1994, which adds another £612, bringing your total lifetime electricity bill up to £12,854.

ENERGY

Energy is measured in joules, which are named after the Victorian physicist and brewer James Prescott Joule. If you take into account all the oil, gas, coal, wind, wave, solar, nuclear and other fuel and power generated or imported by Britain every year, our annual consumption of energy comes to 9.875×10^{18} joules. Or if you prefer, 9,875,000,000,000,000,000 joules a year. This figure is hard to invest with meaning and saying that it is enough to keep 3.13 billion 100-watt light bulbs lit for a year doesn't help much. Nearly all of this energy comes from the Sun, which produces an inconceivable 3.86×10^{26} joules every second. Only two-billionths of this falls on the Earth's surface and only two-thousandths of that falls on Britain. That is equivalent to 956 billion 100-watt light bulbs. This doesn't make it easier to imagine, but it does tell you how many light bulbs you would need if you wanted to replace the Sun over Britain with electric light. If the Sun went out, it would take 300 times more power than we currently use just to keep those lights shining.

A lot of our power use is about replacing sunlight. The most obvious example is light itself, but the power-hungry activities of manufacturing clothes and constructing buildings and heating them are all ways of taking the tropical sunny environment we are adapted to north without having to grow fur. All organic materials on Earth were once elements that chemical reactions driven by sunlight have turned into things like cotton, wood, broccoli, Sir Cliff Richard and salmon. Unlike plants we can't turn sunlight directly into energy so we have to get plants and animals to do it for us.

One of the measures of food efficiency is how many steps there are between you and the Sun. Broccoli turns sunlight into broccoli, then you eat it. Two steps. The Sun shines, grass grows, the grass is eaten by cows, you eat the cows. Three steps. Plankton is eaten by fish, fish are eaten by bigger fish, fish is caught and processed into fish food pellets, farmed salmon eat the pellets, we eat the salmon. Five steps. As between 90 and 98 per cent of all the energy is lost in each step, the daily allowance of 2,245 Calories comes from 37,416 Calories of sunlight if you get them all from broccoli and 173,225,308 Calories of sunlight if all you eat is farmed salmon.

When you put a translucent strip of smoked salmon into your mouth, you are also eating hundreds upon hundreds of other fish and countless millions of plankton. Each step between you and those plankton also has other external energy consequences, from driving to the supermarket to boiling the milk for the trawler captain's cocoa. This can make lowly two-step vegetables just as bad. If one of the two steps between you and the Sun is a plane ride from the slopes of Mount Kilimanjaro, then your green beans are probably more wasteful than eating a hamburger from a cow that has been fed exclusively on smoked salmon.

One calorie is the amount of energy it takes to raise the temperature of 1 g of water by 1 °C. A Mars Bar actually contains 259,000 calories, so to make the numbers less frightening, kilocalories or Calories with a capital

'C' are used. Just running all the processes that maintain your body and keep you alive uses up 1 Calorie a minute. Each Calorie contains 4,200 joules. Power (which is measured in watts) is how many joules are used up every second. Your body uses 70 joules every second, so it runs at 70 watts. In other words, from the moment you are born you must consume enough energy to keep a 70-watt light bulb lit. If the light goes out, you die.

Though this is a meaninglessly tiny proportion of all the energy that the Sun produces, weight for weight human bodies actually produce 10,000 times more energy than the Sun. Life is the most efficient way we have of harnessing the Sun's power. Converting sunlight directly into energy that can be transported and used for other things is very difficult, so usually the results of solar radiation, like wind and waves, are turned into electricity. Currently only 6 per cent of your total energy consumption will come from renewables.

It is much easier to use the energy from sunlight that has been distilled and concentrated by time. Coal, oil and gas are essentially fossilised sunlight. Strictly speaking they are also renewable, just not on a useful timescale. Right now, the Sun is fuelling the growth of plants and microorganisms and the Earth is turning them into coal, oil and gas; they just won't be ready for millions and millions of years. Seventy-six per cent of the energy you consume will be electricity made from fossil fuels. In a lifetime you will also get through 70 tonnes of oil to power all the planes, trains, lorries, buses, cars and vans that will transport you and all the things you need.

There will also be 846 tonnes of coal to heat your house and half a billion watts of gas, which if you set fire to it all at the same time would explode with the force of 119 kg of TNT. The problem with unfossilising all this ancient sunlight is that it has implications for the atmosphere and the way modern sunlight affects the Earth.

At the moment 16 per cent of your electricity will come from nuclear power stations. These don't produce carbon, but they do produce controversy and at the moment the two cancel each other out. Ernest Rutherford, the father of nuclear physics, is often quoted in a comedy way as saying that: 'The energy produced by breaking down the atom is a very poor kind of thing. Anyone who expects a source of power from the transformations of these atoms is talking moonshine.' It is possible that he meant poor in the sense of it being hard to control and make use of, because he also suggested that radioactive decay might be the source of the Sun's power.

For most of human history, the Sun has simply been a magic burning ball in the sky. There were arguments about what was burning, whether the Sun was the chariot of Helios or molten metal or even coal. But, in the absence of a law of conservation of energy – energy cannot be created or destroyed – nobody questioned the Sun's ability to give out huge amounts of energy for a very, very long time without being replenished in any way. Then, in the nineteenth century, once the laws of thermodynamics had ruled out the possibility of perpetual motion machines, it started to be a major problem having one making its taunting way across the sky every day.

The breakthrough came with Einstein's most famous equation: $E = mc^2$. This is one of the foundation stones of modern physics and describes how mass (m) is equivalent to energy (E). In fact, mass is really just a particular form of energy. How much energy is determined by the speed of light multiplied by itself (c^2). This means a tiny mass can represent a huge amount of energy. In a nuclear reaction atoms decay to lighter atoms and the loss of mass becomes heat, light and other forms of energy. If it were possible to reassemble and weigh the bomb that destroyed Hiroshima, you would find that it was less than a gram lighter. Turning 600 mg of uranium-235 – a piece about the same size and weight as an aspirin – into pure energy killed 140,000 people and destroyed a city. This equation also effectively explains how the gigantic mass of the Sun can contain the mind-bogglingly huge quantities of energy required to burn for billions and billions of years.

In a lifetime, you will get through 1.63×10^{11} joules' worth of oil, coal, gas, nuclear and renewable energy. That's 65 joules per second or 65 watts. The energy you get from food provides you with 70 watts. This means that most of the energy you use will come from the simple act of eating and digesting. Using the equation $E = mc^2$, all the energy you use in your life is equivalent to a mass of 0.00484 g. Something so small you would not even be able to feel it on the surface of your eyeball.

EXTINCTIONS

Extinction is part of the history of life on Earth. The background rate for extinctions is about one per million species every year. Occasionally, there are massive disturbances in our planet's ability to sustain life that result in the rate of extinctions rising to 1,000 times the background rate. There are thought to have been five of these in the last 540 million years, which resulted in the extinction of at least 50 per cent of all species.

Establishing the current rate of extinction is very difficult, but estimates put it between 1,000 and 10,000 times the background rate. This means that we are approaching the levels of species loss that saw off the dinosaurs 65 million years ago.

Estimating the total number of species on the planet is also very difficult. So far we have catalogued fewer than two million of them. Estimates for how many remain undiscovered range from between 10 and 100 million. Taking the lowest estimates, 27 species become extinct every day, which means in your lifetime there will be 780,000 extinctions. The best-case scenario is that it will take 13 lifetimes to get through all the species on the planet, which takes you up to the year 3036. In the worst-case scenario, it will take just 100 years.

One of the arguments used by climate-change sceptics is the fact that the Earth has been warmer in the past. This is true, but not in the human past. Whatever we do to it, the planet will be just fine. The Earth doesn't need saving. It has survived supervolcanoes, asteroid impacts, tectonic upheavals, gamma-ray bursts and clathrate-gun methane eruptions and still turned into the beautiful place we first stepped out into hundreds of thousands of years ago. We are the ones who need saving and this is what we really mean when we talk about saving the rhino, the whale, the crested newt, the environment or the planet.

EYES

There is a story about a king who set two rival painters a challenge to produce the most realistic painting. The two painters duly brought their works before him. The first artist revealed his painting – a life-size representation of the king slaying a lion with a sword. The painting was so meticulously done that every hair on the lion was visible, every frozen drop of blood flying off the sword slickly gleaming and wet … The king was very impressed. He turned to the second artist standing beside his own very much smaller painting, which was covered by a cloth. When the king asked him to uncover the painting, the artist replied that he was so ashamed of his modest work that he would prefer to leave it covered. The king became annoyed and ordered him to remove the cloth or else. The painter still refused. Now in a rage, the king snatched at the cloth, but instead of softly draped material his fingers slid across the smooth surface of painted canvas. The second painting was a painting of a small picture covered by a cloth.

What makes this story unlikely is the fact that we have two eyes that enable us to see things in three dimensions. This is probably one of the most obvious facts in the world, but only for the last 170 years.

One of the descriptions of a genius is that he or she is someone who looks at what everyone looks at but sees what no one else sees. Some of the greatest geniuses of all time have puzzled unsuccessfully over the fact that no painting could ever fool you into thinking it was real. Euclid, Archimedes,

Galileo, Leonardo da Vinci and Newton all had a go at the problem. Presumably people must have been aware of the fact that each eye sees a different picture, but no one spotted its significance. It was simply thought you had two eyes for the same reason you have two lungs, two kidneys, two testicles or ovaries – because a spare might come in handy. It wasn't until 1838 that the British physicist Charles Wheatstone had the idea that your brain combines these pictures to make a three-dimensional view of the world. You could say that the third dimension has only been around for 170 years.

Your eyes will work hard all your life, every day from the time you wake up to when you go to sleep again – an average of 16 hours and 45 minutes. Your eyes won't be open the whole time. You blink every five seconds or so – 348,428,776 times

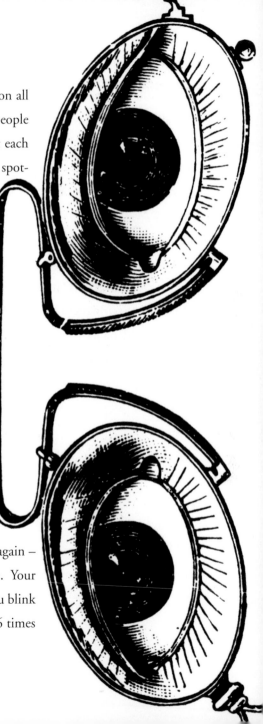

in your life. With each blink lasting 0.1 seconds, you will spend a total of 403 days with your eyes closed while you are awake. The rest of the time – 19,760 days' worth – your eyes will be open and receiving images. The refresh rate of the human eye varies up to a maximum of around 60 times a second, but to produce the illusion of smooth movement films only need around 24 frames a second. Working at this rate, your eyes are going to capture 40,900,000,000 images.

The age of 60 marks the point when the average person needs glasses for distance and reading. Consequently you will own most of your 21 pairs of glasses after your sixtieth birthday. You will visit the optician's 28 times and spend £3,146 on 21 pairs of glasses and contact lenses. The average cost of producing a pair of glasses is £7. The average cost to you will be £148.50, which means that someone is making a colossal average profit of 2,100 per cent.

FARTS

The bacteria in your large intestine produces between 600 and 2000 ml of gas every day, a total of 32,952 l in a lifetime, which will be released at the rate of 26 farts a day. Enough to amuse, embarrass or offend 751,173 lifts full of people. Assuming an average fart length of one second, that's 8.7 days of your life farting round the clock, producing enough gas to demolish a small block of flats.

Though there is a certain amount of debate about how your sense of smell works, it is generally agreed that in order to smell something its molecules must interact with receptors inside your nose. These release G proteins, which stimulate neurons that send messages to the olfactory bulb, where they are turned into the experience we call smell.

If you can smell someone else's fart it is because molecules from their rectum have passed through their anal sphincter, percolated through layers of clothing, wafted towards you and filled your nostrils. There they have dissolved in the mucus membranes of your olfactory epithelium and briefly become at one with your body as they dock with your smell receptors. Then you swallow them.

FILMS

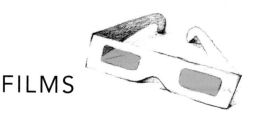

In the 1880s, the explorer, statistician and scientist Francis Galton turned his attention to the fight against crime. Like many Victorians, Galton believed that personality type was related to physical type. Your true nature was betrayed by the shape of your skull, the cast of your features, the cut of your jib. He reasoned that if it was possible to combine lots of criminal faces you could produce a portrait of the average criminal whom all other criminals would resemble. Presumably, the idea was that the police would be able to keep an eye on or arrest anyone who looked a bit like this average criminal. Luckily Galton had just invented composite photography. So, with the full cooperation of Her Majesty's Director of Prisons he amalgamated the photographs of a large number of convicted murderers, thieves and other villainous types. He was surprised and probably a bit depressed by the picture this process produced. Instead of a template of villainy he had a portrait of a rather good-looking young man who hadn't shaved for a while.

In general, the faces we find beautiful are the most average faces, faces that are symmetrical and don't contain any irregularities. The evolutionary argument is that we find such faces beautiful because they are a sign of a diverse and therefore average set of genes. However, while average is good when it comes to choosing someone to combine genetic material with, it is not good when it comes to art.

Big-budget films are not art; they are products just like shampoo or cars. As such they must appeal to as many people as possible. Film studios do this by trying to include all the things the average person likes in every film. Giving people what they want generally consists of assembling a good-looking cast (with nice, regular, average features), putting them in difficulty and then returning everything to normal only better than before. It means that the good guys win, the bad guys suffer and justice prevails.

Making a film begins with someone – usually a producer or a writer – having an idea. The idea is worked up into a concept then into a treatment and then into a screenplay. Along the way the original idea often disappears completely, along with the person who had it. The list of writing credits usually represents a series of hirings and firings as numerous people have a go at producing something that pleases everybody. Then, when the script is ready and enough money has been raised, a small town's worth of people go to work. Once the film is finished, there will be test screenings and a final weeding out of anything that might interfere with the film's success.

Film studios have got better and better at averaging out what we like and giving it to us. While this makes commercial sense it also makes bland, superficially attractive films that we don't love for any longer than the summer they were released in. In September 2008, the IMDb (Internet Movie Database) list of top ten films voted by users of the site only includes one film made in the last ten years and that was *The Dark Knight*, which came out in the summer of 2008.

You will spend 502 days of your life watching 5,609 films, mostly for free on the television. Most of the money you will spend on film will go on summer blockbusters, including £1,072 on cinema tickets, popcorn and giant beverages. You will also spend a further £3,394 buying or renting the film on DVD so you can also watch all the bits the studio cut out – the annoying characters, the dragging scenes and the depressing original ending.

Top of the list of things that the average person wants from a film is a happy ending. Happy endings are a bit like drugs. They make you feel good, but their effects are less potent and the high is shorter the more often you experience them. In order to get the maximum enjoyment from a happy ending you need to have experienced enough unhappy endings to worry about things turning out badly. A healthy balanced diet of films should therefore include independent, European and art-house cinema. Unhappy or ambiguous endings usually have more resonance and stay with us longer. Great films tend not to pander to our weakness for the triumph of good over evil and everything turning out all right in the end. Films that have above-average expectations of their audiences are more likely to become our favourite films over time, which is why the IMDb top ten also includes *The Godfather, One Flew Over the Cuckoo's Nest* and *Schindler's List*.

FISH

Long before Columbus 'discovered' America, Basque fishermen had been returning from the vast uncharted emptiness of the Atlantic with their holds mysteriously full of salt cod. It is impossible to dry and salt cod at sea, so the Basques had to be doing it on land. It took the rest of Europe a surprisingly long time to notice and, in the meantime, the Basques were happily meeting the demands of the European religious calendar that prohibited meat on nearly half the days of the year.

Sadly for the Basques, no matter how jealously you guard it, if your trade secret is a new continent you aren't going to be able to keep it secret for long. By the end of the fifteenth century other European countries, including Britain, were beginning to make their own secret visits to America for fish. When Columbus (and his mainly Basque crew) returned in 1493 he became the first man to publicly announce he had been to America. There is no doubt this really annoyed the fishermen. In fact, a group of English fisherman who had been going there for years actually wrote a letter to Columbus to complain about his intercontinental boasting.

Barring the occasional wood pigeon, rabbit, grouse or pheasant, fish are one of the few animals we eat that have been caught in the wild. The people who catch them for us are the last remnants of our hunter-gatherer past.

When the first hunter-gatherers set foot on North America 14,000 years ago they discovered a continent populated with camels, elephants, mammoths and other improbable animals, like the giant ground sloth and the giant beaver. Within a thousand years they were all extinct. There are various theories for why this happened. The most popular is that the early humans found these huge vegetarians all too easy to spear, trap and stampede over cliffs, and that in the space of 30 generations, crazed on blood and protein, they spread across the entire continent wiping them out. Aside from the evidence, the main strength of this theory is that it sounds like just the sort of thing we would do.

The oceans are not full of fish. In fact, most fish live in the relatively thin layer where sunlight can penetrate. The most productive areas are where the water is shallow enough for light to reach the bottom and where ocean currents meet. Off the south-east coast of Newfoundland, where the Gulf Stream meets the cold currents coming down from the North Pole, there is a large area of shallow water that was once one of the richest fishing grounds in the world. These are the Grand Banks, where the Basque fishermen went to catch their cod. As recently as 50 years ago cod were still being landed that were bigger than the men who caught them and it was thought that the bounty of the sea was limitless.

You will eat just under a tonne of fish in your life, at the rate of 11 kg a year. Most of it will be presented to you encrusted with batter or breadcrumbs. You will eat 392 portions of fish and chips. In the south this will predominantly be cod, but as you move towards the north of Britain it is more likely to be haddock.

The other iconic fish product is the fish finger. Over a million fish fingers are sold and presumably eaten in Britain every day. Of the 476 you are going to get through, some will be cod, but increasingly they are going to be haddock, whiting, pollack or whatever is left in the sea.

In Britain, we only eat four kinds of seafood in significant quantities. These are: cod, salmon, prawns and tuna. Leading the way in turning the last of our hunters into farmers is the salmon and it is increasingly possible to buy farmed cod, prawns and tuna. Perhaps one day all our fish will come from farms, because nearly all of the fish we buy comes from declining stocks that are going the same way as the Grand Banks.

In the 1990s, after 20 generations of commercial fishing, the Grand Banks had been all but fished out of cod. Fishing was banned there to allow stocks to recover, but, nearly 20 years later, they haven't.

At the end of *Finding Nemo*, the charismatic multicoloured and inedible stars of the film save what looks like a shoal of cod from being caught by a trawler. These commercial fish are rude, monochrome and stupid. It seems beyond even the powers of Disney to make us care about the fish we eat. It *is* hard to care about fish. They are fundamentally unsympathetic creatures who live in an alien environment where the general rule of survival is 'If it is smaller than you, eat it!' Perhaps this is why it is possible to go into any supermarket and buy what is essentially an endangered animal, lightly grill it and eat it with a squeeze of lemon. But it is important to care, to read the labels on what you buy, to check that it comes from well-managed fisheries because there are no longer plenty more fish in the sea and no more vast continents out there, over the horizon, waiting to be discovered.

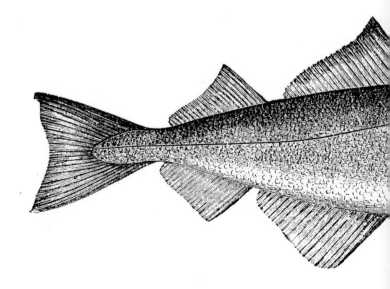

FOOD

We all go through a phase of trying to eat whatever we can pick up and put into our mouth. A combination of taste and the screams of the people looking after us quickly teaches us the difference between food and cat litter. It isn't just about learning what not to eat. During this time we are also taught which foods are acceptable. These tastes are cultural and sometime between the ages of two and three they become more or less set for life. You are unlikely to eat a bowl of black ants stir-fried with rice and garnished with live red ants for lunch. Someone from Thailand would probably be disgusted by the notion of squirty cream in a can. Universal to all cultures is the disgust caused by excrement, putrefaction and other things that make food dangerous to eat. There is also a general lack of interest in eating things that aren't food such as bicycles and light bulbs.

The remarkable thing about your digestion is the fact that it will deal with almost anything you present it with: live ants, squirty cream, chicken vindaloo, crème de menthe, sand ... No matter how bizarre your diet is, once your mouth and stomach have done their work it's all just a thick soup. Your body will extract the useful molecules of protein, starch, carbohydrate, fat, vitamins, minerals and water and pass everything else on.

The thick sludge of nutrients released into the small intestine from your stomach is highly acidic, so the first thing your body has to do is neutralise the acid. In order to do this, the juices from your pancreas, spleen and liver

are all alkaline. They also contain enzymes to break down your food into molecules that can be absorbed.

The 7 m length of your small intestine is where nearly all the nutrients from your food will be extracted. If it were just a smooth pipe it would have a surface area of 0.5 m^2. However, the surface of the small intestine is covered with a fur of tiny structures called villi, which are themselves covered with the even tinier fronds of microvilli. This means that its total surface area is around 250 m^2. While it is good to have lots of nutrient-rich fluid flowing turbulently through the fronds of your microvilli, it would be very wasteful of water, not to mention socially inconvenient, to get rid of what comes out of the small intestine directly. Luckily, you have 1.5 m of large intestine to remove nearly all of this fluid and compact the undigested waste into conveniently sized packages to excrete (usually) at will.

You are going to spend 82 minutes a day eating. Women spend 79 minutes. Men eat more slowly and spend 85 minutes, but the average is 82. If you wanted to get all your life's eating over in one stretch, and allowed yourself eight hours a day for sleep and going to the toilet, it would take you almost seven years of constant chewing and swallowing to get through it all.

You will eat 2.7 kg of food and drink every day; 68,846 kg in a lifetime or just over 983 times your own body weight. Most of this will be useful life-sustaining food, but occasionally you may accidentally swallow something that isn't food, such as an earring. As long as it isn't sharp or toxic and is small enough to fit through the various valves and constrictions along the way, you should be able to put it back into the jewellery box between 24 and 72 hours later.

People affected by pica have a compulsion to eat things that are not food. Their diet is likely to be much more diverse and may well include soil, coal, rubber bands, bicycles, light bulbs, earrings, sand and excrement. Pica is more common in children than adults. The association with pregnancy is a myth. Pica can be very dangerous as it bypasses the disgust reflex that prevents you from eating hazardous substances. Within certain limits, though, you can eat anything. Given enough time and the right tools, it would be easy to break down your house, your car or Nelson's Column into bite-sized pieces and eat them. Seen in this light, Monsieur Mangetout's remarkable feat of consuming an entire Cessna light aircraft was more about sawing, filing and persuading someone to give him a plane than it was about eating.

FREEZERS

In 1845 the explorer John Franklin set out to look for a shortcut to the Pacific along the north coast of Canada. Franklin was the Victorian hero of Arctic exploration and this was his third voyage in search of the North-West Passage. On his first expedition he and his crew had been forced to eat their spare footwear and clothing to survive, which brought Franklin lasting fame as The Man Who Ate His Boots. On his second expedition he had mapped over 1,000 miles of new coastline and now he was setting out with two superbly equipped ships to finish the job. He expected to be sailing the blue waters of the Pacific in a few months, but that summer John Franklin, his two ships and the 133 men who sailed with him disappeared into the ice and vanished.

In 1980, three bodies from Franklin's expedition were found buried on a small island high up in the Arctic Circle. Preserved by constant sub-zero temperatures, their bodies were in pristine condition, as fresh as the day they died over 130 years earlier, less than halfway to the Pacific.

Though food has been frozen for thousands of years to keep it fresh, it wasn't until the 1930s that frozen foods started to become part of the everyday diet. Almost all the innovations that make this possible are down to one man.

In 1912 the 24-year-old Clarence Birdseye was working on the same north-eastern coast of Canada that Franklin's doomed expedition had sailed along two generations before. In his spare time he learned to fish with the Inuit. In temperatures of − 40 °C, the fish they hauled up from holes cut through the thick ice froze almost instantly. Birdseye noticed that when these fish were defrosted they tasted almost as good as fresh and certainly much better than any frozen fish he had tasted before.

The secret was in the speed of freezing. Food at the time was frozen slowly, which allowed large ice crystals to form, damaging the food and making it limp and tasteless when thawed. For the next six years Birdseye travelled about northern Canada by dog sled, working as a fur trapper and meditating upon the subject of frozen food. He arrived in Washington in 1917, fresh from the wilderness, his mind aflame with the dream of providing humanity with a wide range of attractively packaged frozen foods.

By 1923, using some buckets of brine, dry ice and an electric fan, he was flash-freezing waxed cardboard boxes of fish fillets in his kitchen. In 1926 he took the principles perfected in his kitchen and built a 20-tonne fast-freezing machine. In 1929 he sold his company and patents for $22 million.

Bringing a wide range of attractively packaged frozen foods to the nation required many things that are familiar today but which did not exist in the 1930s. Refrigerated transport, freezer cabinets in shops, ice boxes in fridges and ultimately the chest freezer in your garage – Clarence Birdseye is responsible for them all.

Clarence was a slight, balding man with glasses, quite unlike Captain Birds Eye, the ocean-going Santa of frozen food who was invented in the

1960s. In the rest of Europe he is known as Captain Iglo, apart from Italy, where he is Captain Findus.

You will eat nearly 4 tonnes of frozen food. Over 1 tonne of this will be consumed in restaurants, pubs and institutions like hospitals and schools. Though less than 10 per cent of your lifetime's meals will come from places like these, they will account for more than a quarter of your frozen food. Ironically, an innovation designed to make cooking in the home easier is most widely used in restaurants, which buy around 30 per cent of their ingredients frozen.

You will have to carry the remaining 2.5 icy tonnes back from the shops yourself. Once you have popped them in the freezer they should keep just as fresh and pristine as a long-lost Arctic explorer until you are ready to eat them.

FRIENDS

Jean-Paul Sartre wrote that hell is other people. On the other hand, short of inflicting physical injury, solitary confinement is one of the worst things you can do to someone. You will live your life somewhere between the hell of crowds and the hell of solitude.

You will interact with thousands of people in a lifetime but only get to know a few of them really well. The ones you know best will be a very small group of parents, children, lovers and close friends – those whose death would change your world. Psychologists call this your sympathy circle, and studies round the world are remarkably consistent, setting the number at around 12 people. This seems to be more or less the maximum number of people you can care deeply about at any one time. Your general circle of friends and acquaintances is much bigger.

The evolutionary psychologist Robin Dunbar has put forward the idea that the number of people in this larger group is determined by the size of the human brain or, more specifically, of the neocortex, which is the part of the brain responsible for complex thought and reasoning. The bigger the neocortex, the more social connections you can keep track of and the larger your social group. This appears to be true for chimps, gorillas and other apes. Applying the same logic to the size of the human neocortex gives you a figure of 150. There is a lot of evidence for this, and the number 150 keeps cropping up in the average size of hunter-gatherer villages, companies, religious communities and army units. Dunbar has also described this number as being 'the number of people you would not feel embarrassed about joining uninvited for a drink if you happened to bump into them in a bar'.

The composer Erik Satie turned joining people uninvited for a drink into an art form. He was frequently down on his luck and short of money. He used to take an empty suitcase, walk across Paris to Montmartre and go into one of the cafés, where he would wearily and conspicuously put down his case. In his velvet suit, Satie was a distinctive figure. He also had many friends, including Debussy, Picasso, Diaghilev, Ravel, Poulenc, Stravinsky and Cocteau, and he was on nodding terms with every other major artistic figure in belle époque Paris. He never went unnoticed for long. 'Erik, why so sad? And why the suitcase?' To which he would glumly reply, 'I am ruined! Tomorrow I leave Paris for ever!' He would be bought drinks for the rest of the night. The next morning, he would pick up his suitcase and go to a different café. 'Erik why so sad? ...'

Erik Satie's friends knew he wasn't leaving Paris for ever, but they were happy to support him when he was down on his luck. He was a very entertaining man, worth the price of a drink, and when he was flush he spent his money freely. This, after all, is what friends are for – entertainment, understanding, sympathy, love and the occasional loan.

A lot of the people you know could not be

considered friends. People like your plumber, doctor, dentist or old PE teacher. The best estimate of all the people you know at any one time comes from professors Peter Killworth and Russell Bernard. Their idea is to count how many people you know who belong to one particular section of society of a known size, such as postmen or lawyers or people called Dave. By relating your figure to the total number of people called Dave, for example, you can work out how many people you know. They came up with an average of 290 people.

So, 12 people you are very close to, a further 138 you might join for a drink in a bar, and a further 140 you know who aren't necessarily friends. People will be continually moving in and out of your life, so while the 290 remains more or less constant, in a lifetime 1,964 people will pass through this group. This is about 0.0000003 per cent of the world's population.

In the 1960s, the psychologist Stanley Milgram performed a famous experiment to work out how many links between friends it would take to get from you to any random person in the world. He gave a random selection of people a letter addressed to another random person with the instruction

to send it to a friend whom they thought would get it closer to its target. The friend then sent it on with the same instructions. By counting the number of friends in the chain, Milgram came up with the result that gave us the term 'six degrees of separation' and the idea that everyone alive in the world today is a friend of a friend of a friend of a friend of a friend.

What is less famous about this experiment is that it didn't work all that well, has never been repeated and is largely a myth. Fewer than 30 per cent of the chains that Milgram started were completed, and in any case the figures tended towards eight or nine degrees of separation. One of the reasons why Milgram's results were so rapidly and unquestioningly accepted is because it is very comforting to think that we are all just a few friends away from each other. However, even if it is true that Jigme Khesar Namgyel Wangchuck, the Dragon King of Bhutan, is the friend of a friend of a friend of a friend of a friend of yours, this is not much use to you or indeed to him. You are unlikely to be much help resolving Bhutan's border dispute with China and he probably won't be all that sympathetic when you start hassling him in cafés with your panhandling charade about leaving Paris for ever.

FRUIT

Fruit is the only thing we eat that wants to be eaten. Animals run away and hide when they hear us coming. Most plants aren't too keen either and have developed poisons and spikes to discourage us. You might not think that you have to outwit a cabbage to eat it, but you have to steal its seeds and plant them in specially prepared ground, keep the caterpillars off and then chop it up and invent mayonnaise before you can eat it as coleslaw. Fruits, however, are different: being eaten is how they spread their seeds. So it is no wonder they have gone to considerable lengths to make themselves as brightly coloured, attractively packaged and generally delicious as possible.

Fruit represents nature's best efforts to tempt us to eat. Food technologists and packaging designers who create new foods borrow many of nature's tricks. They produce brightly packaged food that is easy to transport, store, prepare and eat. They also add tastes we are unable to resist. We have almost unlimited appetites for things that are scarce in the wild, such as salt, sugar and fat. At one time it would have made sense for us to gorge ourselves on these things whenever we could. Fruits take advantage of this by being sweet and sugars are relatively easy for plants to make. Fat is a little more tricky, while salt is almost unknown at levels we can taste.

This is where the people who design processed food have a massive advantage over nature. They can add all three in huge quantities to make something compellingly delicious and irresistibly purchasable. Fruit has lost the battle to be the most delicious thing in the world and has gone from being a prized source of sweetness and succulent flavour to being the subject of government-sponsored programmes to improve health.

The government guideline of five servings of fruit and vegetables a day is the minimum recommended amount – less than that and you can expect your health to suffer. In setting the figure, the Department of Health was seeking to strike a balance between what is desirable and what is feasible. The Danish guideline is six a day. The French is ten and the Japanese 13. The average British person eats four 80 g portions of fruit and veg a day. You eat slightly more fruit than vegetables – about 2.3 portions. In order to get your five a day, all you have to do is eat an extra piece of fruit. This would add 2.3 tonnes to the 5.46 tonnes of fruit you get through in a lifetime. Getting things to the French level would add another 13.8 tonnes.

HAIR

In order to keep the 12-year-old Rapunzel in her tower, the witch would have to have built it high enough to stop her simply jumping out and running away. Then again, she wouldn't want it too high because, apart from the unnecessary work involved and the danger of making it too conspicuous, she wouldn't want to give Rapunzel the option of suicide. So, the ideal height for Rapunzel's window would have been about 8 m above the ground. Not quite high enough to guarantee death but certainly high enough to really hurt. Assuming that Rapunzel sat right by the window and the witch was able to reach up to grab the end, Rapunzel's hair would have to have been at least 7 m long.

Human hair grows at a rate of 1 cm a month. When the prince vaulted through that window 8 m above the ground, he would have found a 58-year-old woman. This might not have come as a complete surprise. By the

age of 50, 50 per cent of people will be 50 per cent grey. What is actually happening is that hair starts to grow in with no pigment at all and the mixture of white and coloured hairs give the illusion of grey. The prince would probably have noticed the changing character of the rope of hair running though his hands in the last metre or so and been prepared for what he found.

It takes a long period of good nutrition and uninterrupted health to grow beautiful, long, shining tresses of hair. We recognise this and consequently find great hair attractive. Conversely, having no hair at all is not particularly desirable. Baldness is largely inherited. If you are a man and your father is bald, then you have an 80 per cent chance of going the same way. However, if your 60-year-old father has a full head of hair your chance of baldness drops to 20 per cent.

But while male baldness is perceived as something that puts women off, it is surprisingly common. Surely evolution should have got rid of it long

ago? However, most men go bald after they have found a partner and passed on their genes. It is also possible that women are not that bothered by baldness. Female baldness is comparatively rare which may be an indication that men are more superficial about hair and that bald girls have found it much harder to get a partner and pass on their baldness genes.

Despite the other disadvantages, a bald woman would save a huge amount of time and money on haircare. A recent survey by Boots suggests that the average woman spends around £24 a month on shampoo, conditioner and home styling products and just over £300 a year at the hairdresser, which comes to a total of £37,000 in a lifetime. At the rate of 41 minutes a day, she will also spend nearly two years in round-the-clock washing, styling and restyling. Men, in contrast, men spend an average of one minute a day on their hair. Just over a fortnight's worth of haircare in a lifetime. They also spend a lot less money on hair products, with just £9 a year or £750 in total. While the enormous disparity in these figures reflects the fact that women's hair statistics suffer the same biases as those for shoes, no one would dispute that men are less bothered about their hair. Men also have a tendency to steal their female partner's salon-quality shampoo and conditioner, which may also skew the figures.

In order to grow hair long enough to reach the ground while she was still young enough for the prince to be enchanted, Rapunzel would have to have had special quick-growing, fairy-tale hair that never needed to be washed. No matter how well you look after it or how long you wait, your hair is never likely to grow as long as Rapunzel's. Each of the hair follicles on your body grows for a set period of time, sheds the hair and grows another one. The length of the growing phase determines the length of your hair. Most of your body hair is on a short growing cycle, which is why you don't have Rapunzel armpits. The hair on your head grows for between six and ten years before falling out, giving you an average hair length of between 72 and 120 cm. To keep your hair shorter than this you will need to cut off about 10 m in a lifetime. The longest head of hair in the world is the result of the rare combination of having hair follicles stuck in their growing phase and never having a haircut. The resulting 6.3 m of hair belongs to a Vietnamese man called Tran Van Hay. He is 71.

HANGOVERS

The alcohol/mood graph is a subtle curve, like a breaking wave. In small amounts, alcohol is a stimulant. It makes you feel fantastic and drinking more will make you feel even more fantastic until you reach the crest of the euphoria wave. But as the concentration of alcohol in your blood rises above a certain level, it starts to act as a depressant. If you drink more it will not make you feel better, instead it will cancel out the euphoria and start to drive you down the face of the wave. You cannot drink your way back on to the crest; drinking more will just deepen the plunge into depression, dysphoria and unconsciousness. And when you resurface …

The amount of alcohol in your body is measured by taking the weight of pure alcohol per 100 ml of blood. You can expect to feel the stimulant effects of alcohol at between 20 and 30 mg per 100 ml blood. Your euphoria will increase until you reach about 55mg, before the depressant effects start to kick in at 60 mg. In order to surf the euphoria wave, you need to keep your blood alcohol between 50 and 60 mg.

The effect of drinking on your blood alcohol level depends on your metabolism, what is already in your stomach and how much water you contain. The amount of water in the human body varies widely from person to person and also between the sexes. However, if a 76 kg person who is 53 per cent water tinctures themselves with one 8 g unit of pure alcohol, their blood alcohol will rise 20 mg. If you are using 12 per cent wine, you should drink 2.75 units or 229 ml in the first hour to get your blood alcohol up to the magic 55 mg level. As your liver disposes of one unit an hour, you will need to drink another 83 ml of wine every 60 minutes to keep yourself at the optimum level.

As the euphoria buzz is greater the faster you ascend the curve, you should probably drink down the first 229 ml in one go, set a timer for an hour and prepare your next 83 ml dose. This will work. You will feel nicely, happily drunk and silly for the first hour or so and then relaxed, conspiratorial and mildly overaffectionate for the next, and be fast asleep while the depressive effects of clearing the alcohol from your body are at their height.

But there will come a time when you forget to take your funnel, measuring jug, kitchen timer and pocket calculator out with you. You lose track of how much, or even what, you've had. You feel fantastic and you want to feel even more fantastic. Alternatively, you feel terrible and you want to feel even more terrible, or you remember and you want to forget, or you don't want to be bothered by rational thought, you just want to have a good time.

And then you resurface …

Every year, 29 million working days are lost to hangovers, which means the average person has a hangover bad enough to miss work every two years. So, you will live 32 days of your life as a vomiting sack of pain and many hundreds more wearing the bilious stain of the night before across your eyeballs and tongue.

Some of the symptoms of your hangover are caused by congeners. These are the biologically active compounds that give drinks their character. Generally, the more character a drink has, the more congeners it will contain. Brandy has the most, followed by red wine, rum, whisky, white wine, gin and vodka. Congeners can include other alcohols such as methanol, which your body breaks down into formaldehyde, more commonly known as embalming fluid. While this might explain why a schooner of brandy will make you feel worse than the same amount of vodka, most of the damage comes from the alcohol itself. In order to break down alcohol and flush it from your body, your liver turns it into acetaldehyde. Unfortunately, this is almost as toxic as embalming fluid. As your liver is very efficient, it manages to turn nearly all of the acetaldehyde into acetic acid (vinegar basically) so it can be flushed from your body. The tiny proportion of acetaldehyde (less than 1 per cent) that escapes is what gives you your hangover.

Though you will feel the effects of your hangover mainly as a thumping headache and churning stomach, these are just the most noticeable symptoms. Acetaldehyde poisons and kills muscles, damages internal organs and may cause mutations to DNA. The effects of a bad hangover can last for years and there is growing evidence that acetaldehyde is a factor in cancer, liver disease and dementia. There is a good reason why hangovers feel like some sort of attempt is being made on your life.

'I will never ever drink again' is one of the most frequently broken promises we make to ourselves. The problem is that when you are climbing the fun part of the alcohol/mood curve you feel invincible, like things could only ever get better and better and better ...

ICE CREAM

Until recently, ice cream was a luxury food enjoyed only by the elite. Emperors, tsarinas, pharaohs, pashas, caliphs, hidalgos, burgraves, sultans, sultanas, maharajas, kings, infantas, queens, mikados and kaisers exercised the machinery of state to have snow and ice brought from the frozen extremities of their dominions so that cold desserts could be enjoyed in the middle of summer. Ice cream was only a status symbol in hot weather. Presumably, in the depths of winter, when the capitals of Europe filled with snow and anyone who could lean out of a window could make it, ice cream had no value at all.

From the middle of the nineteenth century, ice cream became more widely available, but it remained a treat food to be enjoyed on days out, holidays and special occasions. After the Second World War there was a boom in frozen food which brought with it a network for transporting, selling and storing things below 0 °C. Suddenly, being frozen, the thing that had made ice cream so impractical, so unique and so prized, became an obvious advantage. Unlike other foods, ice cream is improved by freezing.

It really isn't much fun to eat ice cream when you are cold, which is presumably why the general public did not go out and make ice cream from snow in the bitter northern European winters. As well as having access to a transport system for frozen goods that does not rely on you being the head of state, you also have an insulated cupboard in your house that is as cold

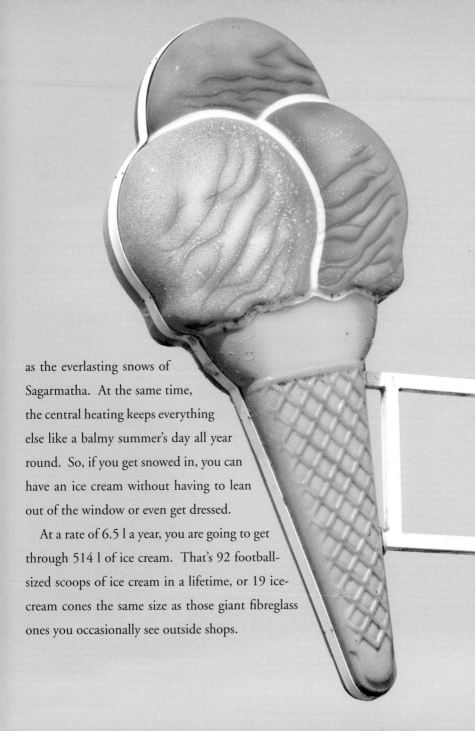

as the everlasting snows of
Sagarmatha. At the same time,
the central heating keeps everything
else like a balmy summer's day all year
round. So, if you get snowed in, you can
have an ice cream without having to lean
out of the window or even get dressed.

At a rate of 6.5 l a year, you are going to get
through 514 l of ice cream. That's 92 football-
sized scoops of ice cream in a lifetime, or 19 ice-
cream cones the same size as those giant fibreglass
ones you occasionally see outside shops.

INSURANCE

Insurance began as a benign and really rather wonderful way for ship owners to spread the risk of transporting goods over the treacherous oceans. Each would pay a little into a common fund so that when a ship was lost the owner would not be ruined. That was a long time ago and now there are entire buildings full of people thinking up new ways to make you worry about your possessions being stolen, crashed into, springing a leak, or catching fire and burning down.

Over your life you will spend £42,582 on insurance. A figure that truly represents the sum of all your fears.

Insurance companies are really just betting shops where you gamble on personal disasters. A house is burgled every six minutes, which is a frightening thought, but when you consider the number of households in Britain (21 million), this means you are likely to be burgled once in your life. The average value of goods taken in a burglary is £200.

IRON

There are many versions of the legend of King Arthur but most include someone drawing a sword from a stone and becoming a mighty ruler. There is also usually a lake involved somewhere, which a sword is either thrown into or taken out of.

The ability to draw metal from the stones of copper, tin and iron ore gave you the ability to fashion a blade 3 ft long in a world where everyone else was armed with stone pen-knives and shards of glass. It is no wonder that the people with swords became mighty rulers. Later, the almost magical process of tempering was discovered. The colour of a steel blade will change from yellow to brown to purple to blue as it gets hotter. By carefully judging the temperature from these colours and then cooling it rapidly by plunging it into cold water, you can change the structure of the metal. If you do this correctly, you will have in your hands a weapon that is flexible, resilient and immensely strong. A sword that could shatter your opponent's lesser blade and cut him in half with a single stroke – the kind of sword that creates legends.

It is tempting to look back at the history of the world and divide it up into neat periods of time. Stone tools are thrown away at the end of the Stone Age and replaced with bronze until the Iron Age comes along. In reality these ages don't come to an end, they form the layers of our civilisation and we mark the period where the new ages begin. We are now surfing the crest of the Information Age as it breaks over the Nuclear Age, the Plastic Age, the Steam Age …

Iron, which we mostly use in the form of steel, is still fundamental to our way of life. Almost everything we use either contains steel or has been made, cultivated, harvested or transported using steel at some point.

Britain uses nearly 27 million tonnes of iron ore and steel every year. Of this, 12.6 million tonnes will be in manufactured goods like fridges, washing machines, cars, trains, buses and ships. The rest will go to the construction industry: pipes, wires, beams and railway tracks. In a lifetime your share of Britain's iron will come to 35 tonnes. The scrap value of this is currently around £7,350, a figure that is going to increase dramatically in the future.

Though the world has vast reserves of iron ore, like everything else on this finite planet, they are running out. It is estimated that this could happen in as little as 60 years from now. When it does, we will be living in the Scrap Iron Age.

JUNK MAIL

Every year, 17.5 billion pieces of junk mail are produced in Britain: 550,000 tonnes of paper, made from 3.3 million trees, using 16.5 billion l of water.

Your annual share is 288 pieces, and in a lifetime you will receive 22,847 items of junk mail. In terms of weight, that's 1,795 copies of this book. Enough to brick up your front door four and a half copies deep.

Junk-mail lists are compiled from the edited electoral roll, harvested from company mailing lists, gathered from the Internet or put together from all these sources by specialised companies. Nearly one-third of companies keep no records of where their mailing lists have been bought, borrowed or 'harvested' from. Unsurprisingly, therefore, the lists tend to be inaccurate. After you die, you will receive another 80 notifications that you have won a guaranteed prize, been preapproved, carefully selected or invited to take advantage of an exclusive opportunity.

To reduce the 4.5 trees' worth of paper you will almost immediately throw in the bin, you can have yourself taken off the edited electoral register by getting in touch with your local elections office. You can also register with the Mailing Preference Service, the Royal Mail Door-to-Door Opt-Out and the Direct Marketing Association 'Your Choice' scheme. It isn't simple, but you will find all the advice you need on www.stopjunkmail.org.uk.

KISSING

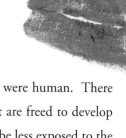

We were walking upright millions of years before we were human. There are many advantages to walking upright: the forefeet are freed to develop into versatile, tool-using hands, you can carry things, be less exposed to the sun, wade in deeper water, reach higher foods, see further and also make love face to face while standing up. There are at least ten theories about how one or a combination of these advantages drove the change from four legs to two – but the ability to have sex up against a wall is not one of them. Our more or less unique capacity to do this means that kissing is also more or less unique to humans.

For hundreds of thousands of years, we have had the lips, upright posture, flat faces and small teeth that make kissing possible and enjoyable. However, the kiss appears to be a relatively recent invention rather than an innate piece of behaviour. The Rig Veda comes from a 3,500-year-old oral tradition that was written down in India for the first time about 2,000 years ago. It contains the earliest mention of something like a kiss – a sort

of nose/cheek rubbing/sniff that is thought to have developed into kissing in time for it to have been brought back to Europe by Alexander the Great's soldiers.

Kissing is an invention still in the process of spreading around the world. In the seventeenth century, European travellers were astonished to find that kissing was unknown in parts of Africa, most of the Far East and the Polynesian islands. Kissing in public is still taboo in many countries, and in both China and Indonesia there have recently been moves to ban the modern and unhealthy 'Western' practice of kissing.

In Britain, we take kissing for granted. According to a recent Internet poll, the average British person spends 54 days of his or her life kissing. This was widely reported in the papers, none of whom bothered to calculate that this would work out as two minutes and 42 seconds kissing every single day of your life and that if each kiss lasted just one second that would be one kiss every nine minutes, 24 hours a day, 365 days a year for 79.1 years. An

American survey came up with a more reasonable figure of 336 hours (two weeks) of kissing in a lifetime.

Most of your kisses will be just one step up from a handshake in terms of intimacy. However, most of the actual time you spend kissing, you will be locked in an embrace that is just one step away from sex. In a study of 1,041 students at an American university, over 50 per cent of the men said they would have sex without kissing, compared with less than 15 per cent of the women. Though they are prepared to do without it entirely, men associate kissing more strongly with sex, which is why straight men rarely kiss their friends whereas women can generally kiss anyone without embarrassment.

Nearly two-thirds of both men and women in the study had occasional experiences where they felt very attracted to someone only to have the passion die at the first kiss. The exchange of saliva containing sex hormones and genetic information may help us choose a mate, though the information is getting to you at an embarrassingly late stage. There is a need nowadays to find an evolutionary explanation for everything. So, kissing has to be a means of mate selection and a way of strengthening the pair bond. It is more likely that these are just incidental bonuses to the fact that kissing is fun. As for it being a uniquely human activity, there are plenty of animals that could kiss or have sex up against a wall if they wanted to, it just hasn't occurred to them yet.

LAND

Pretend an apple is the Earth and cut it into four equal pieces. If you eat three of these, you will be left with the area of the Earth not covered by water in the form of oceans, seas, ice sheets and lakes. If you take your remaining piece and cut this into four and eat three of those bits, you will be left with the 6 per cent of the Earth's surface that is not too steep, too dry, too cold or too hot for agriculture. Alternatively, you could just stick two first-class stamps on an apple. These two stamps are equivalent to the area on the Earth's surface we rely on for food. In fact, only one of the stamps is actually being used to grow crops. The other stamp represents all the land that could be arable land if it wasn't covered with jungle, rainforest, nature reserves, golf courses and out-of-town shopping centres.

Your share of the remaining stamp comes to a square of land with sides just under 47m long. From carrots to cigarettes, everything you consume that has been grown in the ground comes from a plot of land that would easily fit inside the average supermarket.

If you stick another two and a half first-class stamps on your apple you will have the land that we use for pasture. Your share of this comes to a square with 73 m sides. Even added together, the area of the Earth's surface you depend on is only about the size of a football pitch. Every year, as populations rise, your portion of land gets smaller. By 2050 it will have shrunk by around 30 per cent. If a 6-ft man shrank by the same amount he'd be 4 ft 2 in.

In Britain there is one person for every 3,778 m^2. If we were all distributed evenly we would only be about 60 m apart, so you would still be within easy shouting distance of your neighbours. Seventy per cent of the land in Britain is suitable for either crops or animals. This is enough for each of us to have a small square farm exactly 51.44 m wide and long. When Britain was self-sufficient in food, most of us were farmers eating whatever would grow near our homes, unaware of foreign delicacies such as the banana or fresh green beans in the middle of January. We also ate less meat. Our modern standard of living means that your land now has to be spread all over the world. There are onions growing out of it in Tasmania, cattle graz-

LAUGHTER

In 1704 Alexander Selkirk fell out with his shipmates and was marooned on one of the uninhabited Juan Fernández islands 1,000 miles off the coast of Chile. He remained there totally alone, catching goats with his bare hands and sleeping with wild cats to keep the rats away at night, for four and a half years. On his return to Britain he was interviewed by the journalist Richard Steele for an article that would provide the inspiration for Robinson Crusoe. While describing his experiences, Selkirk told the story of how he had chased a goat rather too enthusiastically over a cliff and followed it, all flailing arms and shaggy haired, into the void. When he recovered consciousness he was surprised not to have broken any bones. When he stood up he realised that he had landed on the goat. It cushioned his fall,

saved his life and became dinner for the next few nights. Steele laughed and remarked that there must have been many occasions for humour on the island. Selkirk fixed him with a lonely eye and replied: 'Mr Steele, laughter is a shared pleasure.'

And so it is. You are 30 times more likely to laugh in a group than when you are on your own. Laughter tracks are never used in films, which are meant to be watched with an audience, but they appeared very early on in the history of television, an acknowledgement that TV will often be watched alone. Laughter is communal and the laugh track is there to create the illusion that you are not alone. Who knows, the time may come when your TV is capable of actually projecting a holographic audience into your living room to make the illusion even more convincing.

Though we associate laughter with humour, only about one laugh in five is actually about something funny. Laughter is more commonly a way of releasing social tension, expressing friendliness and signalling that you are not taking offence. Many animals share this kind of laughter. Even rats have been found to exhibit a special kind of squeak when they are play fighting.

As with all types of emotional expression, you laugh less as you grow up. A baby will start to laugh between three and four months. A toddler will typically laugh between 300 and 400 times a day. As an adult this will go down to about 15 times a day. This means that up to the age of 20 you will laugh around 1,344,290 times. The remaining years of your life will only bring forth another 323,572 laughs.

The average total is 1,667,862. Studies of laughter have shown that women laugh more than men. Both women and men are likely to laugh more when listening to men. Perhaps this is why most comedians are male. Unfortunately for female comedians, both women and men are less likely to laugh when a woman is speaking. This at least explains why there are many more bad male comedians than female ones.

As well as laughing less as we grow up, it appears that we are laughing less as a society. Research by the German psychologist Dr Titze concluded that in the 1960s we used to laugh for 18 minutes a day while we now laugh for only six minutes. This may mean that things were funnier back then, we watched less television and we spent more time in social situations. It may

HA! HA! HA! HA! HAA!
HA! HA! HA! HA! Ha! Ha!

also mean that there was a lot more social awkwardness and more anxiety and tension to be released.

LAWYERS

One of the recurrent themes in Greek tragedy is how far you should take things when you have been wronged. Should you revenge yourself on the husband who has betrayed you by murdering his new wife, her father and your own children?

The *Oresteia* by Aeschylus is particularly bloody. Agamemnon sacrifices his daughter and takes up with Cassandra. In revenge, his wife, Clytemnestra, kills Agamemnon and Cassandra. When Agamemnon's son Orestes returns he avenges the death of his father by killing his mother and her lover. By murdering his mother Orestes has released the Furies – mythical beings who punish the crime of killing a parent by pursuing you to the ends of the Earth, driving you mad and destroying you. Just when things look worst for Orestes, the goddess Athene appears and tells everyone to calm down and sort things out like civilised people by going to court. Which they do. Orestes gets off, the Furies are appeased and everything ends in an atmosphere of common sense and mercy.

Aeschylus was a great supporter of Athenian democracy and its new legal system. Unfortunately, once they had a legal system, the Athenians began suing each other. There isn't a Greek play with the theme 'Have you had an accident recently that wasn't your fault …?' However, the misuse of the law to sort out petty grievances by taking people to court is sent up in later Greek plays, especially those of Aristophanes, who was himself constantly being sued by people he had made fun of.

The law is a way of resolving disputes and righting wrongs without getting into a fight or waiting for the goddess Athene to descend from the clouds to sort it all out. It means that in order to protect your property and your rights you don't have to be physically superior. Though, of course, those who are physically superior traditionally make the laws.

Criminal law generally covers all the things that the government will try to settle on your behalf using the police, the courts, prisons, fines and other

punishments. This part of the legal system comes out of your total tax bill and will cost you around £516 a year or £40,864 in a lifetime. The rest is civil or common law and it will be largely up to you to take the initiative and meet the costs to right your own wrongs.

Almost everything you do will be within the framework of the law. This is most obvious when you sign a contract to take out a store card, open a bank account, buy and insure a house, and extend the warranty on a washing machine. In fact, everything you buy, from your house down to a newspaper, will involve some form of legal contract. The law also provides boundaries and rules for how you drive, dress, walk along the street, talk to people, listen to music and everything else you are likely to get up to. Naturally, you will spend your whole life breaking these laws, driving too fast, dropping litter, running naked into the sea, shouting at people in the street and listening to music too loud. It isn't much fun living in countries where these rules are rigidly enforced and you might be sent to prison or whipped for minor transgressions. In Britain, as long as you aren't too conspicuous, don't alarm or endanger people or cost them money, you will probably get away with it.

One of the strengths of our legal system is that it is based on precedent and has evolved to fit the needs of society. Presumably MPs wearing armour in the Houses of Parliament and people hanging beds out of windows were once significant problems, so these are still against the law. The disadvantage is that precedent-based law is inherently conservative. Systems that are based on a notion of rights (as in Scotland) are able to react more quickly to change. In either system there are sometimes arguments about whether something is illegal or not. Arguments like these, which travel up through the hierarchy of our courts through the House of Lords and on to Europe, are very lucrative for lawyers.

In common with all the professions, you pay lawyers wages. In 2008, British lawyers earned a total of £15 billion. That's £247.50 for every person in Britain. Sometimes you will pay a lawyer directly (buying a house, making a will), sometimes less directly (taking out a credit card, insuring your house). In a lifetime, Britain's lawyers will cost you £19,583.

Having a legal system might mean you no longer need an intimidating physical presence and a reputation for extreme violence to get justice, but you will need a deep purse – deep enough to contain at least £60,447.

LIES

We start to lie as soon as we start talking. If we learned to talk earlier we would start lying earlier. To begin with, we are very bad liars. In order to lie well you must be able to imagine what is going on in other people's heads. For the first few years of your life, you won't have even the basic concept that your mind is separate from everyone else's. You assume that everyone knows what you know. Around the age of three or four you begin to understand that you can know things without other people knowing them too. From this it is only a short step to learning that you can make people believe things you know are not true, which is the essence of a lie.

Without a theory of mind, you would be unable to empathise with other people, guess what they are thinking or how they feel or predict how they might react. Without these skills, living and working with other people is almost impossible. Without them you would also be unable to lie. We are very good at lying and very bad at being able to tell when we are being lied to. By the age of five you will already be able to lie well enough to deceive most adults. As an adult around one-third of all the conversations you have will involve some kind of deception and you will tell two important lies a day. So that's a minimum of 57,782 lies in a lifetime.

Lying is one of the most important social skills. We all have an idea of what we are like, which differs from what we are actually like. The lies we tell and are told enable us to preserve the illusion of who we think we are.

The most embarrassing and hurtful moments of our lives are usually when these lies are exposed, either inadvertently or maliciously by other people or through our own stupid behaviour.

Bringing people together and exposing the lies they have been telling each other in front of a studio audience is a staple of daytime television. Increasingly, these programmes seek to establish the truth by using lie-detector tests. Polygraph tests, which essentially measure how anxious you are about answering certain questions, have been shown to be no more reliable than the techniques used by medieval witchfinders. The same appears to be true for more sophisticated brain-scan tests, which claim to be able to tell when you are accessing real or fabricated memories.

Lie-detector tests only have any currency at all because we are so bad at being able to tell when people are lying to us. Surprisingly, knowing some-one well doesn't make you any better at being able to spot their lies. In fact, people in long-term relationships are particularly bad at being able to tell when their partner is lying. This may be one of the reasons they have managed to stay together for so long.

THE LOTTERY

Life is a lottery. The ejaculation that created you contained around 400 million sperm, each one different and only one of which could fertilise the egg. The odds against you being you are 400 million to 1.

In the 79.1 years of your life you will be exposed to all sorts of dangers. The odds of dying by the following causes are:

Car crash	84 –1
Being run over	626 –1
Tripping on stairs	2,400 –1
Plane crash	5000 –1
Falling out of a building	6,300 –1
Drowning in the bath	11,300 –1
Lightning strike	80,000 –1
Being buried alive	81,500 –1
Bus crash	104,100 –1
Firework	341,000 –1
Tram crash	1,874,000 –1

The odds on winning the lottery are 14,000,000 to 1, which means that even travelling by tram you are more likely to be accidentally killed on the way to collect your winnings than you are to win in the first place.

LOVE

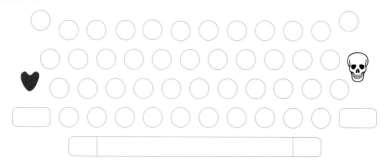

From the point of view of a storyteller, coming up with an idea for a good love story is not about finding an interesting way of bringing two people together, it is about how to keep them apart. By and large, the love stories that endure are the ones where the obstacles are still plausible today. In *Pride and Prejudice*, Elizabeth Bennet and Mr Darcy are prevented from getting together by Lizzie's belief that he is a swine. Then she finds out he has a heart of gold and a large country estate. In the main, though, love stories of the past tended not to turn on subtle internal obstacles. Writers simply took advantage of the rules and laws of society and had the parents of the girl object to the boy. So, there are a lot of love stories where the young man has to get around the girl's parents. This may involve secret meetings, dressing up as a priest or being engaged to give music lessons to the girl's mother who falls for him but then the father is kidnapped by pirates ... The story will end in a wedding if it is a comedy or everyone committing suicide by mistake if it is a tragedy. If you were feeling particularly adventurous you might have your lovers married to other people. But as adultery was punishable by death, and divorce was more or less impossible, these stories always tended to end badly.

This was the situation for thousands of years. Parental word was law and marriage was for life. Romance and love were for the young and came to an end pretty much with marriage or death. However, over the last century there have been such upheavals in morality and what is legally and socially acceptable that both love stories and the concept of love itself have changed utterly. There are still parts of society where the old rules apply, but for most of us, if the only thing keeping the lovers apart is parental disapproval or the fact that they are already married, it isn't enough to make an interesting story.

In modern love stories, the couple can't get together because the woman turns out to be a man (*The Crying Game*), the man is pretending to be a woman (*Some Like it Hot, Tootsie*), one of them is dead (*Ghost*), they are working through some modern angst that friendship and love are incompatible (*When Harry Met Sally*), or the boy has been bitten by a radioactive spider and is too busy using his superpowers to fight crime ...

We will go to crazy lengths to overcome the obstacles that get in the way of love. The language of love shares words with the language of mental illness: 'crazy', 'mad', 'fool', 'addiction', 'obsession'... This link predates the functional MRI scanner by thousands of years, but when you put someone who is in love into one of these machines you find that, in the early stages, love lights up the same areas of the brain as obsessive-compulsive disorder. In the case of the lovesick, anxiety is linked to being with or not being with a particular person rather than checking that the front door is locked or the light is off.

People in the first flush of love also experience the same simultaneous drop in the neurotransmitter serotonin, accompanied by a suffusing of the body's pleasure centres with dopamine, that goes with addictive drugs (and eating chocolate). Love really is an addiction that makes you crave another person and think about nothing else other than your next hit. This craziness and addiction mean that love is a useful theme for storytellers because it makes people do weird things we can identify with.

But the love story will only work if we understand why the people want to be with each other so badly in the first place. In general, this means that the male audience has to fancy the woman and the female audience has to fancy the man. Over the years there has been a lot of research done in this area. The results are never particularly surprising. Both men and women find intelligence attractive. Women like men who have money and are kind. Men are prepared to compromise on wealth and kindness in favour of youth, physical beauty and large breasts. Physically, women tend to prefer handsome men with taut athletic bodies who are slightly older than they are.

In an ideal world, we would all end up with Brad Pitt or Angelina Jolie. But, unlike stories, we do not end up riding off into the sunset with our perfect mate. One of the things love does is to stop us wasting time on the unobtainable. Love stories place an emphasis on the impossible but in real life we fall in love with the people who are available. Usually, they are people we already know and think might like us. Brain scans of people in love reveal that the parts of the brain associated with critical judgement, negative emotions and assessing other people's intentions do not come into play when they look at pictures of their lovers. This is the neurological evidence that love really is blind. It enables you to see your less-than-perfect love as perfect.

Brain scans of mothers looking at pictures of their children have the same pattern. Maternal love is more or less ubiquitous in mammals. This makes sense as there is a strong evolutionary pressure in favour of something that sends the mothers of everything from voles to giraffes into the jaws of death to protect their offspring. Friendship, pair bonding, religious devotion, all forms of love are likely to be developments of maternal love and this is borne out by the fact that they all show similar brain activity and stimulate the same chemical reward pathways. Romantic love is exceptional in two respects because though you can love more than one child or friend at the same time, full-on, head-over-heels infatuation is usually possible with only one person at a time. Romantic love is also the only kind of love that triggers lust …

So, love turns another person into something you find as addictive as cocaine. It drives you slightly crazy, turns off your critical facilities and makes you want to have sex. This adds up to a mechanism that stops you looking. Given the sheer quantities of fish in the sea, love speeds up the search for the perfect mate considerably by making you focus in on one individual. In the traditional love story, the young lovers, helplessly intoxicated, blind and horny, are carried by love over the one-way threshold of marriage, after which being in love is a bonus but hardly essential. But love isn't just something that is hard-wired into our brains by evolution, it is also determined by culture. *Romeo and Juliet* doesn't just reflect a culture where to go against your family meant doom and tragedy, it helped perpetuate it.

The relationship between behaviour and culture is too complex and dynamic to separate out cause and effect and apportion blame. Whether it is part of the feedback loop that drives change or not, the evolution of the love story certainly illustrates the changes. Countries with traditional views on marriage by and large produce traditional love stories where society/parents disapprove. We don't. All the charm of *Brief Encounter* comes from how antique (and uncommercial) its can't-quite-summon-up-the-nerve-to-commit-adultery storyline feels to us now. But something else has happened at the same time. The last 100 years have seen an explosion in the culture of love. It dominates popular music, advertising, film, television, literature – all forms of culture – in an unprecedented way.

We live longer; marriage is no longer a one-way door. Keeping a relationship going is hard. Love is no longer just what brings you together, it is expected to keep you together. It also breaks you up. Not loving someone would have been pretty slim grounds for divorce 100 years ago. It wouldn't even have been taken all that seriously as a reason for not getting married in the first place. Nowadays, we want the love that got us together to keep us together. Being trapped in a loveless relationship, no longer being in love or being in love with someone else are the commonest reasons for splitting up. This has the knock-on effect of putting people back on the market over and over again in a way that didn't used to happen.

You can expect to fall in love like a mooncalf for the first time at the age of 13 and have your first serious adult relationship at 17, with four more episodes in the rest of your life. Love – the kind you can measure in a functional MRI scanner – lasts between one and a half and three years (just long enough to accompany you on your honeymoon). In total, 13.5 years of your life where you may be unexpectedly reduced to a slavering, love-struck imbecile by the way someone adjusts his or her glasses. One in ten people will have a least three unrequited loves.

The commonest obstacle that real-life love has to conquer is the difficult job of keeping it going year after year, decade after decade. Unfortunately, long-term companionate love is not nearly as interesting to write about as the crazy, impossible, constantly-saving-each-other-from-burning-buildings and defying-society kind of love that doesn't last. The problem with stories is that they give you unrealistic expectations, as the many wives and girl-friends of the actors who have played Mr Darcy over the years will tell you.

MAKE-UP

The myth of Narcissus told by Ovid is the story of a hunting trip gone tragically wrong. Narcissus goes into the forest to hunt stags. Echo, a love-struck nymph, secretly follows him. She is too shy to speak or show herself, but when Narcissus hears her footsteps he calls out, 'Hello!' She is so nervous, all she can do is repeat back to him what he has said. *'Hello?'* 'Who are you?' *'Who are you?'* 'Please keep quiet!' *'Please keep quiet!'* 'Just shut up will you, you're scaring them off!!' *'Just shut up…'* This went on for some time and you have to say that Echo was pretty lucky Narcissus didn't shoot her the moment she finally emerged from the bushes.

By this time, surprisingly enough, Narcissus had rather had enough of Echo so he told her to go away and eventually she did. She wandered off to a lonely glen where she pined away from unrequited love until all that remained was her voice, forever cursed only to repeat back what people say in motorway underpasses and other acoustically reflective places. Narcissus carried on with his hunting. No doubt he had to go much further than he intended, having spooked the stags with all that shouting. He got thirsty, went to a pool for a drink, saw his own reflection for the first time and promptly fell in love with it. He moved forward; his reflection moved forward. He tilted his head; the reflection tilted its head. He moved in for the kiss and the rippling of the water made it disappear. He was heartbroken until the pool became calm again. So there the idiot boy sat, staring at his own reflection until he died of thirst and turned into a daffodil.

There are several versions of the Narcissus myth. In one he is pining for his dead twin sister, in another he is being punished for rejecting a string of female admirers, elsewhere he is cursed by the gods after the man whose love he has scorned impales himself on a sword. All rely on the beguiling power of mirrors. We live in a world of reflective surfaces and cameras. We know what we look like. We are used to seeing our reflection. It is hard to imagine a time when it was only a particular conjunction of sunlight, water and still air that allowed you to catch a glimpse of yourself. Stone Age mirrors made of polished volcanic glass must have been startling, even frightening objects. Up until then, the only place you could rely on seeing yourself was in the eyes of others. In all animals – frogs, fish, goats, horses, tigers, crocodiles, people – the centre of the eye is always a shiny, reflective black. In nearly all languages the word for pupil means 'little man' because close up that is what you see there, a tiny reflection of yourself.

Evidence of make-up goes back almost as far as evidence of human culture and long predates the widespread availability of mirrors, which wasn't until the middle of the nineteenth century. Most of the make-up in the history of humanity has been applied without mirrors, probably by other people. As checking what you looked like was difficult, you would have been dependent on other people's reactions. It must have been a bit like playing that game where you have to guess what is written on your forehead. This may have made you more conscious of what other people thought about your appearance, but it probably also meant that it was both harder to become obsessed with what you actually looked like and easier to assume you looked how you would like to look.

Most of the make-up used today – foundation, mascara, eyeliner, nail varnish, lipstick, blusher, powder – has been available in some form or other for thousands of years. Fashions have swung wildly between the extremes of no make-up through subtle enhancement to total obliteration. There have been times when men and women both wore make-up more or less equally, but there never seems to have been a time when men wore more than women. No matter how much make-up the strutting peacocks of Louis XIV's court wore, the women were wearing more. For all the hoo-ha about the rise of the metrosexual man, only about 8 per cent of the £8.16 billion British cosmetics and toiletries market is spent on male grooming. The average British man will spend £23 a year on cosmetics and toiletries – £1,820 in a lifetime. The average British woman spends more than ten times as much: £246 a year or £19,476 in a lifetime, which is about 67 p a day. Of this 8 p goes on skincare and 29 p on make-up.

Even the heaviest make-up represents a layer a few molecules thick between you and the world. Applying it requires you to look at your own face much as a lover might, paying particular attention to the eyes and the mouth. Even if it is being done while changing lanes on the motorway or rattling along in a crowded tube train, putting on your face is an intimate process. But just because it involves gazing into your own eyes doesn't mean that make-up is about narcissism. For most women it involves a different kind of self-love, something you do for yourself, that you deserve because you are worth it, and the result is about self-confidence and a face you are happy to show to the world.

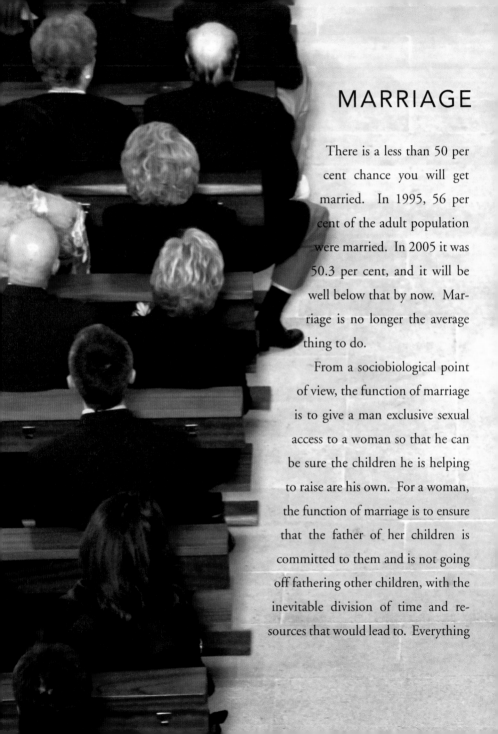

MARRIAGE

There is a less than 50 per
cent chance you will get
married. In 1995, 56 per
cent of the adult population
were married. In 2005 it was
50.3 per cent, and it will be
well below that by now. Marriage is no longer the average
thing to do.

From a sociobiological point
of view, the function of marriage
is to give a man exclusive sexual
access to a woman so that he can
be sure the children he is helping
to raise are his own. For a woman,
the function of marriage is to ensure
that the father of her children is
committed to them and is not going
off fathering other children, with the
inevitable division of time and resources that would lead to. Everything

else – the richer and poorer, in sickness and in health, until death us do part – is no more than you would expect from any friend. This might be a plausible theory of what marriage is for, but you would hope that it isn't uppermost in your mind on your wedding day, and it wouldn't form the basis for very good wedding vows either.

Traditionally, marriages are romantic events. But are they? The essence of romance is uncertainty. Who's that girl? Did he notice me? Will she be there? Will he call? Are we going to kiss? Will you marry me? Romantic stories do not begin with weddings, they end with them. The wedding marks the conclusion of all that uncertainty. An end to all that romance. But, marriage isn't as certain as it used to be.

In the 1970s, you could expect to get married at 26. As the average marriage lasted 37 years you were pretty much expecting to spend the rest of your life with the person you married. Though life expectancy has gone up since then, so has the divorce rate and the average marriage now lasts 24 years. Almost 40 per cent of all marriages will end in divorce after 11 years. Overall, the divorce rate is actually falling by between 2 and 3 per cent a year, but this is probably simply because fewer people are getting married in the first place. The marriage rate is currently falling by 4 per cent a year.

Although there are fewer of them, the cost of weddings seems to go up every year. In 2008 it was announced that the average wedding had finally broken the £20,000 barrier. This widely quoted figure comes from *You and Your Wedding* magazine, which does a survey every year to coincide with National Marriage Week in the run-up to Valentine's Day. Apparently, £7,724 goes on the reception; £3,200 for the honeymoon. The dress will cost £997 and the groom will shell out £1,412 on the ring, the restaurant and the team of sky-diving gypsy violinists for the proposal. These figures are not obtained by dividing the total cost of weddings in Britain by the total number of weddings in Britain, they are obtained by polling 1,500 readers of *You and Your Wedding* magazine. Every national newspaper does a story on this figure every year and they never, ever headline it as 'Readers of *You and Your Wedding* magazine are spending more than ever on their weddings'. The minimum a wedding can cost is £60 for giving official notice that you intend to get married and £43.50 for the ceremony, which includes a marriage certificate. Getting that official piece of paper from the government will cost you each £51.75.

If you take a load of wedding photographs, cut them in two and get a group of people to rank the brides in order of attractiveness and get another group to rank the grooms, it is more or less possible to correctly reassemble the photographs just using these rankings. There will be some exceptions (the result of bad/good photography, personality, wealth, fame), but generally the most attractive bride will be married to the most attractive groom and the second most attractive bride to the second-ranked groom, and so on. The same effect is broadly true for income, social background and education. Now that we have more freedom than ever before to choose to whom we get married, we tend to choose to marry a version of ourselves.

Traditionally, a wedding requires there to be at least one trembling young virgin at the altar making the rite of passage into adulthood and reproductive sex. As recently as 1990 more than 50 per cent of people disapproved of sex or living together before marriage. In the last 20 years there has been a dramatic swing in favour of premarital sex and cohabitation, with more than half of people now thinking it should actually be encouraged. More than 70 per cent of people living together for the first time are not married. The taboo of children being born out of wedlock has also more or less disappeared. In 1974, 5 per cent of children were officially bastards. In 2000 45 per cent were bastards and the term no longer has any connection with the marital status of your mum and dad. There has also been a sharp decline in the importance of marriage as a religious rite. Since 1992 there have been more civil than religious ceremonies and this has increased every year. In 2008 less than one-third of marriages took place within the sight of God.

Marriage is still actively encouraged by the state. A major part of this used to be tax incentives but most of these have gone. There is a 100 per cent inter-spouse allowance for inheritance tax, but this only applies if your estate is worth more than £312,000 and as fewer than 7 per cent of people are this well off, it's not really an issue for the average person. The same applies to the small capital-gains-tax break. More important is the use of marriage to define a relationship in a way that excludes people who are in close relationships but who have not or cannot get married. This creates quite a significant pressure to get married because these rights only become important at the worst possible times. Who gets to make decisions in medical emergencies, who inherits if there is no will, do you get pension rights from your dead partner ...

In 2004, the opportunity to take advantage of these rights was extended to same-sex couples. The obvious thing would have been to change the law so that same-sex couples could get married, but this would have been politically impossible. So, as well as having to create an entirely new legal concept to cover same-sex partnerships, the government also had to be careful never to refer to it as gay or lesbian marriage or compare it in any way to heterosexual marriage for fear of freaking out the country. The groups campaigning for civil partnerships held the view that the rights were more important than the name. The controversy surrounding gay marriage reflects the fact that for a lot of influential people marriage is still a state-endorsed religious institution that has more to do with the sociobiologist's definition of marriage than it does with romance.

Marriage demands some kind of ceremony because it is a legal requirement for the words forming the union to be spoken out loud in front of witnesses. In contrast, a civil partnership is formed when the second partner signs a document. There is no requirement for them even to be in the same room. The whole thing can be done by post. However, it is rare for a civil partnership to be formed without a bit of ceremony. Marriage, gay, lesbian or otherwise – standing up in front of everyone you know and making promises to another person – is still a rite of passage. Unlike the past, couples rarely consider themselves to be making a commitment to the institution of marriage, they are solely making a commitment to each other.

For some people the whole idea of marriage as an institution, as a religious rite, as a social construct with all the baggage of a wife belonging to a husband and having to make a promise to love, look after and put up with someone for ever, is anathema. But it isn't the government or society that decides whether you stay together or not. That is between you and your spouse, life partner or live-in lover. If you go off and father children elsewhere or bear another man's child then your relationship is likely to suffer. The sociobiologist's rules of marriage apply, whether you are married or not.

MEAT

Unlike crops and vegetables, meat goes off quickly. Our ancestors had problems storing meat. If you killed something too big to eat before it went bad, the best way of storing it was in the bellies of your friends and neighbours in the hope that they would return the favour. Cementing friendships and stocking up goodwill is still one of the reasons for inviting people to eat with you, and occasions like these still tend to focus on meat. The bigger the occasion, the bigger and more obviously dead the piece of meat has to be. At Christmas we tend to eat specially reared giant birds such as turkeys or geese, which are brought whole to the table and carved before the admiring eyes of your guests. Other popular feasts may include a whole roast pig or, even more extravagantly, a series of animals of increasing size stuffed inside each other.

The importance of meat as a feast food has diminished as it has got cheaper and easier to come by. Rather than saving it for special occasions, we can now expect to eat meat most days. As an adult, you will get through around 1 kg of meat every week, 3,621 kg in a lifetime.

This is a problem, as raising meat is a very wasteful use of land. Eating too much of it isn't very good for you either. Then there is the moral question. Is it right to kill animals to eat when we don't have to? Hundreds of animals will die to provide you with a lifetime's supply of meat and you are unlikely to have killed any of them yourself.

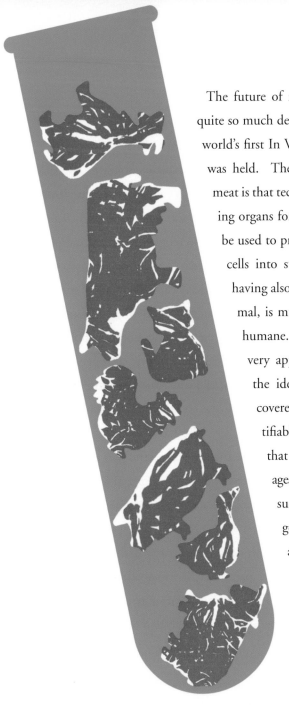

The future of meat may not include quite so much death. In April 2008 the world's first In Vitro Meat Symposium was held. The idea behind in vitro meat is that techniques used for growing organs for transplantation could be used to produce meat. Growing cells into steaks directly, without having also to grow a sentient animal, is much more efficient and humane. It might not sound very appealing, but neither is the idea of mechanically recovered meat or the unidentifiable paste of body parts that goes into most sausages. In vitro meat may well succeed because we have got used to not thinking about where our meat has come from.

MEDICINES

In 2005, Fabrizio Benedetti, a neuroscientist at the University of Turin Medical School, published the results of an experiment in which he deliberately caused people pain for several days. His volunteers had the circulation in one arm restricted using an inflatable cuff, and were given pain relief with morphine. After about a week, he secretly switched the morphine to salt water. None of the volunteers noticed. The salt water provided just as much pain relief as the morphine. Given what we know about the placebo effect, this isn't very surprising. Benedetti repeated the experiment and found that if he added naloxone – a drug that stops morphine from working – to the salt water it no longer worked. The surprising conclusion is that the salt water was eliciting the same biochemical response from the body as morphine. This gives momentum to the idea that the effects of placebos are more than just imaginary.

The idea that the placebo effect is the only useful part of complementary and alternative medicine is not popular with practitioners or users of CAM. It suggests that the therapists are frauds and their patients idiots. However, no one is immune to the placebo effect and it actually appears to work better if the therapist truly believes in what he or she is doing. Putting the placebo effect – the useful part of CAM – to good use raises all sorts of practical and ethical issues for medicine. The study of placebos and what they tell us about the interaction between body and mind is still a relatively unexplored field. In future it may lead to the reintroduction of the concept of doctor as healer and change the way we experience health care. At present, aside from CAM, the major influence of the placebo effect is felt in the marketing of medicines.

Adverts build on and feed into our cultural ideas about illness and medicine. Headaches are glowing red spots between your eyes, or tiny men using pneumatic drills on your temples. Stomach acid is the glowing magma chamber of a volcano, only inside your chest; colds are dripping taps or battalions of runny noses, sore throats and chesty coughs all done up in Napoleonic uniforms attacking you on the way to work. These are not medical descriptions of ailments, but they are memorable and reflect what being ill feels like.

The cures portrayed in advertising are no more accurate. The cold sufferer having taken his medicine scatters the regiments of headachy coldiness with his briefcase. Glowing blobs of honey soothe sore throats, ghostly wisps of menthol clear blocked noses, liquid antacid firemen abseil down your throat and quench the fires of heartburn, the man with the pneumatic drill is karate-chopped, the throbbing red spot between your eyes turns a calming blue so that you can get on with your day …

These work as advertising because they make convincing promises about how effective your medicine will be. It is a bizarre, not to mention annoying, fact that convincing advertising plays a role in the effectiveness of your medicine. Expensive, branded products that promise to send active ingredients quivering into the centre of the pain target may actually be more effective than exactly the same ingredients in a plain box without the mental image to go along with it.

In Britain, unlike in the United States, drug companies are not permitted to advertise prescription drugs to the general public. We are, however, being subtly affected by drug advertising. Numerous studies have shown that medicines are more effective if the doctor believes in them. This may account for an odd effect that occurs when new drugs are introduced. New drugs are heavily marketed to doctors. Consequently, they are likely to be prescribed with a high level of confidence. As time passes, the glow of advertising fades and so does the enthusiasm of the doctor and, with it, the effectiveness of the drug. When a new drug for the same thing is introduced, it is naturally marketed as better. This has an impact on the doctor's faith in the original drug. In a typical example, a drug might be 80 per cent effective in the general population when it comes out, which may drop to 50 per cent when it is superseded. The drug is the same, the patients are the same, the ailment is the same; all that changes is the doctor's level of enthusiasm.

These subtle factors will have an impact throughout your life. In total, you are going to get through 2,291 packs of medicines. Of these, 1,214 packs will be heavily advertised over-the-counter medicines, to which you will add your own expectations to the active ingredients, at a cost of £2,963. The remaining 1,077 will be relatively anonymous medicines prescribed by a doctor. While you may pick up a few clues from the weary, unenthusiastic way your doctor hands over the prescription, you will have little idea about what you have been given.

You will know the name, of course, which will be a combination of medical syllables like am, para, neuro, co, non, pro, anti, myc, phen, dol, cil or dine, which will have been used to inspire confidence and also to give a clue as to what the medicine might do. We all have a basic understanding of what these syllables mean, which is why Neurocil or Vagiphen are never likely to be used as drug names. The colour of the pill may be another clue. As we attach certain emotions to different colours, this is used to market pills to us. Red, orange and pink are stimulating. Blue, yellow, purple and green are calming. Painkillers tend to be red. Prozac is blue and white. Viagra tablets are blue, but this may be for other cultural reasons.

As for the actual contents and effects of your medicines, without testing them for yourself you will just have to trust you aren't being lied to. There are some things that do not respond well to medicine. Things like colds, back pain and stress. The NHS could save a lot of money by offering appropriately coloured sugar pills and other placebo treatments for these ailments. There is the ethical problem of having doctors lie to their patients, but as placebos are more effective if the doctor believes the treatment is real it would be better for them not to know anyway. In fact, for placebos to work, they would have to be kept secret from everyone more or less. If they were being used now, would you even know?

MILK

Like all mammals, at the start of our lives all we eat is milk. Unlike any other mammals, humans continue to eat and drink milk after they have been weaned. The average British person will consume milk in some form almost every single day. A total of 11,782 pints. Enough bottles to fill a doorstep 530 m long. This doesn't just make you exceptional in the animal kingdom, it also makes you different from most humans.

The rest of the world doesn't drink much milk. In fact, most humans do not even have the ability to process milk in these sorts of quantities. In order to digest milk fully you need to produce an enzyme called lactase. In most people this is controlled by a gene that switches itself off before adulthood. Without lactase, drinking milk causes a build-up of the milky sugar lactose, which can cause all sorts of digestive problems. In Britain, 95 per cent of people are equipped with a different gene that does not turn off. You will continue to be able to digest milk fully all your life, which means that unlike most of the world you can pretty well drink as much as you want.

Up until about 7,000 years ago, no one had this gene and humans probably didn't drink that much milk. When a genetic mutation increases the chances of survival, it gets passed on. The first people with the new gene would have been the first people to have access to a food source rich in proteins, carbohydrates, fats and vitamins, which unlike water was not infected with parasites and which unlike crops was available all the year round. Anyone without the gene who tried to copy them would have suffered bloating, stomach cramps and spectacular diarrhoea and would have had a much harder time surviving the northern European winters. The ability to drink milk was such an advantage in northern Europe that it quickly spread, but only to places where it was an advantage. This is why fewer people in southern Europe have the ability to digest milk properly and explains why fresh milk is available in every corner shop in Britain but can only be found in obscure corners of larger southern European supermarkets.

Both the ability to drink milk and its production have spread with northern European peoples. The biggest milk producers in the world are Europe, the USA and Canada. Britain is the ninth biggest producer of milk in the world, despite being only the twenty-second biggest country.

Life isn't much fun for a dairy cow. A cow will typically suckle a calf for 8–12 months and will produce up to 1,000 l of milk a year. A dairy cow, however – fed on a concentrated diet and demand-feeding a milking machine – will produce around 6,500 l a year. Dairy cows have their first calves at about two years old. For a few days after the birth the cow only produces colostrum – a milk-like substance rich in antibodies, vitamins and minerals that cannot be sold as milk. The calf is taken away as soon as the proper milk comes in and the cow is milked 2–3 times a day for the next ten months. In order to keep up milk production the cow will be impregnated again within three months of giving birth, with only a short break in milking before the next calf is born, and the cycle begins again. It is hardly surprising that the average dairy cow lives for just five years compared with a natural lifespan of between 20 and 25 years.

After it leaves the cow, the milk is pasteurised and then homogenised by forcing it through tiny holes at high pressure, which breaks up the fat molecules and stops the milk separating. The layer of cream floating on the top of unhomogenised milk is the first thing to go off and will turn the whole bottle within two days, even if it is kept in a fridge. Homogenised milk can last up to three weeks. The downside of homogenisation is that it makes the molecules of fat small enough to be absorbed directly through the walls of your intestines, which may or may not cause allergies and heart disease. Nobody is quite sure yet, but scientific opinion is moving in this direction. Another controversial aspect of milk is calcium.

Milk contains a lot of calcium, which is one of the reasons we are always being encouraged to drink more of it. Getting enough calcium is important for building and maintaining your teeth and bones. Calcium also plays an essential role in blood clotting, your nervous system and regulating your heartbeat. Your bones are where you store calcium. Up until the age of 30 or so you will be building bone, but after 30 you will slowly lose bone minerals. How much calcium you take in will affect how quickly this happens. Osteoporosis – weak, porous bones – is the result of losing calcium faster than it is being replaced. The strange thing is that osteoporosis is much more common in countries with a high milk consumption, such as Britain, than it is in countries like China where much less milk is consumed. In fact, the highest rates of osteoporosis in generally dairy-free Asia are found in Japan, where milk is becoming part of the national diet.

There is no consensus of opinion on why this is. While milk does contain a lot of calcium, it also contains protein, and digesting protein leaches calcium from your bones. People in countries with milky diets also tend to eat a lot of meat and as a result may be eating too much protein. The Western diet may also be an indicator of the sedentary, indoor Western lifestyle that is not good for any part of your body.

Whatever the case, we no longer need milk to get us through the long hard winters and living longer subjects us to all sorts of new risks such as osteoporosis and heart disease. At the moment, the benefits of drinking a small amount of milk still outweigh the possible disadvantages of drinking too much. However, the jury is still out on this question and things are certainly more complicated than the beaming smiles and milky moustaches of the 'Got Milk' campaign might suggest.

MONEY

In 1817 Squire John Mytton turned 21 and inherited one of the largest fortunes in England. His country estate at Halston Hall near Shrewsbury was worth over £4 million and brought in an annual income of more than £700,000 in today's money. He immediately set about the task of spending it all.

He was a man of uncontrollable desires with the cash to do pretty much whatever he wanted. At the height of his career as the greatest hellraiser of all time, Mad Jack Mytton was getting through five bottles of vintage port a day, living with his 2,000 dogs, which he fed on champagne and steak, and 60 cats, some of which he had dressed in footman's livery. His own wardrobe contained over 150 pairs of riding breeches, 700 pairs of boots, more than 1,000 hats and nearly 3,000 shirts. Along with the cats and dogs, his horses had the run of the house and his favourite, Baronet, would often sleep with him in front of the fire. He would ride his pet bear, Nell, into dinner to frighten his guests. Once it turned nasty and ate part of his leg. His life was a series of drunken brawls, stupid dares, carriage crashes and riding accidents from which Mytton emerged unscathed, laughing and handing out fistfuls of cash. By 1830, his estates sold and all the money spent, he fled to France to escape his creditors. After setting fire to himself to cure a bad case of the hiccups, Mytton returned to England, where he died in a debtor's prison at the age of 38.

Most of us will not have the luxury of being handed our lifetime's supply of money at the age of 21. In total you will earn £1,100,282, but you will only get hold of this a small amount at a time. When you are working you can expect to come into it at the rate of £479 a week, but the average rate across the whole of your life is just £267.50 a week.

You will spend nearly all of this mon- ey without ever getting to see it, let alone touch it. That is hardly surprising because money is not so much a thing as an idea, and the story of that idea is the story of how it has become more and more abstract.

The earliest form of money is commodity money, which is just one step on from bartering. The word 'salary' comes from the salt used to pay Roman soldiers. Salt, sugar, rice, cigarettes, opium, jewels, precious metals – anything both movable and valuable can be used as commodity money. Coins are a way of standardising an amount of precious metal with the logos of the state as a guarantee. The milling that still exists on the edges of £1 coins was invented by Isaac Newton when he was Master of the Mint to prevent people from shaving off gold and silver. As well as being inconvenient and risky to carry around, commodity money suffers from a problem of losing value through use. Millions of pounds' worth of gold and silver must have been worn away and lost in the pockets and sweaty hands of the public.

Commodity money was replaced by representative money, which has no value in itself but can be exchanged for something that does. Every £1 in circulation was matched by an equivalent amount of gold at the bank. Up until 1931, when Britain abandoned the Gold Standard, you could in theory take your £1 note to the bank and demand its value in gold.

The money we have now is fiat money, £1 is worth a £1 because the government says it is. Though bank notes still carry a message from the Queen – 'I promise to pay the bearer on demand the sum of five pounds' – it is unclear what you would be given if you tried it out. A newer £5 note presumably.

In order for our complicated economy to work, money has to be able to flow around quickly and easily. Most of the money you will spend will be electronic and have no more physical form than an arrangement of electrons on a hard disk somewhere.

Every year the Office for National Statistics carries out a survey of household spending. Taking the figures from this, the average cost of living your life in Britain will come to £781,336. ONS figures give the median weekly income before tax as £457. The median is similar to the average but is less prone to being massively skewed by the relatively small number of people who earn huge amounts of money. Taking this figure gives a lifetime income of £1,100,282. Taking off £201,181 for tax still leaves £117,765 that isn't accounted for in the household spending figure. The household spending survey is not intended to be a strict balance sheet of income and expenditure and it does not include the various crazy expenses of our lives such as weddings, dream holidays and stupid gambling sprees. It also doesn't fully take into account credit and how much we spend on debt.

Credit is a way of spending your lifetime's earnings before you have earned them. In this sense, it is the exact reverse of saving. It makes sense to use credit to buy a house you could never afford otherwise, and that you will (probably) be able to sell at a profit. It makes less sense to use a credit card to buy 150 pairs of riding breeches you don't need because you simply can't wait to own them. Britain owes £54.9 billion on credit cards. Between the ages of 18 and 79.1 you will have a constant credit-card debt of £1,174. Like Squire Mytton, you will spend your whole life living beyond your means and at 16 per cent APR it will cost you £11,477 just to pay the interest.

NAILS

In 1952 a 14-year-old boy called Shridhar Chillal from Pune in western India read about a Chinese priest who had grown the fingernails on one hand to over 57 cm. Shridhar decided that this would be an easy record to break. In theory, as fingernails grow at a rate of about 3 mm per month, which is 1 cm every 100 days, he expected to be able to break the record in 1,140 days. A little over three years. So, he stopped cutting the nails on his left hand.

Unfortunately, several other people also had the same idea at the same time and their nails grew faster than Shridhar's. For the next 30 years the record was passed from one hideously curly-nailed hand to the next. The Chinese record fell to a man in Delhi, who lost it to a man in Calcutta with fingernails over 140 cm long. Year after year, Shridhar held his nerve and bided his time in what is probably one of the slowest races in history. Every week he was gaining on his opponents by a fraction of a millimetre. A momentary lapse of concentration, a single broken nail, could put him years behind the pace. Finally, after 31 gruelling years, Shridhar took the world record in 1983. His nails were then over 295 cm long.

Rates of nail growth vary greatly from person to person. It slows with age and is faster in the summer than in the winter. Working with your hands can stimulate blood flow and make your nails grow faster, but then again it can have the opposite effect. Letting your nails grow longer than normal probably has an effect too. It is therefore very difficult to arrive at an average figure that reflects nail growth over a whole life.

However, if you never cut your nails and they grew at the same rate as Shridhar's you would add about 2.6 cm of nail on each finger every year. At the end of your life you would have a 205 cm nail twirling out of each finger. As your toenails only grow half as fast, each of them would be only 102 cm long. Walking, doing anything, would probably be impossible so you would be forced to spend the days watching television through the giant rakes of your feet and trying to push the buttons on the remote control with your nose. In order to prevent this from happening, you will cut your nails 1,424 times, trimming off a total of 30.7 m.

Shridhar Chillal held the world record until 2000. By this time his nails had reached a length of 615 cm. The strain of constantly carrying the extra weight around had caused nerve damage in his left arm, and because of the way the body is wired up, not using his left hand for 48 years had also caused him to go deaf in his right ear. His nails hadn't stopped him having a successful career as a government press photographer, getting married and having children. But, now retired, he wanted to be able to hug his grand-children and get a decent night's sleep without having to worry about the 6 m of keratin growing out of his left hand. He cut his nails.

There seems to be something in human nature that constantly drives us to take things to a crazier new level. The world record is now held by someone growing the nails on both hands. It seems inevitable, though, that somewhere, right now, someone is lying on their back, biding their time, being waited on hand and foot, trying not to scratch themselves, as the nails on their hands *and their feet* move them slowly towards world fame at the rate of 0.19 mm a day.

NAPPIES

Freud believed that adult neuroses and personality disorders may be arte-facts of childhood sexuality. According to his sexual drive theory, in each development stage children satisfy their libidinous desires in different er-ogenous zones while the reactions of their parents and society teach them how to behave as adults. If things go wrong as you progress through the five stages of psychosexual development, you can become overly anxious or fixated on a particular stage. This may lead to all sorts of problems.

Initially, you are polymorphous perverse, which means you can gain sex-ual enjoyment from anything, though you almost instantly enter the oral phase, where you enjoy sucking at the breast. As you start to gain control over your bowels and sphincters you become anal. After this is the phallic phase – boys become obsessed with their penises and girls develop penis envy. These are accompanied by the Oedipus and Electra complexes – the unconscious desire to kill one parent so you can sleep with the other. Then there is the latent phase where nothing much happens at all, the lull before the storms of the genital phase, where adult sexuality begins to emerge.

The term 'anal retentive' was coined by Karl Abraham, one of Freud's pupils, to describe behaviour where the parents have been overzealous in their toilet-training and the child has complied by becoming possessively retentive of their faeces. This leads to stubborn, compulsively tidy, perfectionist behaviour in later life. On the other hand, if you are too lax about the toilet-training, you may end up with an anally expulsive child who is careless, defiant, disorganised and excited by their own and other people's faeces. Either way, if you make a mess of toilet-training, you can really screw up your children. You will send them out into the world riddled with neuroses, strange desires and fetishes that will make them prey to blackmailers for the rest of their lives.

If Freud's ideas seem provocative now, it is hard to imagine how they went down a hundred years ago. It isn't surprising that there have been many millions of hours of research done on the lingering effects of toilet-training on adult life. However, there is no evidence that children actually go through oral, anal, genital, phallic and Oedipal development stages. Neither is there any basis for the idea that your experience of breastfeeding or toilet-training has any effect on your behaviour as an adult. Ultimately, one result of Freud's work has been to provide a lot of reassuring evidence that you aren't inadvertently going to warp your child for life with baby wipes and a potty.

Whether his theories are useful or not, Freud is still important because he was pretty much the first person to attempt an explanation for why we behave the way we do that was not bound up with the concepts of sin, heaven and hell. A secular explanation for why there is so much violence and suffering in the world alongside the kindness, altruism and self-sacrifice that also belong to human nature. What drives our imaginations and emotions? Why do we want the things we want? Why do we fall in love?

As for your legacy …

Disposable nappies are so durable that no one actually knows how long they may take to break down. The current thinking is at least 500 years. If Elizabeth I, Ivan the Terrible, Nostradamus and Sir Francis Drake, not to mention Sigmund Freud, had used disposables, their nappies would still be with us. The landfill from disposable nappies is one of the most enduring things you will leave behind – 5,000 of them.

Making the waterproof polythene outer layer and the water-repellent liner uses up 2,500 pints of crude oil. The fluffy insides are mainly wood pulp, which will come from 4.5 trees. Manufacturing all the disposable nappies you will need uses up over twice as much water as washing reusable ones. They will also use up three and a half times the energy, 90 times as much non-renewable raw materials and produce over 60 times as much waste. So it isn't surprising that they will also cost you a lot more – £900 compared with £200 for buying and cleaning washable ones.

NUCLEAR POWER

In 1922 Howard Carter peered through the small hole he had made in the door of Tutankhamun's tomb. 'Do you see anything?' asked Lord Carnarvon. 'Yes', replied Carter, 'I see wonderful things.' For nearly 4,000 years the tomb had remained undisturbed – a series of chambers filled with everything the young pharaoh would need in his new life beyond the stars: chariots, ostrich-feather fans, boats, folding beds made of gold, weapons, jewellery and wine.

To get to the tomb Carter had ignored numerous seals and dire warnings about the consequences of breaking them. He would not have taken these seriously, and why should he heed the curses of a defunct religion or fear the wrath of a dead god? For him, the unbroken seals with their warnings were signs that what he was after was still there. But what if he had come across the tomb with no knowledge of the Egyptian culture of death and what the tomb might contain? Suppose he had come across this substantial and obviously important structure hidden in the desert. What it contained must be important because it was built like a safe. Would he pay any attention to the curses written on the walled-up tunnels? *Enter here and you will be struck blind, your hair and teeth will fall out, your flesh will melt from your bones, you will die and your children will die and a great evil will be released into the world ...* Would he seal it back up and walk away or would it just encourage him to dig faster towards what must be a great treasure indeed?

Nuclear power works by turning mass into energy according to Einstein's equation $E = mc^2$. The Sun works by nuclear fusion, where the change in mass is created by two atoms coming together to produce an atom lighter than the combined weight of the original two atoms. Nuclear fusion does not produce nuclear waste. Unfortunately, the atoms refuse to come together until you heat them up to the same temperature as the Sun. Doing it without heating them up is what is meant by cold fusion. Nobody has managed to do that yet. The other approach involves making a sun in a box so that it can never touch the sides of the box. Nobody has managed to do that yet either, at least not for more than a few millionths of a second. So, instead, power stations use nuclear fission.

In nuclear fission, you fire a neutron at an atom, which makes it too heavy to exist any more. It splits into two atoms lighter than the original atom. The drop in weight releases energy and more neutrons, which hit other atoms that then become unstable, split, produce more neutrons and so on until there is a massive explosion. In order to stop this happening, nuclear power stations intercept enough of the neutrons flying around to slow down the process so that the bomb takes 20 years to go off rather than consuming an entire city in a blinding instant.

The tiny reduction in mass that produces this huge amount of energy also produces nuclear waste. The only attractive thing about nuclear power is that it gives us electricity without producing carbon. At the moment, 16 per cent of all the electricity you use will have been produced by nuclear fission. Whether nuclear power can ever be made safe enough and cheap enough to meet our energy needs without killing us all in the process, we will still have to deal with the nuclear waste we have already produced.

Since the first nuclear reactor was opened by the Queen in 1956, Britain has accumulated 470,000 cubic metres of nuclear waste. If it was shared out equally, that would be a lump the size of a large shoebox for everyone living in Britain, and every year it gets a little larger. The next generation of nuclear reactors will produce waste that is even more radioactive. Despite more than 50 years of nuclear power, the problem of what to do with the waste has yet to be solved. The only countries currently building long-term storage facilities are Finland and Sweden. Britain is still looking into the problem and at the moment your lump of waste is simmering away in a temporary storage facility.

Eventually it will be put in a very deep hole where it can be kept safe from terrorists, cavers and archaeologists for the next 250,000 years. There are a lot of arguments about where the hole should go and also how it should be protected from being accidentally dug up again 10,000 years from now. Building warnings into the fabric of storage facilities is a priority for the engineers designing them. As well as easy-to-understand symbolic representations of nuclear physics (!), suggestions have included cartoons of people opening waste containers then falling over dead, and surrounding the site with 8 m tall basalt monoliths, carved with screaming faces based on Munch's painting *The Scream*, alternating with faces representing disgust. The idea being that facial expressions will be something we have in common with our descendants.

What seems to be a touching level of concern about the archaeologists of the future is really an acknowledgement that we have to mark the mess we are leaving behind now while we are still organised. Should our civilisation fall, no one is going to waste time on the future while the present is turning to dust. You can dig up the past in the average suburban garden: kitchen middens, coins, flint tools, pot shards, bones and teeth, but accidental survival is not a coveted form of immortality. Deliberate communication with eternity and the future is an act of hubris that usually only pharaohs, kings, emperors and other despots can afford. Nuclear-waste storage has to outlast the tomb of Tutankhamun and the pyramids by a quarter of a million years. The engineers working on these facilities are designing something to survive further into the future than humanity stretches into the past. Something that may in fact outlast all memory of our culture. 'My name is Ozymandias, king of kings: Look on my works, ye Mighty, and despair!'

ORGASM

The *Romance of the Rose* was written nearly 800 years ago. This medieval French allegorical poem of chivalry and love contains the following advice to lovers: 'One should not abandon the other, nor should either cease their voyage until they reach port together ...'

Why do we have orgasms? For men anyway, the answer is generally thought to be pretty straightforward. It is a reward for ejaculation and a way of encouraging you to mate and pass on your genes. Things are different for women. The evolutionary conundrum is, if women can conceive without orgasm, what function does it serve?

The female orgasm has consumed entire careers. There are dozens of theories. The two front-runners are that orgasm somehow sucks up sperm and that by making sex a shared pleasure, it builds a bond between partners. In order for something to have an evolutionary explanation it has to make passing on your genes more likely. But straightforward reproductive sex is not the easiest way for women to have an orgasm. In fact, the opposite is true. For the majority of women, orgasm is pretty much a reward for not having penetrative sex, which more or less rules out any evolutionary theory straight away. This is what led the anthropologist Donald Symons to conclude that female orgasms have no function at all. His idea is that a woman's ability to have an orgasm is pretty much an accident. A by-product of the way we develop in the womb.

For the first eight weeks, the embryo has no gender: it has nipples and a genital tubercle. Male foetuses retain non-functional nipples and the genital tubercle becomes a penis capable of orgasm. Female foetuses develop milk-producing nipples and the genital tubercle becomes a clitoris, which just incidentally retains the potential to give sexual pleasure. The female orgasm is therefore a happy by-product of the male need for an ejaculatory penis. If this is true, in one sense at least men are responsible for all female orgasms.

While this could be taken as a dilution of the female sexual experience, what it really does is separate the female orgasm from childbearing, which is surely a liberating thing. In fact, insisting that the female orgasm must have some sort of reproductive function helps perpetuate the myth that only orgasms produced by penises in vaginas count, and that other ways of giving a woman an orgasm are somehow cheating. Breaking the link between reproduction and orgasm means better sex for women.

A study of 20,000 Australians found that 95 per cent

of the men had had an orgasm the last time they had sex. Only 69 per cent of the women did. Applying these percentages to a lifetime's worth of sex (5,037 times), men will have 4,785 orgasms, women 3,475.

For men, the most enjoyable part of sex ends with orgasm, while for women it may just be the beginning. Female orgasms can happen one after the other, be more intense and last for longer. The average male orgasm is four seconds long. The average female orgasm is 20 seconds long. To stretch the allegory of the *Romance of the Rose* to breaking point, for the man the voyage of sex is about *not* reaching port for as long as possible and staying aboard ship thinking about the offside rule, while the woman is enjoying herself ashore in one port after another. A man's 4,785 orgasms will last 5.3 hours. The woman's 3,475 will last 19.3 hours. Almost long enough to fly to Australia.

PEE

Most of the craters on the Moon have names. The small ones have been given common first names like Susan or Charles, but the big ones are named after specific people, usually scientists, particularly astronomers. The most prominent crater, the big one on the bottom, is named after the Danish astronomer and alchemist Tycho Brahe.

Tycho wore a false nose made of silver and gold because one Christmas his real nose got sliced off during a drunken duel in the dark with swords. He also employed a jester who lived under his dining table, and owned a pet elk that died when it got drunk and fell down some stairs. Despite a lot of this sort of thing, Tycho is principally famous for the meticulous astronomical observations that earned him a crater on the Moon. That, and dying because he was too polite to excuse himself from a banquet and go for a pee.

Alfred Hitchcock's rule that 'The length of a film should not exceed the endurance of the bladder' applies to many things. The length of films, plays, award ceremonies, bus journeys and banquets. The need-to-pee graph follows an exponential curve in that it can take a couple of hours to reach the point where you know you need to pee and then only a matter of minutes before you become desperate. Your bladder fills at a rate of about

1 ml per kg of body weight a minute, with 1.26 ml the average. You start feeling the urge to pee when it is 75 per cent full. Assuming Tycho Brahe had an average-sized bladder (500 ml), it would have taken five hours of banqueting to get to this point.

Taking in excess fluids, especially diuretic fluids like wine, can increase your production of urine tenfold. Contemporary accounts suggest that Tycho was fairly knocking back the wine that evening, so his bladder could have been at 75 per cent after just 37 minutes. Once the bladder reaches 100 per cent capacity, voluntary control becomes very difficult. Under normal circumstances you have up to 99 minutes, but if you are drinking heavily you may have as little as 13 minutes to find a polite way to withdraw from the banquet or risk drenching the jester sitting under the table. The bladder can hold about twice its normal capacity before it will burst and the suggestion is that by a titanic act of will and leg-crossing, Tycho Brahe took himself into this dangerous yellow arena of suicidal politeness.

The relentless water clock in your lower abdomen that means you can never be more than 99 minutes from a toilet is powered by your heart. As blood flows around your body it collects waste products from the metabolic factories contained in your cells. A quarter of the blood pumped by each heartbeat goes to the kidneys to be cleaned and turned into urine by millions of tiny structures called nephrons that make up the Malpighian pyramids.

Doctors and anatomists are not well represented on the Moon. Instead they have left their names all over the human body. Each nephron within the Malpighian pyramids consists of a Bowman's capsule, which filters waste from the blood at an incredible rate – around 125 ml per minute or 180 l a day. If this went straight to the bladder you would have to pee every three minutes. However, each nephron also has a loop of Henle that reabsorbs water (178 l of it a day) and concentrates the urine.

As the bladder fills beyond the crucial 75 per cent mark, the extra stretching of the bladder muscles starts to send messages to a part of the brain called Barrington's nucleus, which tells you to do something about it. When you have made the necessary excuses and arrangements, you notify Barrington's nucleus, which sends a message to Onuf's nucleus in the lower spine to release the external urinary sphincter. At the same time, it orders the muscles of the bladder to contract, forcing out the pee. Sadly for Malpighi, Bowman, Henle and Onuf, many of the parts of the body they discovered are being renamed to make them more systematic and easier to learn. So, the Barrington's nucleus, named after F. J. F. 'Snorker' Barrington (1884–1956; liked the zoo and yachting), is now more commonly known as the pontine micturation centre, which sounds as though it is run by the council.

If you ever get into an argument about whether pee flows because of gravity or because it is forced out of the body by the bladder, all you have to do is to stand on your head and pee. This will be much messier if you are a woman. Peeing is one of the many points of conflict between men and women. A man's ability to pee standing up gives him more options but also certain responsibilities regarding accuracy, discretion and the toilet seat. As the average man needs to make four standing visits to the toilet every day and only one seated, it makes sense for a man living alone always to leave the seat up. However, if a man and a woman live together, the balance shifts. Between them they now make six seated visits compared with four standing. The toilet seat should stay down. If there is another man in the house, the balance swings back in favour of standing visits (eight to seven) and it is now just common courtesy for the woman to make sure she leaves the seat up and for men to get annoyed that she inconsiderately leaves it down.

Having to sit down to pee means that women are much more vulnerable to the filthy toilets that men so blithely pee all over. It is now possible to buy a sort of disposable origami funnel called the p-mate that acts like a paper penis so women can pee standing up and – they make this their main selling point – write their names in the snow.

There are a lot of euphemisms for pee: wee, tinkle, spend a penny, powder my nose, see a man about a dog, number one (as number two rhymes with poo it should surely be a number three), but pee is in itself a euphemism that comes from the first letter of piss. Piss is slightly vulgar because it is rather too onomatopoeic. This also means that it is one of those ancient words that appears in languages all over the world, though the onomatopoeia is not universally vulgar.

Because it contains the waste products of metabolism, urine also contains information about your health. We all do a certain amount of urinalysis on a daily basis when judging the colour of our urine and adjusting our fluid intake accordingly. Alchemists deceived by the golden colour used to waste a lot of time trying to turn pee into gold. Very dark or no urine is a serious indication that something is wrong. When Tycho Brahe finally got away from the banquet and tried to pee, he couldn't. This is what made him think that he had damaged himself in some way. But, short of doing something unpleasant with superglue, no matter how polite you are it isn't really possible to hold out until your bladder explodes.

For nearly four centuries the widely accepted explanation of Tycho Brahe's death was that he had overstrained his bladder, which became infected and so 11 days later he died. In 1991 the Danish ambassador to the Czech Republic was given a present by the director of the National Museum in Prague. It was a small box containing Tycho Brahe's moustache. Unsure what to do with it, he presented it to the Tycho Brahe Planetarium in Copenhagen, which promptly had it analysed by a man called Bent Kaempe. He discovered it was loaded with mercury, which confirmed the long-held suspicion that Brahe had been murdered.

About a year before the fatal banquet, Tycho had taken on Johannes Kepler as an assistant. While Tycho had decades' worth of astronomical data, he didn't have the mathematical skills to work out the orbits of the planets. Kepler, who incidentally was prevented from making his own astronomical observations by his weak eyesight, did have those mathematical skills. It should have been a perfect partnership, but Tycho, who had a permanently enlarged right eye from a lifetime of peering through instruments, was not about to just hand over his life's work to the highly ambitious and frankly rather irritating younger man who was constantly trying to get his hands on it ...

Mercury can cause irreversible kidney damage, leaving the pyramids of Malpighi in ruins, Bowman's capsule a wreck and Henle's loop clogged with weeds – the products of metabolism build up in the blood and poison you. This is what would happen if you couldn't pee. You would die. Then Kepler would steal all your data and use it to formulate his laws of planetary motion, upon which Newton would base his law of universal gravitation, which 282 years later NASA would use to put a man on the Moon.

Kepler loved the Moon. In 1611 he wrote a science-fiction novel about a journey to the Moon. When he was the imperial mathematician to the court of the Holy Roman Emperor Rudolph II King of Hungary and Bohemia, he used to go into the palace gardens at night to pee in the bushes and look up at the Moon. Presumably, with his weakened eyesight it was the only heavenly body he could see. He has a crater there too: it's a 260-mile Moon-buggy drive from the landing site of *Apollo 12*.

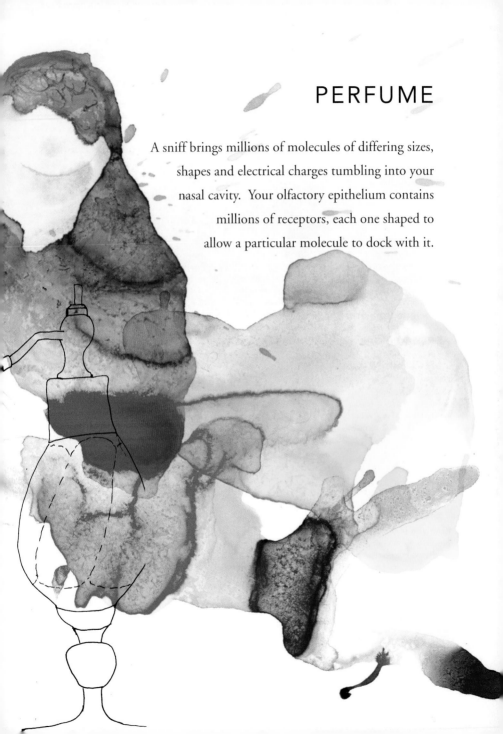

PERFUME

A sniff brings millions of molecules of differing sizes, shapes and electrical charges tumbling into your nasal cavity. Your olfactory epithelium contains millions of receptors, each one shaped to allow a particular molecule to dock with it.

When a molecule of camphor docks with a camphor receptor it triggers a signal unique to that molecule. In this case the smell of mothballs.

This may not be how we smell at all. It might turn out that the mechanism for smelling is completely different. This theory is simply the best guess at what might be happening based on the available evidence. It cannot be used to predict how differently shaped molecules will smell. It does not explain why molecules with nearly identical shapes can smell very different or indeed why molecules with very different shapes can smell very similar.

Smell remains the least understood of all the senses. A complete theory of smell would enable us to design molecules to create specific smells in the same way that we manipulate the frequencies of light to produce different colours. We would also be able to predict what combinations of different molecules might smell like in the same way we can predict how different musical notes make harmonies. Most of the research in this area is being funded by the perfume industry. At the moment, coming up with a new perfume is a haphazard process of mixing scents and concocting new molecules for professional noses to assess. 'We must add woody notes and balance it with a marine zestiness!' But doing this without any real idea about how smell works makes it a hit-and-miss affair.

Recently, researchers have found a way of predicting the rather vague concept of 'pleasantness' from a molecule's structure. Compact, heavy molecules smell better than light, spindly ones. This seems to hold true for humans all over the world, which contradicts the established belief that our responses to smells are cultural and are acquired in childhood, like a taste for rancid yak butter or fermented fish sauce. Being naturally attracted by some smells and repelled by others is useful, leading us to ripe fruit and away from rotting meat. This would give enough of a survival advantage to enable built-in feelings about smells to evolve. Tastes do vary across cultures, but the fact that you like smelly cheese or anchovies does not necessarily mean you like the smell. There is no perfume company developing an aftershave with the great smell of Camembert.

One of the worst things you can smell of is yourself. We have become extremely intolerant of even the faintest whiff of body odour. Once you have washed and rinsed away your natural smell and applied deodorant to prevent it reappearing, you can choose what you would like to smell of. This is one of the subtlest forms of lying we engage in. Several studies have shown that our natural smell contains information about our genes. We prefer the smell of people who are not related to us. The less genetically similar someone is to you, the more likely you are to be attracted by their smell, which makes for better mating choices.

You will be aware of this smell and it exerts an influence over you because you either like it or you don't. The mechanism appears to work in the same way as your affection for ripe strawberries and your distaste for rotten fish. In the popular consciousness, the idea that smells can influence our decisions is linked with pheromones. However, pheromones – and whether they even exist in humans – are an altogether weirder and more controversial phenomena.

The term pheromone was invented in the 1950s to describe the chemical signals that insects use. These aren't simple messages that the insect decodes and decides to act upon, but something that triggers a certain preprogrammed behaviour. A tiny quantity of sex pheromone released by a female silkworm moth will cause every male who detects it from up to 10 km away to be irresistibly drawn to her. A crushed ant releases alarm pheromones that instantly alters other ants' behaviour, making them aggressive and better able to fight off a threat. These frenzied ants may also release propaganda pheromones that make enemy ants attack each other uncontrollably. Similar mechanisms have been observed in plants. When damaged, some plants release pheromones that trigger the production of tannins in other plants; these make them bitter and less attractive to the foraging animal that damaged the first plant.

Some mammals have been shown to use pheromones. Signal pheromones produced by male rats function as neurotransmitters in female rats, eliciting a lordis response. Which basically means that the female rats immediately and involuntarily adopt a mating position. This is similar to the advertising campaign for Lynx, which suggests that if you wear it women will be uncontrollably attracted to you. The massive success of this campaign indicates that men at least are prepared to believe that smell can make people do things. Lynx does not claim to contain pheromones, but there are numerous products that do. These are nearly all aimed at men, who seem to be more interested in the short-term benefits of this kind of deception. If you are going to buy one of these products, you should consider that if there was any evidence they worked, they would probably be illegal.

Mammals such as rats, pigs and elephants that have been shown to use pheromones have a tiny extra set of nostril-like tubes inside their noses called a vomeronasal organ (VMO). These react like smell receptors, recognising pheromones and sending the signals to the brain, where they take effect. The problem for human pheromones is that while humans have a VMO, it isn't connected to the brain or in fact to anything. This suggests that we evolved from something that did use this organ, but the ability has been lost somewhere along the evolutionary road.

Despite this, evidence is accumulating that humans do respond to chemical signals that we sense in the same way as smells, though we may not be able to smell them. In one study, people were asked to smell two sweat samples collected from people who had been watching either funny films or scary films. Though they weren't able to discern any difference in the smell, they were nevertheless able to sort the samples into scary and funny. It seems that you really can smell fear; what is more surprising is how your brain reacts when you do. In another experiment, cotton pads were taped to the armpits of novice skydivers. Scanning the brains of people while they sniffed the carefully extracted odour of terrified armpit showed that, though they had no idea of what they were smelling, there was increased activity in the parts of the brain associated with fear.

Human body odour is mainly produced by the apocrine glands in the skin. These are associated with hair and are particularly concentrated in the groin and armpits. Though you will have had them since you were born, your apocrine glands will only start to function at the onset of puberty, which suggests a link between body odour and sex. There does appear to be some sort of airborne chemical communication going on, though no one can quite agree how or why it happens.

There is a lot of anecdotal evidence that women living together tend to synchronise menstrual cycles. This effect has also been observed in experiments where the women never meet but simply have each other's sweat applied to their top lips. In a different study, women who had male sweat applied to their upper lips had more regular periods and reported feeling less tense and more relaxed. Men also seem to be able to tell which stage of her menstrual cycle a woman is in. A study of strippers and lap dancers found that women earned double the tips when they were ovulating. Pheromones may also have a small influence on the age girls start menstruating. Girls living in a household where their father is present have their first period an average of three months later than those who have less contact with their dad.

Isolating what might be responsible for any of these effects from the 2,000 components that make up human body odour is very difficult. Our smell is also a result of complex interactions between numerous glandular secretions and the bacteria that live on us. Freshly produced apocrine fluid has no smell. This doesn't develop until the microorganisms concentrated in these areas go to work on them, which explains why your smell changes the longer you go without a bath. Humans have more productive apocrine glands than other primates, which indicates that smell may be more important to us than it is to any of the animals we are closely related to. We are the naked, smelly apes.

When we choose which tiny little bottle contains what we want to smell of, it is likely that we unconsciously come under the sway of our own pheromones and pick something that subtly enhances our natural body odour. We have done this in a remarkably consistent way throughout history. Though new fragrances are being invented all the time, they usually depend on ingredients that have been popular for thousands of years and are rarely dramatically different from established perfumes. Many of the biggest-selling perfumes have been around for more than 50 years, such as Mitsouko (1919), Chanel No 5 (1921) and L'Air du Temps (1948), and these were themselves based on scents that had been popular for generations.

In a lifetime, the average woman will spend £1,680 on perfume. The average man will spend £971. The average person spends £1,302, 75 per cent of which will be spent in November and December. Fifty per cent of women and 34 per cent of men receive perfume as a Christmas present. Unless you have been consulted, this is a case of someone deciding what you should smell like, which is a curiously intimate decision to make on your behalf.

PERI●DS

Most animals do not go through the menopause but remain fertile their whole lives. One explanation for why humans are different is called the grandmother hypothesis. This has its roots in our hunter-gatherer past. Unlike most animals, humans collaborate to provide their community with food. There is therefore a delicate balance between the number of people providing the food and the number of people eating it. Children come at a high cost as they can't work and also hinder their mother's ability to work. The menopause means that not only are there fewer children, there are also more women not actively involved in nursing children who can help gather food. Therefore, children with non-reproductive grandmothers stood a better chance of survival. And so, the menopause evolved.

In the womb, there are up to 7 million eggs stored in the hundreds of thousands of fluid-filled follicles that cover the ovaries. They begin to deteriorate and dissolve back into the body even before birth. Then, there are less than a million and these will dwindle to about 300,000 by the time a girl reaches twelve. Like the menopause, periods are more or less unique to humans. All mammals build up a lining in their uterus to receive the egg, which is usually reabsorbed unless the egg is fertilised. In humans, around two-thirds of this lining is reabsorbed and the rest – about 35 ml – will take an average of four days to flow out of you. As yet, no one has come up with a sensible explanation for why humans have periods and other animals don't.

Menstruation is less of a cultural issue in this country than in other parts of the world, but it is still more or less a taboo subject. If you did not already know what a period was, you would have no idea what tampon and sanitary-towel advertising was selling. On the one hand the adverts are about hiding your period and reinforcing taboos. On the other, they're about liberation and having a good time while skydiving, waterskiing or straddling things in tight white trousers. In a lifetime, you will discreetly dispose of 12,000 sanitary towels or tampons, hopefully by bagging and binning them rather than flushing them off to cause all sorts of problems elsewhere. All in all, your periods will cost you £854. Surprisingly, unlike other essential items, sanitary protection is subject to VAT, which will add another 5 per cent, or £43. VAT is also a feminist issue.

Allowing for an average of 1.9 pregnancies, you will ovulate 446 times, produce 15.6 l of blood and spend 1,784 days having your period. In your late forties, you will only have a very small number of eggs left. Ovulation slows, then stops, accompanied by a hormonal upheaval on a similar scale to puberty and adolescence 39 years before. By 51, the reproductive part of your life will be over. The average age to become a grandmother is 54.

PETS

As you get older, time appears to speed up. This is partly because your perception of time is related to the amount of new information you have to process. As you get older, there is less and less novelty to deal with. One of the simplest ways of introducing an element of randomness that will constantly refresh your life with new experiences is to get yourself a pet. The amount of randomness you feel you need will determine the kind of pet you choose.

There are 27 million pets in Britain today, which means that the average Briton owns approximately 0.44 of a pet. You are most likely to opt for 0.44 of a cat or a dog, which will provide a socially acceptable amount of havoc – the destruction of homework, soft furnishings and personal items, the odd pool of sick, the inevitable turds … Every once in a while your cat will bring you something nearly dead at three in the morning. After a frantic chase around the house you will corner it in the kitchen and try to bring its life humanely to a close with a frying pan. More rarely, your beloved spaniel will come lolloping out of the bushes with a severed human hand in his mouth.

On occasions like these, the traditional role of the pet as companion pales into insignificance compared with his ability to slow down time and open up new areas of experience: police stations, coroner's inquests and a frisson of excitement whenever you let him off the lead in the future.

Strictly speaking, a pet should have no useful function at all. As soon as you start eating your canary's eggs for breakfast it has become a working animal and you are a farmer. The less useful a pet is, the higher its status, which is why so many celebrities accessorise themselves with pointless dogs.

The highest-status pets of all are the ones that take a lot of effort to look after, either because they are difficult to keep alive, like rare tropical fish, or are actually dangerous, like lions and tigers and bears. Perhaps this is why there are more tigers being kept as pets in the USA than there are wild tigers in the whole world.

Small animals, usually rodents like gerbils, hamsters and guinea pigs, are traditionally children's pets. As children provide more than enough randomness on their own, it makes sense to give them something in a cage, and animals with short lifespans are a good way of introducing the concept of death. If you have two in a cage, there is also the possibility – given the difficulty of sexing small animals – that your children's pets will take on the job of revealing the potentially embarrassing miracles of sexual reproduction and birth in explicit furry detail.

All of these things should be taken into consideration because having a pet costs money. Feeding Britain's pets costs over £1.7 billion every year – more than half what the UK spends on foreign aid. In your lifetime this amounts to £2,219 on pet food. When you add the cost of buying (£679) and insuring (£496) them, an average lifetime's worth of pets will cost you £3,394.

However, aside from companionship, teaching children about sex and death, slowing down time and proving that you are really hard or really rich, pets also make you healthier. Pet owners are less likely to suffer from stress, have lower cholesterol and suffer fewer minor ailments. This is going to be important to you as you near the end of your life and the years start whizzing past like weeks.

PHONES

Civilisation advances at an ever-increasing pace. The wheel, the plough, agriculture, bread, metalworking, money, writing and other wonders of civilisation took thousands of years to spread across the world. Writing was particularly slow. The printing press – the crucial innovation that brought the written word to the masses – only came along 5,000 years after writing. Even now, 20 per cent of the world's population are illiterate and unable to use this 5,500-year-old technology. Though the written word is unlikely to be superseded, our reliance on it for long-distance communication is quickly being replaced by the telephone. The first telephone exchange was only built 130 years ago, and the first truly commercial mobile phones have only been around for 40 years. But already nearly half the world's population have a mobile.

In a lifetime, you are going to spend 7,494 hours on the phone. With eight hours off every day for sleeping and leafing through the phone book, that is 468 days of doing nothing else. To this you can also add another 40 days for the time it will take you to send and receive 77,834 text messages. Because you will do it practically every day, using the phone is one of the most expensive things you will do in your life. It will cost you £39,036.

In the early days of the phone it was thought that, like the telegraph, every town would have one or two phones, which people would queue up to use. Phone boxes, which these days have more to do with heritage than they do with communication, are the increasingly rare relics of this idea. Connecting everyone to the phone took nearly 100 years. In the 1990s, BT ran a series of adverts promoting the rather vague message 'It's good to talk.' This reflected the fact that, as everyone was now connected to the phone network, the only way to increase revenues was to get people to use it more. Mobile-phone companies have reached this point much more quickly. Already there are 74 million mobile-phone connections in Britain. This is 13 million more than our population.

To keep revenues growing, as well as encouraging us to talk longer and more often, we are also being sold content for our phones. You will spend a further £1,305 on games, ring-tones and music. Then, of course, there is the handset itself. Currently people change their mobile every 18 months. If you get your first one at 14, you can expect to get through 43 in a lifetime.

The current average cost of manufacturing a handset is £63. Which is £2,709 for all 43. In the past, as part of the drive to get us all on the phone, handsets have been heavily subsidised. Now they have us hooked, the prices are bound to rise.

Mobile companies are working hard to shorten the replacement cycle of mobile handsets. In Japan, the average is down to six months. The ultimate aim is to get the cycle down to three months to coincide with the seasons, which means you would get through 260 phones. While this might seem absurd now, it is no more absurd than the whole notion of mobile phones was 30 years ago.

You may have spent hundreds of hours with it pressed to your face talking slightly louder than is necessary, and it may have been no more than arm's length from your body for a year and a half, but you are unlikely to get sentimental about your phone. Unlike other items that gain character with wear, phones just get scratched and lose the sleek, glossy good looks that made you choose them in the first place. Though they will contain your whole life – all your family, friends and lovers, music, pictures and other sentimentalia – these can all be easily reincarnated in the shiny body of your new phone. The old phone is most likely to end up in a drawer, like the 30 million other perfectly usable phones in drawers all over Britain.

Mining the minute amount of South African gold used in the main circuit board of just one phone generates 100 kg of waste. Your phone also includes copper from Chile, magnesium, iron and aluminium from China, arsenic from Peru, beryllium from the USA, lithium from Australia and tin, cobalt and tantalum from Congo. Tantalum is a key ingredient of the low-voltage components that shrank the breeze-block-sized phones of the 1970s to more manageable proportions. Eight per cent of the world's tantalum reserves are in Congo and the boom in tantalum prices more or less paid for the Congolese civil war that claimed hundreds of thousands of lives. All the materials in your mobile phone have a human and environmental cost. Though it is possible to reduce these by recycling your phone, by far the best thing is to use it for as long as possible and then hand it on to someone else.

The biggest market for used phones is in those parts of the developing world not reached by landlines. Mobile phones are often the only method of communication and new phones are very expensive because companies don't make enough money from calls to subsidise the handsets.

Producing each of your 43 handsets takes a global effort. Thousands of people will be involved in mining materials and thousands more will manufacture its 400 components. These will be transported from all over the world to the factory, probably in the Far East, where hundreds of nimble-fingered workers will assemble your phone so that it can be shipped 3,000 miles to your outstretched hand. Then you will be able to take advantage of a global network of wires, masts, computers and satellites orbiting in space to connect with one of the other 3.3 billion mobile-phone users. It doesn't matter where they are or even if they can read and write. If you have their number, you can tell them, 'I'm on the train!'

PIGS

While making *The African Queen* on location in East Africa, the director John Huston employed a local hunter to supply the production with food. The filming conditions were extremely tough and the cast and crew looked forward to their nightly barbecues. But then the police turned up and arrested the hunter. Local people had been going missing. It seems that they were the source of the delicious 'long pig' that the hunter had been supplying them with. While this story may not be true, the thought that Humphrey Bogart and Katharine Hepburn have been feasting on human flesh certainly adds something to the experience of watching the film.

Of all the animals we eat, the pig is the one most like us. An adult pig is much the same size as an adult human and the internal organs are very similar. Pig and human hearts are almost identical, which is why it is possible to repair a human heart with a valve from a pig's. We also share a lot of the same parasites, which is why it is particularly important

to kill them all by thoroughly cooking or curing pork before you eat it.

You are going to eat 325 g of pig a week. In a lifetime, that's 1,340 kg of pig meat. As only 50 per cent of the pig is meat we eat, that could come from one colossal 2,681 kg pig the size of a mobile home, but more realistically from 26 individual pigs.

Nearly two-thirds of all the pigs you eat will come from outside the UK. Imported pigs are cheaper. Some of this difference is down to feed prices: in the Netherlands and Denmark feed producers and pig farmers belong to the same cooperatives, so feed bills are much lower. The other reason is that we pay our farm workers more and treat our pigs better. In fact, nearly half of the pigs you eat will have been raised in conditions that would be illegal in Britain.

Wild pigs have been extinct in Britain for centuries and there have been several unsuccessful attempts to reintroduce them. Both James I and his son Charles I released wild boar imported from Germany in the hope of re-establishing them for hunting. In Europe, the wild boar is one of the few animals you can hunt that will fight back. When you couldn't find anyone to fight a duel with, the next best thing was to go out and hunt a boar.

A pig can be a formidable adversary. All pigs have canines that never stop growing. These become razor-sharp tusks that are sharpened against each other like carving knives whenever the pig opens and closes its mouth. Understandably, domestic pigs usually have their tusks cut back to harmless stumps. The wild boar, however, is armed with a set of weapons that can eviscerate a horse. Medieval noblemen hunted boar with specially bred dogs. You would follow these on horseback into the forest and hope that if they cornered a boar you would be able to get there before all your dogs were dead. Often two kinds of dogs were used. Your bay hounds would keep the boar at bay and sound the alarm. Then your catch hounds, usually a form of pit bull, would latch on to the boar and bring it down.

Traditionally, as a nobleman, you would now be expected to get down from the relative safety of your horse and approach the squealing, rugby-scrum-sized clot of fur and blood and teeth to dispatch the boar with a small dagger. If things went wrong and the boar managed to charge, you would hopefully also be equipped with a boar lance. A boar impaled on a simple spear has the power, and the determination, to force itself all the way up the shaft and kill you, so a boar lance is equipped with a crossbar to stop this from happening. If everything goes well, you should have a nice set of tusks or perhaps a whole head to mount on the wall as a testament to your manhood. Something you certainly couldn't do with your opponent in a duel.

Despite the failure of several kings to reintroduce the wild boar, there are now small numbers of them living wild in southern Britain. They have reintroduced themselves, probably by escaping from farms. Though they can be dangerous to people, you

can minimise the risk by not chasing after them with horses and dogs.

The similarity between pigs and humans is exploited in numerous ways. If you want to study the way a human body decomposes in the grave, bury a pig. If you want to test the effectiveness of a new bullet, shoot a pig. All over the world trainee forensic scientists are visiting faked-up murder scenes and determining how and when the pig victim died. Pig carcasses are also routinely burned in mocked-up house fires to help with the unravelling of human tragedies.

One of the most disconcerting things for emergency workers who have to deal with the aftermath of fires is the smell. The fact is that roasted human smells very much like roasted pig. You might not be able to tell the difference, especially if you are returning tired and hungry after a hard day filming in the East African bush.

THE PILL

The contraceptive pill works on the simple principle of convincing your body that it is already pregnant. In the past, women could expect to be pregnant or breastfeeding pretty much all the time between puberty and menopause. Adjusting for lifespan, it is estimated that hunter-gatherer women had approximately 160 periods compared with the average woman of today, who has about 450.

Not having periods is one of the side effects of the pill. The decision to package pills so that they are taken on a monthly cycle of 21 days with seven days off was essentially a marketing decision. The pill stops ovulation and also prevents build-up of tissue in the uterus. In the week off, when either no pills or placebo pills are taken, the rapid drop in hormone levels prompts the small amount of tissue that has grown to be shed. Biologically, it is not a period at all. The people who developed and marketed the pill knew that building in an artificial period would make it less controversial.

The pill is currently the most popular form of contraception. Twenty-seven per cent of women between the ages of 16 and 49 are on the pill and each of these 3.8 million women will take an average of 7,812 pills in a lifetime.

The next stage in the development of the pill is already happening. Women using implanted or injected contraception like Norplant, Mirena or Depo-Provera often go for years at a time without periods. Recently oral contraceptives that give you a 'period' every three months have become available and it seems likely that this trend will continue. However, amidst all the arguments for and against medicating away the period, there is a curious side effect of the pill that is often ignored.

In 1995, a Swiss biologist called Claus Wedekind got a group of men to sleep in T-shirts and then had a group of women smell the T-shirts and pick the ones that smelled the best. He found that most of the women preferred the smell of T-shirts worn by men genetically dissimilar to them. This made sense, as genetic diversity makes for healthy offspring. However, some of the women preferred T-shirts worn by men who were genetically similar to them. These women had one thing in common. They were all on the pill. The conclusion Wedekind came to is that by tricking your body into believing it is pregnant, the pill also affects the kind of person you are drawn to. When looking for a mate, you are looking for someone who is not related to you. When you are pregnant, you seek out family who are more likely to look after you.

This has a number of implications. If you get together with someone when you are on the pill, it may be harder to conceive with them when you stop taking it. It is also possible that you won't find them quite as attractive. In other words, when you come off the pill, the man of your dreams may turn out to be a stinker. As yet, no research has been done on the correlation between the pill and divorce.

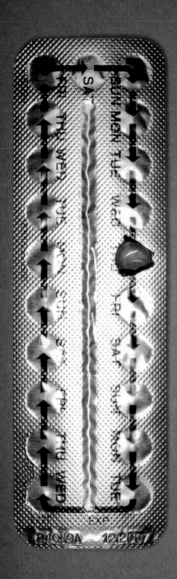

PINEAPPLES

In the 1670s the English philosopher John Locke was writing his *Essay Concerning Human Understanding*. In this, he set out his idea that at birth the human mind is a blank slate and that all our ideas, principles and opinions are based on our experience of the world. For one of his illustrations of the principle that there are sensations you cannot know without experiencing them, he chose the pineapple: 'Let him try if any words can give him the tastes of the Pine Apple and make him have the true idea of the Relish of that celebrated delicious Fruit.' The pineapple was famous at the time. An exotic mystery beyond price. When the king ate one in 1668 it was practically a national occasion. He carved the fruit himself and fed his court favourites the chunks. Locke's readers would have seen drawings. They would have read descriptions and gone to bed only to be kept awake by envy, a feeling of social inadequacy and the watering of their mouths. Unless they were a close personal friend of the king or prepared to take a year out of their lives to make the round trip to the West Indies, they would never know the taste of the pineapple.

When St Paul's Cathedral was finished in 1710 its clock towers were topped with golden pineapples. By the end of the eighteenth century, you could actually buy a pineapple. At a cost of £5,000 each in today's money, they were much too valuable to be eaten and were put on display to slowly fill the great houses with the smell of rotting pineapples. In the early nineteenth century, the socially ambitious could hire a pineapple for parties. A guest who cut themselves a chunk could ruin a family. However, by the 1850s costermongers were selling pineapple in the streets – 'A taste of paradise, a penny a slice!' – and the pineapple finally lost the last remnants of its mystique when it started to be tinned in the 1880s.

Up until recently, most pineapples sold in Britain were Smooth Cayennes. Despite their name, Smooth Cayennes are viciously spiked and have the disadvantage of remaining green even when they are ripe. In the 1970s, scientists working at the Pineapple Research Institute in Hawaii came up with the Gold. The Gold is much sweeter, less spiky and goes gold when it is ready to eat. Arguments over who owned the rights to the Gold meant that it didn't appear in the shops until 1996. Once it did, pineapple sales took off.

In your lifetime, you will eat just under 100 pineapples: 277 tins of pineapple rings or chunks, 54 actual whole pineapples and another 13 or so as juice. Though this is more pineapple than any other British person in history, it is still a small enough amount to count as a luxury. Like all tropical fruits, pineapples are generally produced by low-paid workers in appalling conditions. You might not be the king of England, but the disparity between you and the person who grows your pineapple today is probably greater than that between Charles II and any of his subjects 340 years ago.

POO

The dog poo you see on the streets is about 50 per cent of all the dog poo produced. The average human produces four times as much and there are eight times as many of us. If all the humans in Britain pooed in the streets, there would be 64 times as much. Imagine this, and you pretty much have the situation before sewers were invented.

Solving this problem becomes crucial if you want to have towns or cities. The earliest known sewers date from about 4,500 years ago with the Harappan civilisation of the Indus Valley in what is now Pakistan. Clean water was taken from wells. Dirty water was sluiced away in covered stone channels and most houses had flushing toilets. In contrast, apart from a brief period under the Romans, Britain did not reach this degree of sophistication till the Victorian age.

By 1850 there were 2.3 million people living in London, producing 460 tonnes of poo every single day. The city was awash with human excrement. Year after year, the problem grew worse and nobody did anything about it until something happened that finally forced Parliament to act. It wasn't the city's 200,000 overflowing cesspits. It wasn't because every time you crossed the street you had to step over mingled streams of raw sewage, blood from slaughterhouses and toxic waste from factories. It wasn't even the thousands of people dying every year from cholera and other sewage-related diseases. No, it was the smell.

London had always been smelly and by 1858 it was the biggest, smelliest city in the world. Summer had always been the worst time, but the summer of 1858 was particularly hot. Thousands of tonnes of poo fermented and bubbled in the sun. The smell was so overpowering that people couldn't work during the day or sleep at night. Down by the gently steaming waters of the Thames, antiseptic curtains were hung in the windows of Parliament and MPs debated through scented handkerchiefs. Two years earlier, the same MPs had dismissed plans for new sewers as being unnecessary and too expensive. After the Great Stink of 1858, work began almost immediately on a complete sewage system that was to become the model for cities all over the world. Things might have been very different if Parliament had been on a hill.

The poo you put into the sewers will already have undergone a certain amount of treatment. Food only takes about seven hours to get through your stomach and small intestine. Your large intestine is the slowest part of your digestive tract. If you are healthy, it will take between 16 and 65 hours for the remains of your food to reach the toilet. On the way, nearly all the water will be removed, which reduces the amount of poo you produce every day to about 200 g. A lifetime's worth is about 5 tonnes. The same weight as five small cars. This is just 7 per cent of the 69 cars' worth of food you put in the other end. When things go wrong with your digestion this figure may rise close to 100 per cent and it will feel as though all 5 tonnes are coming at once.

You will spend an average of 95 minutes a week on the toilet, or 271 day in a lifetime. You will use up 8,701 rolls of toilet paper and use over 1.5 million l of water to flush it all away on its final journey to the sewage-treatment works. The attraction of the flush toilet is the fact that once you flush it, it is gone for ever, it's as if your poo never happened. There is a good reason why we find poo disgusting, because eating it will make you very sick. Most sewage in Britain is treated to stop this happening. In the later stages of treatment your poo will have turned into a thick sludge. This is 99.9999 per cent free of pathogens and full of nutrients. To prevent the degradation of farmland and close the nutrient loop, about 70 per cent of sewage sludge produced in Britain is used in farming. There is a fair chance you will be getting some of those nutrients back.

Poo is an embarrassing and often taboo subject. When we talk about it, we tend to use words like bowel movement, poo, number two, motion and stool. The problem with this is that in certain situations the facts lose all their impact. When the UN or the WHO state that 40 per cent of the world do not have access to proper sanitation, what they actually mean is that 2.6 billion people are having to shit in the streets every day. That between 10 and 20 per cent of all deaths are caused by eating shit. That every 15 seconds a child will die from drinking shitty water – 166,413,744 in your lifetime. Perhaps if we were forced to live with the smell of it, we would do more about it.

POTATOES

Potatoes are not just the most popular vegetable, they are the most poisonous. As little as 2 kg of potatoes can contain enough poison to kill you. Over the course of your life you will eat 7,435 kg. That's enough poison to kill 3,717 people.

Potatoes belong to the same family of plants as deadly nightshade and contain the toxic alkaloids solanine and chaconine, which interfere with your neurotransmitters, causing delirium, hallucinations, paralysis and death. These compounds are not damaged by heat and they are not water soluble. So, washing and cooking has no effect on them. Too much of anything will kill you. However, there is a difference between something like salt or water that is good for you in small quantities but can be harmful if you have too much and something that is active in your body in a way that isn't good for you in any quantity. The World Health Organisation advises that there is no safe minimum level of solanine or chaconine in food. In fact, if the EU had existed 400 years ago, the potato would never have got past Novel Foods Regulation (EC) 258197, which requires all new foods to undergo safety testing. We would be living in a world where the Irish potato famine never happened, chip-pan fires would be unheard of and students' airing cupboards would be filled with grow lamps and hydroponic spuds to supply illegal mash parties.

Luckily, you are unlikely to want or even be able to eat 2 kg of potatoes in one sitting. Even if you did, you would probably be affected by a burning sensation in the mouth and stomach cramps before you ate enough to kill you. This is partly why the WHO is not about to ban the potato. The other is that it simply isn't practical to ban crisps, chips, latkes, croquettes, mash and all the other variations of the potato. The only solution to the problem is to try and minimise the damage.

Many plants produce poisons to protect themselves. We don't eat the dark green leaves of the potato plant because they contain enough poison to be dangerously, inedibly bitter. Being eaten isn't much of a problem for the tubers until they are brought to the surface. As soon as this happens, they start making themselves as toxic as possible to discourage humans and other foraging animals. At low levels, the flavour of toxic alkaloids is an essential part of what potatoes taste like. However, in sunlight, solanine levels can quadruple every 24 hours. Green patches are a sign of high toxin levels. The whole potato (not just the green bit) is affected and should probably be thrown away.

Bearing this in mind, the best way to store potatoes is to trick them into believing they are still under the ground. Lure them into a false sense of security in a cool dark place … until the time comes to peel off their skins, chop them up and lower them slowly into the boiling oil.

READING

There are two kinds of knowledge. There is all the information you carry about in your head, then there is all the stuff you don't know that is stored somewhere else. A lot of the knowledge you use is stored in other people's heads. If you are in a long-term relationship, a lot of the things you need to know just to make your day-to-day life work are probably stored in your partner's head: how to use the washing machine, how to set the video, the name of that Greek restaurant you went to. We also have to seek out other people to access the knowledge stored in their heads. The doctor to find out what that strange swelling is, the lawyer to find out how to make a will, the car mechanic to find out why your car is pulling to the left. When you or one of these people come up against something they don't know, they will have to go and look it up. In the simple act of looking up the correct tyre pressures for your car, the mechanic is accessing the vast body of knowledge that has accumulated in the 5,500 years since the presumably simultaneous inventions of reading and writing.

In our nomadic past, all the knowledge you needed to survive could be contained in your head and the heads of the people you lived with. If writing had existed it would have been just another thing that had to be carried around. Settling down, cultivating crops and domesticating animals made it possible to create a body of knowledge that would not be destroyed or lost whenever you had to move on to the next hunting ground or pasture.

The technologies required to share knowledge across the generations have developed very slowly. The first language-based writing system emerged about 8,000 years after agriculture, and the movable-type printing press another 5,000 years after that. In between, thousands of books had been written in hundreds of languages, preserving the thoughts, histories and discoveries of vanished civilisations. Books on clay tablets, the shells of turtles, the teeth of whales, scrolls of papyrus, bound sheets of vellum, gigantic codexes of thick paper ... Most of these books got lost or were destroyed by war, natural disasters or human incompetence. What survived was extremely valuable and as such tended to accumulate in the libraries of pharaohs, kings, emperors and the Church.

One aspect of the Renaissance was Europe's rediscovery of the knowledge buried in these libraries. The invention of the printing press meant that alongside old knowledge, new knowledge could be spread more widely and more quickly. The English Newton built his laws of motion on the work of the Italian Galileo who was influenced by the Pole Copernicus who owed a considerable debt to the Arabs Muhammad ibn Jabir al-Harrani al-Battani and Nasir al-Din al-

Tusi. Though books were becoming more widely available, they remained too expensive to own except by a tiny minority. In any case, books aren't much use if you can't read. Shakespeare's plays and sonnets, everything by Keats, Byron, Shelley and Wordsworth, and the novels *Robinson Crusoe*, *Pamela*, *Tom Jones*, *Tristram Shandy*, *Frankenstein* and *Pride and Prejudice*, were all written in a country where the average person was illiterate.

Reading has only been an activity the average person is capable of for less than 200 years. In the mid-nineteenth century, 50 per cent of women and 33 per cent of men could not even sign their own names. Eventually, partly prompted by industrialists who believed that British illiteracy was bad for business, the Education Acts of the 1870s were passed. These were designed to provide an education for all children between the ages of five and 13, which finally ensured that the majority of people would be able to read whatever books they got their hands on if they wanted to. Reading as a leisure activity rose sharply as the cost of reproducing the written word fell, reaching a peak in the second half of the twentieth century before television started to dominate our leisure time.

Nowadays, with books cheaper than they have ever been, reading for pleasure is in decline. More than 40 per cent of British people do not read any books at all, ever. The average person spends a total of six hours a week reading: 11 minutes a day on fiction, 6 minutes on non-fiction, 2 minutes on reference books, 17 minutes on newspapers, 5 minutes on magazines and 7 minutes reading online. In total, just over two years of reading in a lifetime. In comparison, you will spend 8.7 years watching TV.

As entertainment, books have probably had their golden age. They won't ever completely die out, they will always be there for the people who want them, along with travelling minstrels, bards, plays, radio, film and all the other ways of telling stories that used to be more popular than they are now. But the thing that makes books different from these other forms is that books are how we learn to read and write. The average British adult has the same reading skills as the National Curriculum expects of the average 14-year-old. Less than 40 per cent of the population are reading at the level you would expect of the average school-leaver. In a world where access to stories, entertainment and communication no longer relies on the written word, literacy is getting harder to teach and maintain.

Whatever the format – clay tablets, papyrus and squid ink, vellum and ox blood, a quill dipped in venom, PDF, JPEG, HTML/internet.co.doc – writing is still the most durable way of preserving knowledge and reading is still the most efficient way of retrieving it. This is just as likely to be true in 3009, when being able to read will give you access to 6,500 years of human knowledge. Somewhere among the great works of art, football scores, unified theories of everything, new ways of killing people, accounts of voyages to distant worlds and recipes for macaroni cheese will be the correct tyre pressures for your 1,000-year-old Toyota Avensis estate.

RELIGION

Stories are one of the ways we make sense of the world. They take basic human drives and play them out in fictional universes. Each time has its own stories, its own fictional universes with their own obstacles and opportunities, and though these change, the ineradicable desires and emotions of the human heart that drive the characters remain remarkably similar over thousands of years. A classic is usually a story whose truths about these desires and emotions transcend their fictional universe in a way that resonates with future generations.

One of the best-selling books at the beginning of the twentieth century was written by a man called Ranger Gull. Ranger decided that as his real name sounded like a pseudonym, he would be better writing under a pseudonym that sounded like a real name. So, in 1903 a book called *When It Was Dark* by the altogether more likely Guy Thorne appeared. Despite the publisher's boast that it was 'The most daring and original novel of the century!' (not much of a claim just three years in), sales got off to a slow start. But *When It Was Dark* proved to be one of those books you only have to sell one copy of – the rest is about making sure that each bookshop has a massive stack of them just inside the door and nobody gets trampled in the rush. Your initial reader tells all his or her friends. They tell all their friends and so on until the laws of chain reactions, exponential growth and infectious diseases set off a popular cultural landslide. The future General

Montgomery of el Alamein, who was 16 when it came out, listed *When It Was Dark* as the most influential book in his life. The Bishop of London was so enthusiastic that he gave a sermon about it at Westminster Abbey and later editions carry a 200-word excerpt encouraging people to buy 'this remarkable work of fiction'.

When It Was Dark tells the story of how an evil Jew from Manchester blackmails an adulterous academic from the British Museum into faking up a tomb in Jerusalem with an inscription by Joseph of Arimathea. Joseph was the man who gave up the tomb he had bought for himself so that Christ's body could be laid there. In the inscription, Joseph confesses that after the Crucifixion he had a change of heart and secretly moved Christ's body to this new tomb. When the fake tomb is discovered, the bad news spreads quickly round the world. Christ didn't rise from the dead! The Resurrection never happened! Christianity is all a lie! The result is the TOTAL BREAKDOWN of civilisation all over the world. Crime, violence, looting, bands of men raping women in the streets ...

It is easy to believe that the average British person at the beginning of the twentieth century was not all that different from us. They had aircraft, trains, cars, ocean-going liners, telephones and electricity. You can pick up photographs and look them right in the eye. Apart from some repugnant attitudes to class, women and race, which are not exactly unknown today, the differences appear to be largely a matter of collars, coats and hats. But the people in those photographs turned *When It Was Dark* into a best-seller. They bought it, read it and recommended it to their friends. The scenario played out in the book was as plausible to them as being eaten by a shark is to the readers of *Jaws*. Though the book was derided in some circles, the general public had no problem with the belief that Christianity and the literal truth of the Gospels was the only thing restraining our bestial urges and holding society together.

The book sold steadily through the real darkness and chaos of the Great War, was made into a film in 1919 and continued to sell strongly enough for new editions to be produced well into the 1920s. But before that decade was over, people had stopped reading *When It Was Dark*. It went out of print and has remained more or less forgotten ever since. Reading fashions change. People probably didn't stop buying *When It Was Dark* just because they came to a sudden realisation that a belief in the Incarnation and Resurrection was not the only thing preventing Western civilisation from blowing up. But it is this ludicrous premise, among other things, that makes *When It Was Dark* almost comically unreadable today. The fact that, not so long ago, the majority of people found it entirely plausible puts a distance between us and them that has nothing to do with time and is a measure of how much the status of religion has changed in Britain over the last 100 years.

This has little to do with church attendance, as the average person does not go to church. It is possible that the average person has never in fact been a regular churchgoer. In the mid-nineteenth century, the population of Britain had grown so rapidly that politicians were worried about there being enough space in churches to fit everyone every Sunday. The results of the religious census they carried out in 1851 horrified them: it revealed that a mere 39 per cent of the British population went to church. Taking into account the people who went more than once means this figure may actually have been as low as 24 per cent. In 1903, the year *When It Was Dark* came out, it was 19 per cent and the decline has been slowly accelerating since then to the current figure of 6 per cent, which takes into account churches, mosques, temples and all other places of worship.

But regular attendance for religious worship is only one of the reasons for going to church. In the average month, around 11 per cent of the population will visit a place of worship for a funeral, wedding, nikah, shadi, carol service, Eid celebration, bar mitzvah, bat mitzvah or other service, which means that the average person goes to church every nine months or a total of 105 times in a lifetime.

Though empty buildings are powerfully symbolic, the most significant change for religion in the last 100 years has been in the nature of belief. It is hard to imagine the general levels of religious belief that sustained the success of *When It Was Dark*. In contrast, the best-selling novel of the early twenty-first century is *The Da Vinci Code*, which is based on the premise that the Church has been lying to us for the last 2,000 years.

The reader of 1903 would probably have been outraged by the smash-hit bestseller of 2003, but not in a way that sold lots of books. It is doubtful whether General Montgomery would have considered it the most influential read of his life. No doubt the Bishop of London would have hated it, not least because the climax takes place in the Temple Church, which is in his diocese. The current Bishop of London takes the view – forced upon many religious leaders by the state of religious belief in Britain these days – that anything that might get people interested, no matter how silly, must be accommodated.

In 1999, a survey by the Catholic newspaper *The Tablet* and the *Daily Telegraph* found that only 45 per cent of people believed that Jesus was the son of God. This jars rather with the 2001 census in which 72 per cent of people said they are Christians. This means that potentially 37 per cent of people who feel they are Christians do not have the basic knowledge required to fully understand or be outraged by either *When It Was Dark* or *The Da Vinci Code*.

RUBBISH

Nearly everything you buy is either going to be thrown away or flushed down the toilet. Every year Britain produces 335 million tonnes of waste – that's 5.5 tonnes each or 437 tonnes in a lifetime. About 9 per cent of this will be produced directly by you, which means that in a lifetime you will personally put just under 40 tonnes of waste in the bin. You will also flush around 5 tonnes of waste down the toilet.

Most of the waste you produce will have been dug up from a hole in the ground, made into something that you will have until it is broken, eaten, has gone off or out of fashion, then it will be put back into the system to be burned or buried in a different hole in the ground. About 27 per cent of the waste is intercepted at the point where you throw it away and is made into something else. In 1997 we recycled about 7 per cent of our waste; now it is around 27 per cent, which saves the same amount of carbon as taking 3.5 million cars off the roads. However, recycling is still pretty much a minor eddy in the economic current that ultimately draws everything down into landfill, incineration or dispersal.

Occasionally, things are too beautiful, useful or interesting to throw away. They defy entropy and are passed from generation to generation, turning up on *The Antiques Roadshow* or making their way into museums and art galleries. Alongside the things no one could bear to throw away in the first place are things that were thrown away or lost a long time ago, which civilisation has now changed its mind about and decided to keep for ever in a climate-controlled building.

Eventually, we will have dug up everything. Though there are vast resources of raw materials, we are using them at an extraordinary rate. In the last century we used more natural resources than in all the human history that went before. It is estimated that in the next 60 years we will have dug up all the gold, silver, zinc, uranium, tin, lead, copper and iron, as well as the more exotic metals such as indium, gallium, germanium, hafnium and rhodium that are essential for building microchips, solar cells and catalytic converters. Nobody is quite sure what will happen then, but it is bound to involve digging all our rubbish up again.

SALIVA

You produce two kinds of saliva. The slightly thicker kind is produced slowly all through the day to keep your mouth moist and supple. But, when you think you are about to eat you quickly start to produce a much thinner, watery saliva that helps turn the food you have chewed into a slippery mass you can easily swallow. Both kinds contain enzymes that get to work on the starches and fats you have eaten and start digesting them in your mouth. In total you will produce 750 ml of saliva a day. Enough to fill a wine bottle. If you had a big enough cellar, in a lifetime you could lay down 25,348 bottles of spit.

SALT

Elephants have a culture in that their children learn patterns of behaviour from their parents and in turn pass them on to their own children. Like all animals, elephants need salt to survive. The elephants living on the slopes of Mount Elgon in Kenya have a problem getting enough salt. The peculiarities of the local environment mean that the soil and plants contain almost no salt at all. Luckily, the rocks that make up Mount Elgon contain rich salt deposits. But while other animals can lick salt from these rocks, the shape of their mouths means the elephants have to do things differently. Using their tusks, they gouge out from the cliff lumps of the soft, salty rock, which they pick up using their trunks and eat. Generations of elephants have passed this trick on to their children and over thousands of years they have carved out huge caves that follow the salt deposits hundreds of metres into the mountainside.

For us, salt only became a problem that had to be solved when we settled down and became farmers around 13,000 years ago. Up to this point, we had been getting just the right amount of salt from meat, but with an increasingly vegetarian diet, we had to find additional sources of salt for both ourselves and our livestock.

Blood, sweat and tears taste of salt. We are 60 per cent water and all of it is salty. In our bodies, the salt we consume becomes electrolytes – solutions that conduct electricity – which our body uses in myriad ways to keep our cells inflated, control blood pressure and regulate how much water we drink and how much we pee. Our nerves and muscles are electrical tissues and also rely on electrolytes to function properly. This is why if you dilute your saltiness too much by drinking large amounts of water your whole body will cease to function properly and you will die. Around about 10 l of water in half an hour will do the job.

Conversely, if you have too much salt you will also die. About 1 g per kg of body weight is the fatal dose. There is a good reason why salt water makes you throw up.

The importance of salt to maintain health and preserve food made it one of the key commodities of the ancient world. As it is an essential requirement of life, rulers and governments have traditionally established a monopoly over salt production and trade. Grievances about unfair salt taxes played a key role in the American War of Independence, the French Revolution, the fall of imperial China and the end of British rule in India.

Nearly 10 per cent of the Raj's tax revenue came from salt and it was illegal for anyone other than the government to manufacture it. In 1930, Gandhi set out with 78 followers on a 240-mile march to the sea to make salt. Twenty-three days later he stood on the shores of the Arabian Indian Ocean with 50,000 people, held up a handful of salty mud and proclaimed, 'With this, I am shaking the foundations of the British Empire.' This moment is now seen as one of the turning points in the Indian struggle for independence.

The fact that we can't do without it, and that for most of our history getting enough of it has been a problem, means that we tend to eat too much salt. The average person needs around 4 g a day to survive, which amounts to 113 kg over a lifetime. However, you are actually going to consume more than twice as much: 237 kg, which is an average of 8.2 g a day.

In an effort to reduce the health problems such as high blood pressure, osteoporosis and stomach cancer that come from eating this much salt, the government has recently recommended a maximum daily consumption of 6 g. This would give you a lifetime total of 173 kg. While this is well below the amount we actually consume, it is also well above the amount we actually need. The government might just be setting itself a realistic target, but it is also showing us how little it feels we can be trusted to take their advice.

Cutting down on salt means putting up with blander food for a few weeks while your palate readjusts. It is notoriously hard to sacrifice even a few weeks' pleasure for a potential health benefit years down the line. The best thing is not to start at all, but unfortunately, like the salt-mining elephants of Mount Elgon, you probably learned your salt-eating habits from your parents. And, just like the elephants, you are using them to dig yourself a hole in the ground.

SANDWICHES

The idea of putting something between two slices of bread is as old as bread itself. In Spanish they are known as *bo-cadillos*, in Sweden *smörgås*, in Finnish *voileipiä*, in Italian *panini* and in Germany *belegte brot*. In Britain, they used to be called simply 'a bread and meat'.

The popular legend is that John Montague, the 4th Earl of Sandwich, was so loathe to leave his cribbage that he had his salt beef brought to the gaming table. So as not to get grease on his cards, he had the meat put between two slices of bread. What evidence there is contradicts this story. Though he came from an illustrious family, Sandwich was not rich. He worked hard and rose through the ranks of government purely on merit at a time when govern-ment figures were expected to pay their own way. In the 1760s, when sandwiches started to be called sandwiches, Montague was First Lord of the Admiralty, a Cabinet min-ister and one of the principal Secretaries of State. He is known to have worked extremely long hours and often had to eat meals at his desk. Far from being the snack of a greedy aristocrat too lazy to get up from his card game, the sandwich is named after an overworked government official who spent too much time at the office.

No doubt his colleagues in government – Viscount Sackville, the Earl of Halifax, Lord North, the Earl of Euston and Lord Shuldham – also ate at their desks, but Sandwich is such a good name, the cheese sackville or the prawn halifax never had a chance. It is such a good name that as our habits of overwork and eating on the go spread across the world, 'sandwich' is becoming the international word for anything between two slices of bread.

You are going to eat 189 sandwiches every year of your life. A total of 15,029. You will make and eat over half of these at home. A quarter you will make and put in a lunch box. Buying the remaining quarter in shops will cost a total of £5,733. An average of £1.67 a sandwich.

SCHOOL

You will spend most of your life doing the same things over and over again. On your first day at school you will be introduced to the concept of going to the same place every day at the same time in more or less the same clothes to do more or less the same thing surrounded by the same people who will turn on you if you step out of line …

Over the course of 1,800 days you will be taught the essential skills of reading, which will enable you to access 5,500 years' worth of accumulated human knowledge, and writing, which will enable you to add to it. You will also be taught the number system and brought up to date in various different fields of knowledge so that you don't waste time later trying to invent a smallpox vaccine or prove that the Earth goes round the Sun. As well as the sciences, you will also be exposed to history so that you have some notion of how we got to where we are, the arts so that you can join in and sport because it is good for you.

You will spend 14 per cent of your life at school and you will be taught many things; whether you will learn or remember any of them is up to you. In order to check how you are doing, the government has made it a statutory requirement that you are tested along the way in maths, reading, writing, spelling and, later, science. In all, 11 sets of tests. If you include the mock exams, by the time you leave school at 16, you will have sat 29 exams and countless other small tests and assessments.

Just as importantly, during your years at school you will also be learning how to behave. In theory, school is a safe, nurturing place to learn the consequences of being late, lazy, aggressive, timid, smelly, obnoxious, criminal and all the other things that for better or worse will determine whether you fit in or stand out. The punishments for breaking the rules of school are all milder versions of the consequences of breaking the rules of society. You are obliged to attend school until you legally become an adult on your sixteenth birthday. After this, breaking the rules will have adult consequences.

In order to give you the chance to be interested in everything modern civilisation has to offer, school is a time when you will do a lot of things for the first and often only time. Things like: dissecting a cow's eyeball, throwing a javelin, having your dinner money stolen, sitting in detention, burning hydrogen with a squeaky pop, reading Shakespeare, going on a cross-country run, having a fight, being charged up on a Van de Graaf generator, smoking a cigarette, playing a musical instrument, writing an essay about *Animal Farm*, learning a foreign language …

If you like any of them, you might end up doing them for the rest of your life.

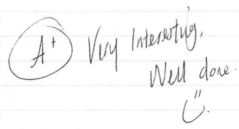

SEX

The one thing all your ancestors have in common is that they had sex. You are the result of 3.8 billion years of winning a mate, having sex with them and successfully raising at least one child who was able to do the same. Of course, your ancestors have only been doing this in human form for the last 250,000 years or so. Your lineage stretches back through time via a huge range of forms some large, some small, some furry, some scaly. Forms that made it through the asteroid impacts, the supervolcano eruptions and other catastrophes that have befallen the planet, right back to slime and the origin of life itself.

When we talk about the origin of life, what we really mean is the origin of something that was able to make copies of itself. The origin, in fact, of genetic material. If you like, you can consider yourself as merely the current envelope of a genetic chain letter that got going 3.8 billion years ago. You might want to explain to your date that the desire you feel rises from a feeling of responsibility to your ancestors to forge the next link of the chain with the best possible partner. You should also tell this lucky individual that your ancestors will reward both of you by flooding your brains with dopamine and endorphins at the crucial moment ...

If you ask people how often they do this, they tend to give unreliable answers. If you ask men and women how many people of the opposite sex they have had sex with, you will get different figures for men and women.

Now this is clearly impossible. The only thing you have found out is that men exaggerate. One way round this problem is to ask instead, 'When did you *last* have sex?' If you ask enough people you can use these figures to work out an average for the whole population. When these calculations are done you get a figure of 1.55 times a week. Traditionally it is the woman who has the 0.55 of sex and the man who worries about this. If 1.55 seems like a ridiculously high figure you are probably older than 30. If you find it depressingly low you are probably in your twenties.

Statistics on sex – particularly the average number of times and the average number of partners – can be wildly misleading because the average includes subsets of people who are having so much more sex than the rest of us. This pulls the averages up. Before you get envious of those rock stars and millionaire playboys, by far the most significant group is prostitutes doing it out of economic necessity. Contrary to their clients' delusions they are probably not enjoying it much. A report in 2002 from the universities of East Anglia and Manchester estimated that British men spend an estimated £770 million a year on prostitutes. A 2008 survey by the *Observer* found that 18 per cent of British men have visited a prostitute. For the men in this subset this represents £11,533 in a lifetime. The non-financial costs are beyond calculation.

The reason people are likely to lie about their sexual behaviour is thought to be because in this area – more than any other – we want to appear to be normal. So, what is a normal amount of sex? If a statistician ever asks you,

'When did you last have sex?' you could tell them that you lost your virginity at the age of 16.6 and have sex 1.55 times a week, which comes to 5,037 times over a lifetime with 8.8 different people. Sex surveys are a popular way of selling newspapers, magazines and books, but sex surveys are also important and useful in all sorts of unfrivolous ways such as the control of hepatitis, syphilis and HIV. So, perhaps it would be better to tell the truth, contribute some useful data and, if you are a man, try to keep the boasting to a minimum.

SHOES

Up until recently you would expect to get years, perhaps even a lifetime's wear out of a pair of shoes that you would take to the cobbler for regular servicing in much the same way as you would take a car to the garage. Now, mass production in countries with low labour costs means that shoes are cheap enough to be disposable and are often constructed in a way that makes repair impossible anyway. Two million pairs of shoes are thrown away every week in Britain; 104 million pairs a year. In a lifetime, you will own and throw away 136 pairs of shoes. These will have cost you £7,369.

From time to time, a fashion house will do a survey of women's shoe-buying habits and these always come up with very much higher figures than this. The average woman, they say, owns between 40 and 50 pairs of shoes at any one time. She spends over £500 on ten new pairs of shoes a year, which costs her £30–40,000 in a lifetime. It is true that women spend a lot more on shoes than men, but if these crazy figures were correct then sales of women's shoes alone would be over £10 billion, when the total British shoe market is worth only around £5.5 billion.

This could be a genuine mistake and it may be coincidental that the figures are always overestimates. If you were cynical, then you might be suspicious of surveys commissioned by people who sell things overestimating how much of that thing we buy. You might feel their aim is to reset the idea of average behaviour to a higher level to encourage you to spend more

... But only if you were cynical. Like being a chocoholic or a soap addict, not being rational about shoes is often celebrated as a forgivable sin. But it is only forgivable up to a certain point. Imelda Marcos said: 'They went into my closets looking for skeletons, but thank God, all they found were shoes, beautiful shoes.' In 2001, as part of her attempt to rehabilitate herself, she opened a shoe museum in Manila, still unaware that for most of the world the shoes *are* the skeletons in her closet – 1,060 pairs of them, all size eight and a half.

SLEEP

Though you will be unconscious for one-third of your life, you won't really mind because the other two-thirds would not be worth living otherwise. You will also have a vague notion that something important to do with memory, brain development and general body maintenance is going on during those lost hours.

The traditional theory is that something that forces us to spend eight hours out of every 24 lying unconscious and vulnerable could only be justified if it gave us a vital advantage for dealing with the challenges of the world while we are awake. The search for this crucial biological function has not been a great success so far. The answer may be that there simply isn't one, which means we may not need to sleep at all.

Each of your 28,891 nights of sleep will have a similar structure. Stage-one sleep, when you are drowsily brushing the boundary of proper sleep, is the hallucinatory state known as hypnagogia. This can last for a long time if you are in a distracting environment like an airport departure lounge or a car. In more peaceful surroundings, or if you are very tired, you will pass quickly though hypnagogia and slip into a light stage-two sleep. After about 15 minutes, your breathing and heart rate will slow and you will enter the slow-wave sleep of stage three. After about an hour you will be totally submerged in stage four – deep slow-wave sleep, the deepest sleep of the whole night.

Slow-wave sleep seems to be the kind of sleep your brain craves the most. The more sleep-deprived you are, the quicker you will descend to stage four. You might feel refreshed waking from a 15-minute nap, but being hauled from the depths of slow-wave sleep after a hour can be unpleasant. You will feel sick and groggy and it may take up to half an hour for the effects of sleep inertia to wear off. Left alone, after about 90 minutes of deep sleep, you will resurface to a state of near wakefulness and have your first episode of REM (rapid eye movement) sleep.

REM sleep was only noticed and described in the 1950s. Attaching electrodes to the heads of sleeping people to try and find out what was going on in their brains during REM was the beginning of modern sleep research. The different stages of sleep are characterised by the different waves they make on an EEG. In stage two, you find sleep spindles – tight little scribbles that look like springs – and K-complexes, big, isolated, sharply pointed zigzags. In stages three and four you have delta waves. These large, slow, regular waves are rarely found in a waking state except in young children and intoxicated adults. In contrast, your EEG during REM is almost the same as when you are awake. REM is closely associated with dreams. To stop you acting out your dreams, your muscles are somehow disconnected from your brain, though your heart rate, breathing and body temperature will all fluctuate as if you actually are doing the things you are dreaming of. Over eight hours, you will have between four and five 90-minute cycles of slow-wave and REM sleep. Even at the rate of just one dream per cycle, you will have over 130,000 dreams in a lifetime.

There has been a lot of research into what REM and dreaming might be for, with a particular emphasis on memory. However, people can adapt to having no REM sleep at all. For instance, if you are on antidepressants you may go for years without REM sleep and have a perfectly normal memory. Research into the more opaque area of slow-wave sleep has been no more fruitful and although important biological processes undoubtedly do go on while we are asleep, none have been found that justify losing 26 years of your life.

There is also no adequate explanation for how some animals, most notably dolphins, can go without any sleep at all. Dolphins are famous for sleeping with one half of their brain at a time, but this is only detectable with sensitive instruments. It might be better to describe what they do as resting, because they remain functionally awake, responsive and equally coordinated on both sides of their body. Depriving them of this rest doesn't seem to have any effect either. They remain just as able to perform all the complicated tasks we make them do to prove their intelligence.

One of the pre-eminent researchers in the field of sleep argues that the reason we have been unable to come up with a crucial biological function for sleep is simply because there isn't one. Jerry Siegel from the University of California in Los Angeles has suggested that sleep is a response to our environment. It is a way of saving energy and keeping us out of trouble. The sleep patterns of other animals would appear to support this. Giraffes, who must forage constantly for food and avoid predators, sleep three hours a night. Lions, who once they have eaten have nothing else to do for the day, sleep 14 hours. Fur seals exhibit REM and slow-wave sleep when they are on land and then rest dolphin-like with no REM for weeks on end when they are living in the sea. Back on dry land they go right back to a normal sleeping pattern without the slightest sign that they have any sleep to catch up on.

The evidence suggests that forcing us to do nothing, keep out of harm's way and conserve energy for a third of our lives may provide a greater survival advantage than any of the biological benefits that may simply be incidental to sleep. If this is the case, it may turn out that how we feel when we don't get enough sleep is a way of punishing us and making sure that we get to bed earlier in future rather than evidence that vital maintenance work hasn't been carried out. The more sleep you miss, the worse the punishment and the greater the incentive to behave yourself in future. As for REM, Siegel argues that its main function is to stimulate the brainstem in a way that enables you to stay unconscious for hours on end. Rather than evidence of vital maintenance work, your dreams are a kind of internal television to keep your brain occupied.

This means that our eight hours of sleep – which correspond to the eight darkest hours of the night – are simply a way of stopping us blundering about in the dark with our inadequate night vision, falling over, hurting ourselves and getting eaten. Instead, we spend the whole day knowing that we will have to find a safe place to pass those dangerous hours, somewhere we can lie unconscious until dawn.

The idea that sleep is nature's way of drugging you so you can be safely stored for the night is controversial. Any theory suggesting that everyone working in a particular field is wasting their time is likely to be met with resistance and this theory suggests we are all wasting our time – around eight hours every night. However, it does also open up the possibility that we may one day be able to circumvent the mechanisms that compel us to sleep so we can spend those 26 years doing something else.

SMOKING

When the National Lottery was set up in 1994, it made sense to sell the tickets in local newsagents and tobacconists because they are convenient, established local outlets. It also made some sort of sense to sell lottery tickets and cigarettes together because of the link between believing that you will live for ever and that some day you will be rich.

The average life expectancy in Britain is 79.1 years. The average life expectancy for a smoker is 69.1 years. If you are one of Britain's 11,638,346 smokers, then you are essentially gambling with ten years of your life.

The average British smoker gets through 13.97 cigarettes a day or 270,945 in total. As for the dream of one day being rich, these cigarettes will cost £70,852. The average person is not a smoker. The average person's share of all the cigarettes smoked in Britain in their lifetime is 78,424.

Smokers have to deal with a lot of disapproval, preaching and sermonising. However, if you do smoke and are careful, then there isn't really that much to feel guilty about. Working conditions in the tobacco industry are no worse than those in the banana, pineapple and coffee industries. If you are careful not to smoke in front of children or to force others to smoke passively, if you dispose of your butts and ash considerately and if you don't start forest fires, then there really isn't that much to feel guilty about other than the waste of cash on something that damages your day-to-day health and shortens your life.

Every year, smoking-related illnesses cost the NHS £1.722 billion. If you made each of the 11.6 million British smokers pay for this out of their own pockets it would cost them £147 each a year. The duty on tobacco represents about 80 per cent of the price of a cigarette. Every year, the average smoker pays £1,066 in tobacco duty. Once they have paid for their health care there is £919 left over.

This is the other thing that the National Lottery and smoking have in common. They both make a lot of money for the government. Despite this, the government makes considerable efforts to encourage smokers to give up. As each quitter costs the government over £1,000 a year in duty, it is difficult to be cynical about this. The first confirmed link between smoking and lung cancer was established by Dr Richard Doll in 1954. These were only his initial results and the study continued. Fifty years later Sir Richard Doll announced his final results. Though the study proved that smoking will kill you early, the conclusions for smokers are hopeful. Although if you continue to smoke your life expectancy is reduced by ten years, giving up at any age has an instant benefit. If you give up at 30 you regain a full ten years of life. At 40 it's nine years. At 50 it's six, and at 60 it's

three. Three years might not seem like much, but for a
60-year-old smoker this actually represents a 16 per cent
increase in their life expectancy.

If you choose to ignore the opportunity
to be richer and live longer, then
you have a 50 per cent chance of
being killed by cigarettes. Once the cost
of caring for you in your final illness is
taken off, the government will have
made a profit of £48,864,
which it may or may
not have spent
on good
causes.

SNEEZING

The average person sneezes four times a day. That's 115,565 times in your life. Sneezing is similar to vomiting. It is one of your body's ways of getting rid of things that shouldn't be in it. Your sneeze reflex is stimulated when the lining of your nose becomes irritated, which causes the release of tiny protein molecules called histamines. These irritate your nasal nerves. This is the 'ah ah ah ah' part of the sneeze, the bit where you are waiting for your brain to throw the switch that convulses muscles all the way from your groin to your eyebrows, resulting in the explosive 'chooo!'. This will blast 40,000 droplets at 100 miles an hour over the dashboard of your car. Sneezing behind the wheel of a car involves driving with your eyes closed. It is a myth that if you sneeze with your eyes open they will fall out, but it is more or less impossible to keep them open. They will close for less than one-tenth of a second. Even travelling at 70 mph you will only travel about 3 m with your eyes closed. So, unless your sneeze is violent enough to completely obscure the windscreen, you should be OK.

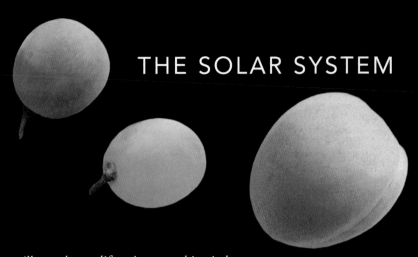

THE SOLAR SYSTEM

You will spend your life going round in circles
but never quite coming back to where you started ...

If you were suddenly gripped by the urge to construct a scale model of
the solar system out of fruit and vegetables, then it would make sense to
choose the biggest thing you could find to be the Sun. Assuming you could
get your hands on a pumpkin 1 m across, you would need to place the white
peppercorn representing Mercury 41 m away. The tiny currant of Venus
would be another 40 m on and by the time you were reaching into your
brown paper bag for the Earth (a large pea) you would be more than 100 m
from the pumpkin. By this stage you would probably be starting to worry
about birds and mice making off with the planets. Can you really be bothered with the 40-minute walk to correctly place a tomato seed representing
Pluto? Perhaps it would be better just to sit down 100 m from the Sun and
eat Mars, Jupiter, Saturn (cranberry, nectarine, apricot) and the grapes of
Neptune and Uranus.

Though it might feel like you are sitting still reading this book, you are in fact moving at fantastic speeds. The Earth is spinning at 600 miles an hour and simultaneously gliding silently through space at over 18 miles a second as we orbit the Sun. The Sun in turn orbits the centre of the Milky Way at over 420,000 miles an hour, and our gently rotating galaxy is plummeting through the universe at nearly 400 miles per second.

Don't ever let anyone accuse you of sitting still. The Earth will spin 28,891 times in your lifetime and you will make 79.1 journeys round the Sun. In the giant Spirograph of the solar system you will trace out a line

SPERM

Men will produce 10 litres of semen in a lifetime. In terms of wallpaper paste, that is enough to hang 16 rolls of lining paper. In terms of sperm, that's 1.2 trillion spermatozoa swimming frantically towards an egg that probably isn't there and more than enough to father a child for every star in the Milky Way.

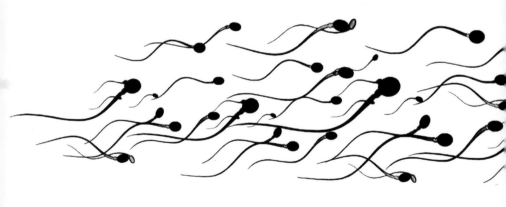

STATISTICS

These are the numbers used throughout this book ...

The world is 4.6 billion years old.

Life emerged 3.8 billion years ago.

Modern humans appeared about 200,000 years ago.

There are now 6,464,750,000 people living on Earth.

You are one of the 60,587,000 people living in Britain; one of the 2.4 individuals living in 24.7 million British households.

You will start to walk and talk at 12 months. You will start school at five. At 15 you will start to drink. In your sixteenth year you will have sex for the first time. By 18 you will have reached an average adult weight of 76 kg. You will begin work at 22. You will have 1.6 children and become a grand-parent at 54. You will retire at 62 and die 17 years later at the age of 79.1. Including leap years, you will have spent 28,891.275 days on Earth.

The you in this book does not exist and no one person lives this life.

Every year 11 billion packets of crisps are eaten in Britain. If you div-ide this number by the total population you get 175, which is how many packets of crisps the average Briton gets through in a year. Multiply by the average lifespan and you get the average lifetime's supply of crisps: 13,842 packets. But this is just one way of being average. If it had been possible to survey a large number of people on their crisp-buying habits, then work-ing out the number of crisps bought that marks the mid-point – with half the population buying less and the other buying more, would give you the median crisp consumption. If you took the commonest number of crisps bought you would have the mode. This would have told you a lot more about Britain's relationship to the crisp; however, it simply wasn't practical for a book like this as that sort of detailed information is not generally available. So, this book contains the meaning of life rather than the medianing or moding.

In many ways an average is a clumsy analytical tool. The average British person does not have two legs or for that matter two eyes, or two arms. But knowing that you have an above-average number of legs and eat less than the average quantity of crisps does tell you something about the population as a whole. Creating this imaginary average you is the most practical way of putting together a picture of how we live our lives in Britain today and how the real you reading this book compares to everyone else.

STOMACH ACID

In the outside world, hydrochloric acid in the same concentration as your stomach acid is classed as a hazardous chemical, which by law must be stored and transported in containers marked with the correct warning signs. It is powerful enough to dissolve most metals, let alone human bodies. If something goes wrong with the thick layer of mucus that protects your stomach, or you produce too much acid, you will start to digest yourself from the inside. At the rate of 2.6 l a day your body will produce enough hydrochloric acid every two months to fill a bath. In a lifetime, you would be able to completely submerge and dissolve yourself in your own gastric juices more than 440 times.

Doctors are prescribing pills at an ever-increasing rate. In 2002 the average GP wrote 64 prescriptions a day. In 2007, this had gone up by 26 per cent to 81. While some of this increase is undoubtedly a good thing – a result of there being more treatments available and more people being treated – some of it is because we would much rather be prescribed a course of pills than a change in lifestyle. That would seem to be our fault, and it partly is. However, when doctors decide to prescribe you something, you have to trust that they are doing the best thing for you. Any external factors that might influence their decision are something you should know about.

Every year, drug companies spend tens of millions of pounds funding all-expenses-paid trips so that British doctors and other health-care professionals can attend conferences and events around the world. The drug companies say their funding of doctors is about education, and doctors say they are not influenced. It would be relatively simple to put this to the test by comparing what doctors prescribe with drug- company funding of trips. However, though the Department of Health requires NHS trusts to make these figures available to the public, fewer than a quarter do. In other countries, drug companies are required by law to declare every penny they spend on funding medical organisations, educational events and individual doctors. In Europe they are only encouraged to do so. In 2008, however, drug companies did agree to make a full disclosure of their funding of patient groups.

According to an investigation published in the *Independent*, in 2007 the National Kidney Federation, the Arthritis and Musculoskeletal Alliance, the National Rheumatoid Arthritis Society, Beating Bowel Cancer, the Royal National Institute for the Blind and the Alzheimer's Society each received up to 50 per cent of their total funding from drug companies. All of these groups are bringing pressure to bear on the government to make new drug treatments more available. A postcode lottery exists because some NHS trusts have more money than others. Curiously, none of these six groups have made an issue in their recent campaigns of the high prices drug companies charge for their treatments.

Indigestion is big business. Every year, 5 per cent of the NHS's £10 billion total drug bill goes on indigestion – £550 million. In a lifetime, you will spend £718. Some of this (£164) will be spent by you personally on over-the-counter medicines. The remaining £554 will be spent by the NHS on extremely powerful prescription drugs such as proton pump inhibitors. PPIs are very effective: they interfere with the enzymes that make stomach acid and can reduce acid production by up to 99 per cent. However, most people do not need this sort of drastic treatment. The *British Medical Journal* recently estimated that every year up to £300 million worth of PPIs are prescribed for people who don't need them. Which means that 70 per cent of the £425 million spent annually by the NHS on PPIs is wasted. Enough to pay for a year's worth of the breast-cancer drug Herceptin for 3,000 women.

STUFF

You live surrounded by the stuff you own. Some of it will be useful stuff. Some of it will be stuff you are planning to make use of one day. Some of it will be stuff you haven't got round to throwing away yet. Perhaps you have even forgotten it is there. Nearly all stuff-related problems stem from the last two categories, which will dwarf and occasionally bury the first – all the stuff you actually need.

Some of the stuff you are saving for the future may well be useful one day but a lot of it will be the result of wishful thinking: fish kettles, size-ten jeans, five-inch heels, ice skates, skis, wool and a dartboard. You would like to be someone who cooks whole salmon, wears size-ten jeans and five-inch heels and enjoys winter sports, knitting and darts, but you aren't and hanging on to it all is a waste of space and time.

You will spend 31 minutes a day cleaning and tidying your stuff and a lot of this time will be taken up with making it seem more important by organising, sorting and storing it. You may have a wonderful workshop, an exquisite sewing basket and a marvellous collection of wellingtons, but if you never use them, they are just clutter. You will spend a year and eight months of your life tending your stuff. But if it isn't helping you to live the way you want, then it is probably just getting in your way, wasting your time or tethering you to the past.

Throwing out stuff is hard. For one thing, it will have cost you a lot of money. In a lifetime, excluding cars, houses, consumables like food and toiletries and services like insurance and utility bills, you will spend £149,960 on stuff: furniture, furnishings, DVD players, DVDs, tents, skis, clothes, carpets, fire extinguishers, musical instruments, woks, gardening tools and fridge magnets. To get rid of things you spent money on means you have to admit to yourself that you wasted the money. It would be better not to buy them in the first place, but that can be even harder.

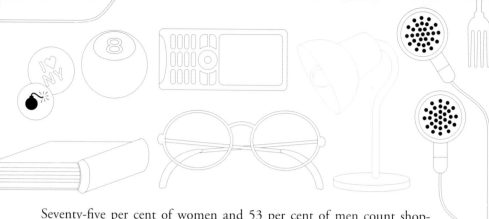

Seventy-five per cent of women and 53 per cent of men count shopping as one of their favourite leisure activities. The average man spends 27 minutes a day shopping, the average woman 40. In a lifetime, the average person will spend 802 days shopping round the clock, more than at any other time in the history of civilisation. Our shopping habits may well be another example of how modern culture hijacks deeply programmed behaviours that helped us to survive in the past and exploits them to ever-crazier levels. Shopping shares many characteristics with hunting and gathering as well as being a highly social activity – interacting with shop staff, friends and other shoppers. It also feels creative. There used to be an empty space, now there's a floor lamp, a clock for the shower, spare slippers in an exciting shade of green or a smoothie-maker that will usher in a new age of healthy living and a slimmer, fitter you …

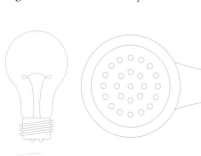

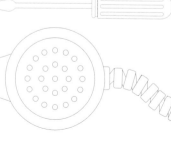

SUCKLING

It comes as a surprise to most
new mothers that breastfeeding is a skill
that has to be learned. What is even more surprising
is that if you have a second child, you may have to learn how
to do it all over again. This is because while you may be a skilled
and confident breastfeeder, your new baby isn't – they have to learn how
to breastfeed too. It is strange that something so essential for survival and
supposedly so natural can be so difficult to learn. After all, other mammals
rarely have this problem. But then, **no other m**ammals have our enormous brains.
Giving birth would be much **easier if women ha**d wider pelvises and babies had
tiny heads. Common descriptio**ns of giving birth bei**ng like shitting a watermelon or
swallowing a baseball reflect the f**act that forcing you**r lovely new baby's head through
the birth canal is the hardest par**t of the process**. Unfortunately for the mother,
having a big brain in a big head is such an advantage that reaching the maximum
size to fit through the mother's pelvis may be one of the things that triggers
labour. In any case, women's pelvises are already more or less at the
optimum size – any wider and it would be significantly harder
to move around. This sets an upper limit on the size of
babies' heads. In order to grow our big brains, therefore, most human brain development has
to take place outside the

womb. This is why human babies
are so helpless and take such a long time
to learn how to breastfeed, while gazelles are sucking happily and running away from lions in a few hours.
It can take a baby and mother up to six weeks to learn how to
breastfeed. In Britain only 48 per cent of mothers are still breastfeeding at
six weeks, which means that most people give up while they are still learning.
During these six weeks you will drink 26.5 l of your mother's milk. To produce this,
your mother will use up 16,537 extra calories – 64 Mars Bars' worth, which would
cost £25. Your first meals will be made specially for you in a way that will never quite
be matched by any others in your life. As well as nutrients, they will also contain a cocktail of ingredients individually tailored to your needs, such as growth factors, hormones
and also antibodies, white blood cells and nucleotides to protect you from infection,
as well as a whole load of other things it would be illegal to put into formula milk.
Formula milk is usually cow's milk that has been modified to contain the same
proportions of nutrients as breast milk. You are going to get through a lot
more of this – around 284 l made up from 43.5 kg of powdered baby
formula at a total cost of £364.56. You will drink your imitation
breast milk from bottles topped with imitation nipples
(made appropriately from silicone), which
will cost a further £20.

SWEAT

Whatever the temperature of your environment, your body does its best to maintain a temperature of 37 °C. As this is the optimum temperature for the molecular interactions and reactions that make up life, there is a real advantage in being warm-blooded and therefore able to keep your body at a constant temperature. The downside is that if your temperature rises or falls just a few degrees either side of this, you will start to die.

If your body temperature drops by just one degree your muscles will go into spasm, fluttering and twitching in an attempt to make heat by shivering. At 35 °C your muscles begin to malfunction. As you get colder, your thumbs will become less opposable. At about 34 °C you won't be able to make them meet your little finger. At 32 °C you won't be able to make them meet any of your fingers and your muscles will be malfunctioning to the point where you can no longer shiver. But, as you will be suffering from short-term amnesia and mental confusion, you probably won't notice. At a body temperature of 30 °C – the same as a beautiful sunny day and just seven degrees below your normal temperature – your major organs start to fail and you will not live for long.

In the other direction, you will start to feel a bit odd at 38 °C. Quite ill at 39 °C and you will start hallucinating at 40 °C. Anything over 40 °C, just three degrees above normal, is life-threatening. At 41 °C brain death begins and by 45 °C it is more or less certain. Anything over 45 °C and you actually start to cook.

In Britain, the mean annual temperature is about 9.5 °C, so to stay alive you need to be an average of 27.5 degrees warmer than your environment. This is not usually too much of a problem as your body is constantly producing heat. Most of it is produced by your liver and by friction from all your muscles, joints, tendons and ligaments rubbing together. Your body can regulate the amount you radiate by controlling blood supply to the skin and you can help out by adding or removing layers of clothing.

But you can only radiate heat if your surroundings are colder than you. If the room is the same temperature you cannot radiate heat at all and if it is hotter you will start to absorb heat radiated from the room. To solve this problem, your body produces sweat. Turning water into water vapour absorbs energy, so evaporating sweat from your skin cools you down. You can produce up to 8 l of sweat a day. However, as you live in Britain and don't take much exercise you will produce an average of just 100 ml. In a lifetime, 2,534 l. Enough to shower for nearly five hours in your own perspiration.

TALKING

People have spent a lot of time trying to teach chimps to talk. Chimps are unable to produce consonants very well and so far no one has been able to come up with an intelligible language that relies on vowels. It's all just 'Oo oo ee ee aaah aah, uh uh uh.' You can get around this difficulty by teaching chimps to communicate with a combination of pictures and sign language. It is interesting that no human has ever managed to learn to speak chimp. Surely with our wonderfully flexible voice boxes and enormous brains this should not be too much of a challenge. The problem is that language has to be based on common experience, which is why a special chimp–human language had to be invented occupying the common ground between people and chimps.

We do not have this difficulty communicating with other humans. There is no human language we cannot learn. No matter how complex its structure or strange its sounds, every language is based on common human experience and can be learned by any human. The average British person is only able to speak one language. The average human can speak two. Luckily, as the other language that the majority of the world's population speaks is English, we can get away with being below average in this respect.

As babies, our voice boxes are very like a chimp's. They are high up in our throats and enable us to drink and breathe at the same time. As you get older your larynx moves down your throat and the ability to breastfeed is replaced by the ability to make complex sounds. The resonant chamber between the larynx and the mouth is what enables you to make all the noises we call language. Unfortunately, it also means that we are the only mammals that will choke if we try to eat, drink and breathe simultaneously.

All the adaptations that enable us to talk have come at a cost. Our short jaws mean that we are unable to chew food as well as Neanderthals, who were able to eat a wider range of foods than us and also get more nutrition out of them. The shape of our voice boxes also constricts our breathing, which means we get out of breath more quickly. The physical disadvantages have been worth it. Our superior ability to pronounce the vowels 'a', 'i' and 'u' and the consonants 'k' and 'g' is one of the reasons we are still around and the Neanderthals aren't.

Though all animals need to communicate with each other to live their lives, only humans have developed complex languages. Without language, civilisation would not be possible. Your life is going to involve millions of interactions that rely on your ability to talk. A certain amount will be purely functional – things like ordering a takeaway, job interviews or asking for directions – but the majority of it will be just idle chit-chat.

There has been a lot of research into

how much people talk and there is no evidence that women talk more than men. In fact, most studies show that women actually talk less, but the difference is very small. The average for both sexes is 80 minutes a day. In a lifetime, four years, two months and 12 days talking non-stop. As most of this will be in conversation with other people, the actual time spent chatting could be twice as much.

Though chatting might feel like a purely recreational activity, even the most banal conversation will have some element of building or maintaining friendships, finding out gossip, learning from other people's mistakes and a thousand other things that could well be essential for your survival. Conversations that don't include any of these elements are so dull that they rarely last for long. There hasn't been much research done on boredom, but it is probably a survival mechanism that kicks in when you feel you are wasting your time on something that is of no use to you.

It might seem strange, therefore, that someone would choose to spend their whole working life talking to chimpanzees. After all, these conversations are apt to run along the lines of: 'Give me a banana, I want a banana, give me the banana, my bottom is itchy, I'm tired, give me a banana ...' But then, we all have the capacity to be interested in things that are of no conceivable use, such as stamp collecting or sudoku. We are also prepared to put up with boring conversations to get what we want – a lift home, perhaps, or maybe some insight into the primate mind that sheds light on human existence ... 'My bottom is itchy, give me a banana. I want the banana. Look, why don't we just drop this tedious charade? If you give me the banana, I will tell you all about what it's like to be a chimpanzee and you can turn that PhD into a Nobel Prize …'

TEA

In his *Confessions of an English Opium Eater*, Thomas De Quincey describes his perfect night in on the drugs. First of all, there is a stern, wild, mountainous landscape with a small valley let into it. In the valley stands a cottage. It is winter: 'Candles at 4 o'clock, warm hearth rugs, shutters closed, curtains flowing in ample draperies on the floor whilst the storm rages audibly without.' The odd hailstone drops down the chimney and hisses in the fire. Thomas sits in an armchair reading a book of German metaphysics and pouring himself doses of ruby-coloured tincture of laudanum from a crystal decanter. Opposite him at the fireside is a beautiful woman with 'arms like Aurora's and a smile like Hebe's'. She is there to make him endless cups of tea.

Tea and drugs are linked in British history. Though tea was known in Britain from the early seventeenth century, it remained little more than a drinkable souvenir brought back from the East until 1662, when Charles II married the Portuguese princess Catherine of Braganza. Tea was the favourite drink of the Portuguese court and Catherine brought the habit to England with her. It quickly became a craze that spread beyond aristocratic circles to the wealthier classes, and began trickling down through the social orders with used tea leaves being sold, used, and sold again. Meeting this new demand was not as lucrative as it might have been, because at the time, tea could only be obtained from China. Now, Britain didn't have anything the Chinese particularly wanted, so the tea had to be bought with silver. To increase profits, the British East India Company began producing opium in India and smuggling it in to China in exchange for tea. The Chinese were strongly opposed to drugs. In one of many decrees they declared: 'Opium has a harm. Opium is a poison, undermining our good customs and morality. Its use is prohibited by law.' The Chinese even wrote directly to Queen Victoria asking for her help to curb the drug trade. The British took no notice and eventually Chinese efforts to stop the trade resulted in the Opium Wars. After Britain won, it forced China to pay for the war, hand over Hong Kong and also sign a treaty legitimising the trade in opium.

Back in Britain, tea was rapidly becoming the nation's second favourite drink after water, pushing beer into third place for the first time in 4,500 years. In order to replace the lost calories from beer, tea had to be very sweet. This brought Britain's other shameful trading triangle into play. Manufactured goods were shipped to West Africa to be exchanged for slaves and the slaves were shipped to the West Indies, where they were worked to death on sugar, cotton and tobacco plantations.

Sitting by the fireside of the cottage he inherited from William Wordsworth, getting quietly smashed on laudanum and nodding off into his copy of Wolff's *Rede über die praktische Philosophie der Chinesen*, Thomas

De Quincey was unlikely to be thinking much about where it had all come from: the cotton of his shirt, the linings of his curtains, the rug on the floor, the tea in the pot, the sugar in the bowl or the tobacco in his pipe.

These days tea is less controversial, though it continues to be an industry that relies on cheap labour. You can do something about this and minimise the post-colonial guilt besides by trying to buy fair trade. Tea requires at least 100 cm of rain a year to grow, and by the middle of the nineteenth century Britain was beginning to grow tea in the rainier parts of the empire – northern India, Kenya and Sri Lanka. This is where most of our tea comes from today, with China and India being responsible for about 50 per cent. In Britain 165 million cups of tea are drunk every day – just under three cups a day each, making us the second-biggest tea-drinking nation in the world after Ireland. Nearly all of these are made with tea bags (96 per cent) and milk (98 per cent). Nowadays, only about one-third of people take sugar in their tea. In a lifetime you will get through 78,681 cups of tea, and as tea bags only cost a penny each this is a modest £787. The 2.5 g of tea in each bag only costs 0.2 p wholesale, so the convenience of having it in a bag adds a considerable cost.

Britain was directly responsible for getting over 25 per cent of the male population of China hooked on opium. Ironically, it was the stigmatisation of Chinese immigrants and their opium dens in the late nineteenth century that led to the first laws controlling drugs. The drugs that are most strictly controlled are the ones that affect national productivity or just annoy people. Health is certainly an issue, but the problems caused by alcohol and smoking demonstrate that they are not enough on their own for something to be done about them. Especially when so many of us enjoy a smoke and a drink.

Tea, the cup that cheers but does not inebriate, is seen as the teetotaller's choice. But tea, though not addictive, is a drug. It has no real nutritional value and makes you feel better. This isn't just because it is hot and wet, it is also full of things that monkey about with your neurochemistry. Things like the psychoactive amino acid theanine, which relaxes you, reduces stress and has mood-enhancing properties, in combination with caffeine which produces effects that are similar to Ecstasy. As with all drugs, there is a spectrum of approval. Seventh Day Adventists are strictly prohibited from drinking tea and coffee, while Mormons are not really supposed to have any hot drinks at all. By and large the rest of the country regard it as an essential and virtuous drink.

On 1 September 1939 Germany invaded Poland. Two days later Britain declared war. There was a frenzy of military mobilisation provoked by Mr Hitler unexpectedly starting the war early. Amid the chaos, someone thought to bring the vast quantities of tea stored in warehouses around the London docks under government control. In the dark years ahead, tea would be vital. Just four days after the war began, the national tea stocks were dispersed to secret rural locations all over the country lest the Luftwaffe reduce Britain's morale to a burning pile of leaves.

TEARS

The first thing you did after you were born was breathe in. The next thing you did was let that breath out with your first cry. That first time is probably the only time you will be happy to hear a baby cry. From then on, looking after a baby is mostly about trying to find out why it is crying so you can stop it. Up to the age of around ten months babies don't really make the connection between their crying and your increasingly frantic efforts to make them stop. Once they do, their crying will start to become manipulative.

Throughout your life, crying will remain one of the most powerful ways you have of communicating with other people and it is given an added force because it is very difficult to fake. As you grow, learn better forms of communication and gain more control over your emotions, you will cry less and less. By the age of 17 the average boy will have cried 4,443 times and the average girl 5,384. The difference between the sexes is even more marked in adults. From the age of 18 onwards, you can expect to burst into tears 30 times a year if you are a woman and nine times if you are a man. In a lifetime, women will cry 7,313 times and men just 4,982.

Humans are thought to be the only animals that cry for emotional reasons, but most of the tears you produce will have nothing to do with sadness or joy. Tears are just one of the many different lubricants that your body makes without which you would be unable to move your eyes, swallow your food or walk without squeaking.

Keeping your eyeballs slippery will take up to 1ml of tears a day. In a lifetime, 73 l. Not quite enough to take a bath.

TEETH

Why are you rewarded for losing your first 20 teeth when it is so important to hang on to the rest? It seems like the wrong kind of encouragement to give children, and like everything else it is getting more expensive.

In 1982 the tooth fairy left an average of 17 p. In 2007 it has risen to £1.05, meaning that you can now expect to make an average of £21 for a mouthful of teeth. That's an increase of 500 per cent compared with the cost of living, which has only gone up by 150 per cent. The tooth fairy now has an annual turnover of £20 million – an impressive figure for a business that has only one member of staff.

Celebrating the loss of baby teeth is almost universal. In many cultures the tooth fairy is a little white mouse. This is thought to be because mice teeth can nibble through steel, never wear out and keep growing throughout their owners' lives. Unlike mice we need to make regular trips to the dentist – at least 156 times in our lives, which comes to 38 hours in the dentist's chair. Minimising the pain of these visits will require 274 tubes of toothpaste and 78 toothbrushes.

TELEVISION

You will spend more of your life watching television than any other single activity apart from work and sleep. The average person spends 157 minutes a day watching TV, so in a lifetime you will spend eight years, seven months and two weeks sitting motionless in front of a television screen. For children who have no jobs to go to, the proportion is even higher. By the age of six, the average child will have already spent a year of their lives watching TV.

There is a perception that 50 years of research on the link between television and violence has failed to come up with anything conclusive; that there may be a link, but no one is sure. The reality is exactly the opposite. The evidence for a link between watching television and violent behaviour is as conclusive as the link between smoking and cancer. As with smoking, the link is both commercially sensitive and difficult to prove as the cause and effects can be years apart. We are also reluctant to take on board the idea that yet another thing we enjoy might be harmful.

We have got used to being suspicious about being told that things aren't good for us. In a way, everything is bad for you. Walking exposes you to the risks of tripping up or being crushed under the wheels of a truck. You have to accept the risks inherent in simply being alive, but usually you have a fair idea of what those risks are and can make choices about the extent you are going to expose yourself to them. Given that you are likely to spend 11 per cent of your entire life watching television it is sensible to be aware of the risks involved.

A 25-year survey of over 700 randomly selected families living in New York found a significant link between the amount of television watched and aggression as an adult. Forty-five per cent of boys who grew up watching more than three hours of television a day went on to commit an aggressive act against another person, and nearly a quarter of this group (11 per cent) had used a weapon to commit a crime. In contrast, only nine per cent of the group watching less than an hour of television a day committed any aggressive acts at all. In women, 17 per cent who  watched more than three hours a day went on to commit an aggressive act compared with the women who watched less than an hour a day.

There was no attempt to log the content of the programmes. It doesn't seem to matter what you watch, the important thing is simply how much time you spend every day watching. The effect of television on the developing minds and bodies of children is particularly marked and goes far beyond a tendency to be aggressive as an adult.

All other things being equal, as little as an hour of television a day for the

under-threes reduces mathematical ability, reading recognition and com-
prehension in later childhood. Every hour of television a day at this age is
also matched by a 9 per cent increase in attention problems and a significantly increased risk of ADHD.

As children get older it is a little harder to distinguish between cause and
effect, but children watching more than one hour a day at 14 were more
likely to have negative attitudes towards education and less likely to do well
in exams. Those watching more than three hours were unlikely to go on
to further education. There is also a correlation between the amount of
television you watch in adolescence and your socio-economic status and
well-being in later life.

TV also makes you fat. In one American study a group of 70 overweight
children aged between four and seven were split into two groups. Over the
space of two years, one group had their TV viewing reduced by half. They
showed a significant reduction in body mass index. Those who continued
as before showed little change.

Not only does television require you to sit still for long periods of time,
it also slows down your metabolism. The effect is more pronounced than
with other sedentary activities such as writing, reading or sewing and isn't
limited to the hours you spend watching. Your overall resting metabolic
rate right now, as you read this book, is directly related to how much television you have watched in the last week.

At the same time, television interferes with your ability to tell when you've had enough to eat. The mechanism isn't fully understood, but one of the effects of watching television is that you will continue to salivate for far longer in response to food than you would normally. The average British person eats their evening meal in front of the television and, it is estimated, consumes up to an extra meal's worth of food every week as a result.

The thing that links these studies is that they are all based on the amount of time spent watching television rather than on the content. It doesn't seem to matter whether it's *Who Wants to Be a Millionaire?*, *Cannibal Holocaust* or live debates from the House of Commons – how much you watch is more important than what you watch. While it is easy to generalise from your own experience – watching television doesn't make *me* fat and aggressive – there is too much evidence to ignore the real possibility that television is a major factor in raising the levels of violence, aggression and obesity in society as a whole.

Your 8.6 years of television viewing will cost you £3,667 in licence fees and around £4,570 for the six television sets you will watch it all on. Not including the cost of the electricity, that's about 11 p an hour.

TIME

In physical time your life will last 79.1 years or, allowing for leap years, 28,891.275 days. Each of those days will feel different, some will seem longer than others, but generally as you get older they will feel like they are passing more quickly. While the summer of your sixteenth year seems to last for ever, the summer of your seventy-sixth flashes by in an instant. Physical time does not speed up, but the world we live in is created for us by our brains out of sensation and memory, which means that the way we experience time can change.

One idea about why time speeds up is that as you get older, each year is a smaller proportion of all the time you have lived so it seems shorter. Your tenth year was 10 per cent of your life. Your fortieth just 2.5 per cent. But this doesn't work, because it suggests that time speeds up most between the ages of two (50 per cent of your life) and 20 (5 per cent), whereas the effect is most noticeable as you move into your fifties (2 per cent), sixties (1.6 per cent) and seventies (1.4 per cent), when the changes in percentage of total life are very small.

Another explanation is that as you get older, you just get more used to being alive. Familiar journeys always seem to take less time and as you get older all journeys start to become familiar. Your sixteenth summer will have been full of new experiences. Sixty summer holidays later, novelty will be more of a challenge. If you do manage to spend your seventy-sixth summer doing things you have never done before it may well feel longer, especially when you look back proudly on all the things you managed to do. Unfortunately, you will probably still be painfully aware that if you had been sixteen it would have seemed even longer.

Fergus Craik and Janine Hay of the Rotman Institute in Toronto recently carried out a series of experiments to test how your ability to estimate short periods of time changes as you get older. In order to stop people simply counting off seconds in their heads, they were given distracting tasks to perform and asked to stop when they thought thirty seconds or one minute had passed. The researchers found that older people consistently underestimated the amount of time. They would work on the trial for a minute, thinking that only thirty seconds had gone by. The results seem to indicate that we do have some kind of internal clock that measures time and that as we get older it slows down.

Having a slower clock makes it feel as if time is passing faster. A minute's worth of life feels like it has gone past in 30 seconds. It is not clear whether this can also make a fortnight feel like a week or a year seem to zip by in six months, but it is probably part of the explanation. These results are backed up by a different study where large numbers of people of varying ages were asked how much faster they feel time is going now than when they were younger. The results were remarkably consistent. In general people felt that time was passing about 1.4 times as quickly as it was when they were half their present age.

The depressing conclusion is that though the amount of physical time you live each day may be the same, as you get older the amount of time it feels like really does get shorter. This means that the midpoint of your life in physical time is not the same as the midpoint of your life in perceived time. In fact, using these figures, by the time you are 20 you will have already lived half your perceived life.

TIME USE

You will spend 27 years of your life asleep, 9.5 years at work and 8.7 years watching television.

This will account for 57 per cent of your life.

You will spend 5.2 years just lounging about the house and 4.7 years eating and drinking.

These five activities will take up 70 per cent of your lifetime. When you add on 2.4 years' worth of washing, getting dressed and personal care, 2.2 years' cooking and washing up, 1.8 years' shopping and 1.6 years' cleaning and tidying, you will have accounted for 80 per cent of your lifespan with just nine activities.

Everything else you do will take up less than a year and a half of your total life.

⭑ Seventeen months of formal education.

⚢ You will spend fifteen months each on looking after children, reading and going out.

⭑ A year on hobbies.

⚥ Ten and a half months doing gardening and DIY.

⭑ Nine months each using a computer and washing clothes.

F	S	S	M	T	W	T	F	S	S	M	T	W	T	F	S	S	M
29	30	31	1	2	3	4	5	6	7	8	9	10	11	12	13	14	15

THE AVERAGE LIFE OF THE AVERAGE PERSON   351

✻ Six and a half months on sport and outdoor activities.

✢ Five and a half months looking after other people's children.

✣ Five months phoning, visiting or being visited by friends and family.

✤ Four and a half months looking after pets.

✥ One hundred and one days on entertainment and culture.

✦ Eleven weeks studying for fun.

✧ Fifty-eight days doing voluntary work.

✩ Fifty-eight days attending religious meetings.

✻ 37 days caring for adults in other households.

✻ 20 days caring for them in your own.

Every four years the Office for National Statistics carries out a time-use survey. The last one was in 2005. Thousands of people over the age of 16 were given diaries to record everything they did every minute of the day for a month. The months were spread through the year to account for seasonal variations and avoided Christmas and Easter to get the best possible idea of a typical day. These diaries were divided into the 29 categories listed above. Anything that did not fit into these was marked as other. An average of 14 minutes a day. In a lifetime you will spend 6,736 hours or 280 days doing other things.

NOVEMBER	M	T	W	T	F	S	S	M	T	W	T	F	S	S	M
WEEK 47	1	2	3	4	5	6	7	8	9	10	11	12	13	14	15

TINNED FOOD

In the ancient world it was widely believed that life generated spontaneously: rotting meat produced maggots, mice would emerge from badly stored grain, mud transformed into eels and old logs rotting underwater came alive as crocodiles. From the sixteenth century onwards, the evidence that all living things were descendants of other living things gradually gathered weight. Maggots come from flies; mice, eels and crocodiles have parents. The final mystery concerned the smallest forms of life – the microbes, germs and infections that made people ill and turned food bad. It wasn't until 1864 that Louis Pasteur conclusively demonstrated that no matter how attractive an environment you create, if it is sealed from the outside world no microorganisms will spontaneously appear. No life will appear until you open the container and let it in. This discovery provided the foundation for microbiology and led to the germ theory of disease and infection that is at the heart of modern medicine. It is also one of the fundamentals of the preservation of food.

All tinned food is pasteurised. Once the food is sealed in the tin it is cooked at a high temperature that kills off all the microorganisms inside. As long as the tin remains sealed, the food cannot go off. It would make sense then for Pasteur's discovery to have sparked off a revolution in tinned food. It didn't. Tinned food had been invented more than fifty years earlier by a French sweet-maker who had entered a newspaper competition to devise a way of preserving food for Napoleon's army.

Though no one understood how it worked, canned food was quickly taken up by armies, navies and explorers. Originally the food was preserved in glass jars, then in metal canisters or cans. Later, the inside of the cans were tinned to stop corrosion from food acids. As the tins were handmade, they were far too expensive for ordinary people to buy. Naturally, this meant that there was a brief period when tinned food became an exciting novelty on the tables of the very rich.

The production is now so highly mechanised and automated that tinned food is some of the cheapest food available. Consequently, though you are going to consume 6,389 tinned canisters of food in your life, they will only cost you an average of 41 p each, or £2,619 in a lifetime. The rising cost of steel means that in future your tinned or canned foods are less and less likely to come in actual tins. In the future you will be tearing open a tin of beans with your bare hands and your tin-opener will become increasingly redundant.

The tin-opener remained uninvented for a long time. The tinned foods served at posh dinner parties in the 1830s had to be chiselled open at the table, while soldiers, sailors and explorers used bayonets, stones or whatever came to hand. The first patented tin-opener appeared in 1855. It was a sort of cross between a bayonet and a sickle and was so dangerous that your tins would have to be opened by a professional operator at the shop. It wasn't until 1870, 60 years after tinned food first appeared, that William Lyman invented the first tin-opener that could be used by an ordinary person without the risk of you severing a limb or splashing the contents all over your dinner guests.

VALENTINE'S DAY

Valentine's Day is the next most expensive day of the year after Christmas. Every year around £2.4 billion is spent on this day alone. That's £39.61 for each man, woman and child in Britain, about ten times as much as it costs to run the NHS for a day.

In a lifetime, you will spend: £1,411 on restaurants and going out, £610 on jewellery, £342 on flowers, £281 on balloons and teddy bears, £155 on clothes, £124 on chocolate, £113 on lingerie, and almost as an after-thought, £97 on cards. In total £3,133. In return, you will receive your fair share of roses, chocolates and candle-lit occasions. There may also be some oddly unromantic gifts that are the result of retailers piling whatever they can on to the Valentine's Day bandwagon. So, you may find your lover communicating their unspoken feelings for you through the medium of coasters or *Grand Theft Auto IV*.

You will also send and receive 32 Valentine cards. This means that there will be at least 47 Valentine's Days when you don't get a card at all.

Thine.

or ever and for ever
My heart dear one
is thine
And soon a ring
shall prove to all
You're mine and
only mine.

VEGETABLES

Vegetable is a vague term that disappears when you try to define it. Pedants who insist a tomato is a fruit and not a vegetable should also insist that everything that started off as a flower, like peppers, aubergines, courgettes and pumpkins, are also fruits. Broccoli, cabbage and brussel sprouts are not vegetables either, they are flower buds. Corn, peas and beans are seeds. Celery and rhubarb are leaf stems. Potatoes, Jerusalem artichokes and sweet potatoes are underground stems swollen into tubers. Carrots, beetroot and parsnips are just roots. Apart from coming from plants, the only defining characteristic of a vegetable is that we consider it to be a vegetable.

Dividing the world into different categories that we all agree on makes life a lot simpler, but these categories are not innate, they have to be learned. Children below the age of five have difficulty just distinguishing between things that are alive, like plants and animals, and things that aren't, like mountains and clockwork toys. The ability to make more sophisticated distinctions such as why popcorn is not a vegetable while sweetcorn is will take years to develop.

You will eat 1,172 g of vegetables a week, an average of two 80 g portions a day. Over a lifetime you will consume 4.8 tonnes of vegetables. This might seem like a lot but it is only the equivalent of two medium carrots a day. Adding another carrot to bring you up to the minimum healthy level would add another 2.3 tonnes. In this case, more is better. Five a day is a minimum requirement and it is almost impossible to eat too many vegetables, as long as you don't batter, deep fry or cover them in chocolate sauce.

Though we are born with a predilection for fat, salt and sugar, most of our tastes are learned and are determined by what we were fed as children. Learning to eat vegetables as a child is not just important for your immediate health, it is vital for your lifetime's eating habits, which have such a profound effect on how well and how long you will live.

VITAMINS

In 1743 Dr James Lind of the Royal Navy carried out one of the first ever medical trials. He had the idea that scurvy was the result of the living body somehow going off and rotting like old meat. Scurvy is not a pleasant thing to suffer from. Your hair comes out in clumps. Your gums recede. Your teeth become loose and fall out. Old wounds reopen, your lips start to bleed, ulcers appear all over your body and your eyes seem to shrink back into your skull. You start to look like a zombie from a horror film. Then, unlike the zombie, you die. Dr Lind believed that the process of putrefaction could be halted and reversed by the use of the right preservative.

So, he rounded up a group of sailors with scurvy and fed them different kinds of popular preservatives. Some were treated like cooked shrimps and fed brine. Some, like gherkins, were given vinegar. Others received cider, presumably for its acid and alcohol content. Another group were given a sort of spicy marinade to eat, and one unfortunate group had a weak solution of sulphuric acid. Finally, possibly following the examples of chutney and marmalade, where the acid from the fruit acts as a preservative, two men were given oranges and lemons. While all the others got worse, the men on fruit more or less recovered.

Nowadays, we know that scurvy is a result of not getting enough vitamin C, which your body needs to make collagen. As collagen makes up about 25 per cent of all the protein in your body and is the stuff that binds all your cells together, the consequences of not being able to make it any more are pretty dreadful. As with most vitamins, your body cannot make its own vitamin C so it has to come from food.

The fact that your body is so good at manufacturing everything else it needs from whatever you eat is why vitamins went undiscovered for so long. In general, people suffering from the effects of vitamin deficiencies were also generally not getting enough food. One exception was sailors on long voyages, who were reliant on preserved foods that had lost all their vitamin C. No matter how well fed they were, they would still get scurvy. Another exception were the otherwise well-fed middle classes of the Orient, who relied on polished white rice. Removing the brown husk of the rice effectively removed B vitamins from their diet, causing beriberi. It was the study of beriberi in the late nineteenth century that gave rise to the notion that certain foods might contain something other than fats, carbohydrate and protein that the body needed and could not make itself.

Without understanding how it worked, Lind's cure for scurvy could not be very effective. When limes replaced other fruit because they were cheaper, scurvy returned because limes contain comparatively little vitamin C. For most of the nineteenth century it was believed that scurvy was caused by low morale and could be prevented by good personal hygiene and sing-songs. By the time of Scott's expedition to the South Pole it was believed that you caught it from eating canned food that had gone off.

The first man to get credit for isolating one of the mysterious ingredients in food that your body so desperately needs was a Polish scientist called Casimir Funk. Sadly, he resisted the temptation to give the world 'Funka-mines' and decided instead to name the molecule 'Vitamine', which is short for 'vital amine'.

Most of us are not polar explorers or engaged in round-the-world voyages. In Britain we are surrounded by such a profusion of cheap fresh food that most of our problems stem from eating too much of it. The notion that any of us should worry about vitamin deficiencies seems ludicrous. But we do worry. Forty-three per cent of British adults take some kind of dietary supplement. Every year we spend £630 million on vitamins and minerals, a figure that represents a colossal lack of confidence in the food we eat. In a lifetime it is going to cost you £822.

VOMIT

In order to get at the nutrients in your food, your body has to turn it into a liquid. Your teeth chop and grind, then the muscular bag of your stomach adds chemicals and churns the whole lot up. This thick soup is passed on to the small intestine for the nutrients to be extracted and absorbed.

You can live without your stomach. You would have to eat lots of small meals – six or seven a day – as there would be nowhere for the food to be stored. As there would be nothing to turn the food into a thick soup pretty much everything you ate would have to be in the form of thick soup to start off with. You would also have to be very careful about what you ate because one of the functions of the stomach is to reject things that might be bad for you and get rid of them as quickly as possible.

You rarely vomit without warning because your body has to get ready for it. The first thing that happens is that your production of saliva increases. This is to protect your teeth from dissolving in your stomach acid. Then the rippling, muscular movements of peristalsis, which normally moves food through your intestines, goes into reverse. This sweeps everything from about halfway along your small intestine back up into your stomach. Then, the muscles in your abdomen squash your stomach, forcing the contents violently up your throat, out of your mouth and, occasionally, your nose. It takes some time for food to travel back from your small intestine, so your first bout of vomiting is likely to be more or less what was already in your stomach. If you carry on, you will empty your small intestine a stomachful at a time. Once you have got rid of all the food you may continue to be sick until all you are producing is bile and other digestive juices.

You will vomit an average of twice a year. At just under 1 l each time you will produce nearly 139 l. Enough to fill two baths.

Vomiting is controlled by your brain and is one of the emergency functions of your body that you are not trusted to make decisions about. Though you can hack into the system and stop yourself from vomiting using drugs, this is only safe when you are sure that the vomiting has nothing to do with keeping you alive, as with reactions to chemotherapy and travel sickness. The importance of vomiting for getting rid of poisons means that it can be contagious. This may well be a survival mechanism from our distant past when we would have foraged in small groups eating similar things. If someone started vomiting because they had eaten something poisonous then it would make sense for you to join in immediately, rather than wait for it to trigger your vomit reflex by poisoning you as well.

Anything that overrides the conscious control of your body has the potential to be hugely embarrassing. But it is probably

a good thing that you cannot turn off
your vomiting reflex. We are such slaves
to social pressures that given the
choice of dying of embarrassment because a tainted
prawn cocktail has
caused you to un-
swallow a four-
course meal,
showering your-
self and every-
one in the three
rows of seats
in front of you
with partially di-
gested food, saliva,
bile, stomach acid,
pancreatic juice, still-
fizzing champagne, mucus
and tomato skins and frankly
ruining the ballet for everybody
... given the choice between that and actually
dying, you might prefer the latter.

VOTING

George Washington did not belong to a political party. Like the other Founding Fathers, he disapproved of them. He felt they were divisive and led to conflict and ultimately stagnation. There were no political parties when Washington became president and he did his best to make sure things stayed that way. However, though everyone agreed who should be the first president, there were the inevitable disagreements about who should get to be the second. Different factions started to form: one around Thomas Jefferson called the Democratic Republican Party, which ultimately became the Democratic Party, and the other around Alexander Hamilton called the Federalists, which, through a slightly more tortuous line of descent, became the Republican Party.

The British party-political system also has its roots in the aftermath of the American Revolution. Up until the 1780s, British politicians might have confessed to Tory or Whig tendencies, but there were no political parties. However, the instability that followed the loss of America created a unique situation that more or less forced political parties into existence as support coalesced around the leadership of two men – Charles James Fox and William Pitt the Younger.

Fox was a staunch opponent of George III, whom he regarded as a potential tyrant. He had strong republican sympathies and supported the revolutionaries across the Atlantic. He took to dressing in the colours of

Washington's army, an army his king was at war with. This would have been controversial if he had just been the landlord of a pub, but Fox was Foreign Secretary at the time. George III didn't like Fox much either. The austere, frugal king disapproved of Fox's gambling and womanising on principle and blamed him for the corruption of his son the Prince Regent, with whom Fox shared a mistress and much else.

Fox didn't spend long in government. George forced him out in a devious move involving the House of Lords that made the 24-year-old William Pitt the Younger prime minister. Much to the surprise of everyone, Pitt, who had been seen as a stopgap appointment to get rid of Fox, kept the job for the next 17 years. Though they were now bitter political rivals, they had once been friends and there was still a lot of common ground. Fox supported Pitt on electoral reform, Catholic emancipation and the abolition of slavery. Fox was a Whig and Pitt also considered himself to be a Whig (he didn't like the idea of political parties either and referred to himself as an Independent Whig). However, there were important differences regarding the monarchy, personal freedom, the army and the right to vote that aligned you with one or the other. Fox's supporters tended to be young radicals and libertines. Pitt attracted older conservatives. Their supporters continued to call themselves Pittites and Foxites long after Pitty and Foxy were dead and these divisions later evolved into the Tory and Liberal parties.

There is something fundamental about the differences between Fox and Pitt that means you do not need to have a deep understanding of late eighteenth-century politics to know which one you would vote for. You probably won't know all that much more about any of the local councillors, MPs and MEPs you vote for in the 39 elections that will be held in your lifetime. It is possible to become knowledgeable enough to compare the health, education, defence, foreign, agricultural and economic policies of the three major parties and decide which is the best one. But, in reality, we tend to vote for the party we approve of most on the basis of a few crucial indicators such as tax, immigration or fox-hunting and assume we also agree with everything else.

In a democracy, the people get to decide. What this actually means is that as one of 71,555 voters in the average constituency you get to play a small part in choosing who will make the decisions for you. The House of Commons sits on around 146 days of the year for an average of just under eight hours each day, with 221 divisions or votes being made. It would be possible to abolish the House of Commons and its 646 MPs and give us all access to a gigantic virtual people's parliament online with seating for 46 million people. As each vote is the result of about five hours of debate, in order to give everything the same level of consideration you would have to spend at least three hours a day on it, and there is a lot more to being an MP than debating and voting. All in all it makes sense to choose someone every four or five years and delegate the decision-making to them.

Elections are only a small part of democracy. In between, we get to keep an eye on what our representatives get up to and exercise the threat of not voting for them next time. What we get to know is filtered, simplified and spun for us by the media. When Alexander Hamilton and Thomas Jefferson were setting up their rival political parties one of the first things they did was to set up rival newspapers. The rise of political parties came at the right time for the steam printing presses and railways of the Industrial Revolution to make large-circulation national newspapers possible. To survive, newspapers must please their readers at the same time as they report the news. So, after the sinking of the HMS *Sheffield* during the Falklands War, the *Sun* ran the headline, 'HMS *Sheffield* Burns out in a Blaze of Glory', while the *Morning Star* had the headline, 'Senseless Sacrifice'.

You will spend 3,102 hours reading 4,654 newspapers in a lifetime and the strange thing is that if the majority of these are the *Guardian* you would have been more likely to have voted for Fox and if they are the *Daily Telegraph*, the chances are you would have chosen Pitt. It is also easy to imagine that these are the papers they would have chosen for themselves.

It is curious that someone who shares your opinions on nuclear power is also likely to share your opinions about same-sex marriages. We predict how well we will get on with people based on their likes and dislikes, their political opinions, their favourite soap opera, newspaper or eighteenth-century politician. Conversely, you don't have to know someone all that well to be able to guess their political affiliations and which paper they read.

Most psychologists believe that there are five aspects to personality: Conscientiousness, Openness, Extraversion, Agreeableness and Neuroticism.

In 2003, John Jost, a psychologist from New York University, collated and analysed data from 88 studies of more than 20,000 people in 12 countries, looking for a correlation between these personality traits and political orientation. He found that while all political viewpoints attract equal numbers of agreeable and neurotic people, the other three traits varied considerably. People who were Extravert (talk about themselves, bad at keeping secrets) and Open (idealistic, receptive to new ideas and embrace change) were more likely to be liberal and therefore more likely to vote Labour, Democrat or Liberal. Those who are less Extravert and less Open but more Conscientious (organised, self-disciplined, responsible and law-abiding) are more likely to be conservative. These traits came out in other ways. Testing groups of self-avowed conservatives found that they tended to prefer simple, unambiguous works of art and also exhibited a greater fear of death.

Part of your personality is inherited, with around 50 per cent of the variation in each of the five traits being determined by your genes. A 20-year study of identical twins by John Alford, a political scientist at Rice University, Houston, Texas, found that identical twins who share all their genes are 80 per cent likely also to share opinions on complex political issues such as property tax. This is much higher than in non-identical twins and siblings who share an upbringing but only half their genes.

The role of personality traits in political opinion is possibly why the formation of opposing political parties is inevitable and may also account for the durability of the liberal–conservative divide: a group that wants change and a group that wants things to stay as they are. Perhaps these groups are predestined to disagree and the genetic element means that you may be a Labour-voting *Guardian* reader or a *Daily Telegraph*-reading Tory from the moment sperm meets egg. If political opinions are partly genetically determined, then changing someone's political views could be a bit like trying to argue their hair blonde. Politics is full of this kind of stalemate. Three of the Founding Fathers of America – including Alexander Hamilton – died in duels fought with political opponents they had lost elections to.

But there is a lot of common ground. Though idealism and realism also face each other across the political divide, we all broadly agree on the kind of world we ultimately want to live in. The disagreements are largely about how to achieve it. After all, Pitt and Fox worked together on electoral reform, the abolition of slavery and Catholic emancipation.

Pitt, Fox, George Washington and John Adams, the man who succeeded him, were right: political parties that have to differentiate themselves in order to survive are divisive. An idea can't be simply a good idea or a bad idea; it is a Labour, Liberal or Tory idea that other parties can only use if they are prepared to be accused of stealing. Political parties also make it possible to have an opinion that you don't need to think about too deeply. The fact that we tend to base judgements on a few key facts rather than on the complete package makes us easier to manipulate. There is a joke about a man who is given the chance to hire one of three women: a Nobel Prize winner, an award-winning novelist and an Oscar-winning film director.

He chooses the one with the biggest tits. In the privacy of the voting booth, the average voter is not making a finely balanced judgement of the merits of the different parties, he or she is often choosing the one with the biggest tax cut.

Our political system does encourage divisiveness, conflict and stagnation. However, it remains the best system we have come up with yet for simplifying the decisions that have to be made about running the country and giving everyone the 1 in 60,587,000 share of the influence that is their birthright. Winston Churchill, who started out a Conservative, became a Liberal Home Secretary and ended up as a Conservative prime minister, said that: 'Democracy is the worst form of government. Except for all the others that have been tried.'

WATER

All life as we know it is dependent on water. This is why, when we look for life on other worlds, the first thing we look for is water. If we ever find life that has evolved without water it will probably be so weird, so alien, that we will hardly be able to recognise it as life at all.

Every drop of the water we depend on has been produced by fire. Hydrogen burns explosively and, when it does, its atoms pair up with atoms of oxygen to form H_2O. The cool blue waters of all our oceans, lakes, rivers and seas were produced in a colossal explosion billions of years ago during the formation of the Sun. On other planets the water has either boiled away or frozen. The presence of liquid water on our planet is one of the unique features that makes our particular kind of life possible.

Water is the most common molecule in the body. Our bodies are essentially a foam of cells filled with water making up 60 per cent of our body weight. You only have to lose around about 2 per cent of your water volume to start suffering from dehydration. Initially there will be headaches and dizziness. Later there will be delirium, unconsciousness and death, but not before the lack of water shrinks your skin to blackened leather, exposing your fingernails down to the roots and pulling your mouth and eyes permanently open. Your lips, nose and gums will all but disappear. Meanwhile, your tongue will swell to enormous size and force itself out between your teeth. It is hardly surprising that thirst is such a powerful instinct.

For most of the 30,000 or so years that modern humans have been living on our notoriously wet islands getting enough water has not been difficult. However, during the Industrial Revolution the growth of cities meant that getting enough clean water and getting rid of dirty water became a major problem. At the beginning of the nineteenth century, epidemics of water-borne diseases such as cholera and poor health caused by drinking water contaminated with sewage meant that the life expectancy in towns and cities was half that in the countryside. The series of Public Health Acts and colossal engineering schemes that solved this problem in the second half of the nineteenth century saved more lives than any of the advances in medicine over the same period. Almost every building in Britain now has its own supply of clean water. The fact that we take this for granted is probably why we waste it so lavishly.

To survive, you have to take in at least 2 l of water a day to maintain your body and flush away the waste products of metabolism. Buying a lifetime's supply of tap water at the current price of 0.19 p per litre will therefore cost you £96. Of course, you will also need water for cooking and washing. Most people in Africa have restricted access to water and are forced to survive on less than 20 l a day. If you did the same, it would cost you £960 for a lifetime's worth. Unfortunately, the average British family will waste more water than this every day just brushing their teeth with the tap running. Your actual domestic water consumption is over 150 litres a day – a total of 3.93 million litres, costing you £7,465.

The ability to waste water so carelessly might seem to be one of the advantages of living in a wet country. Brushing your teeth irresponsibly or obsessively washing your car is not going to affect rainfall in sub-Saharan Africa. Sadly, the 3.93 million litres of water you will get from the tap is just a tiny proportion of the water your lifestyle depends on.

Feeding a cow, milking it, processing the milk, packaging it and transporting it to your fridge uses up 3,087 l of water for 1 l of milk, while 250 g of cheese – which after all is just concentrated milk – takes 7,700 l of water. One slice of bread takes 40 l and 1 kg of coffee an astonishing 21,000 l. This means that a simple cup of coffee and a cheese sandwich actually represents 1,207 l of water, only 200 ml of which will come out of your tap.

The water used in producing, packaging and transporting the food you eat, the clothes you wear and the things you own amounts to around 4,600 l of water every day. A total of 132,568,665 l in a lifetime. This is enough for everyone in Edinburgh, Glasgow and Liverpool to take a bath simultaneously.

Only 38 per cent of the water you consume will have fallen as rain on Britain. The majority will have been used to irrigate fields of cotton, tomatoes, salad or other crops in countries with more sun and less rain than us. Ironically, despite our climate, virtual water is one of Britain's main imports.

Twenty per cent of the world's population has no access to safe drinking water. Meanwhile, in Britain we not only have it piped directly into our homes, we also go out and buy it in the shops. Though bottled water isn't any cleaner or better for you than tap water, it will cost you over 500 times as much. In blind taste tests, people are generally unable to distinguish between their favourite bottled water and ordinary tap water. Despite this, you are going to buy and drink 2,300 l of bottled water at an average cost of £1 a litre. Water that is more about lifestyle than it is about life.

WORDS

Mum is one of the commonest first words. Aside from the fact that young children spend more time with their mums than anyone else, the 'm' sound is one of the easiest sounds to make. You will have been making it more or less randomly for some time before someone, probably your mother, interprets it as a word. In most languages the word for mother begins with an 'm', which raises the possibility that this word comes from babies rather than their parents. Mums became 'mums' because that is what babies called them.

Before your first words, you will have been using all sorts of other ways to communicate: holding out your hands for things, crying, laughing and making babbling noises that imitate the intonations and patterns of speech you hear around you. In this sense, you will have been talking for some time. The muddled boundary between babbling and proper words means that your first word may go unnoticed. But as soon as you realise that you can get what you want much quicker by using words, you will start to learn them really fast.

There are around 250,000 distinct English words, though your vocabulary will contain only about 10 per cent of these, or 25,000 words. These are the words you know without having to look them up. Language is hierarchical. At the tip of the pyramid are basic concept words such as 'fish', which cannot be defined by any simpler terms. At the opposite end there are words like 'Finnock', which is a Scottish word for a juvenile migratory sea trout. We usually don't need this kind of accuracy. There is also a certain social pressure to use simple words, to call a spade a spade rather than a digging implement. So, we will mostly use a functional vocabulary of around 4,000 words.

In a lifetime of talking (around 36,441 hours) at an average rate of 200 words per minute, you can expect to speak 437,292,000 words. You can get a flavour of what you will be saying from the most commonly used words. Your favourite nouns are: time, person, year, way, day, thing, man, world, life. Verbs: be, have, do, say, get, make, go, know, take, see. Adjectives: good, new, first, last, long, great, little, own, other, old. Twenty-five per cent of all the words you speak will be: the, be, to, of, and, a, in, that, have and I.

English is the most widely spoken language in the world. Chinese and Spanish might have more speakers, but English is spoken in more countries and is on its way to becoming the first global language. English isn't a particularly good name for the language any more as it carries the idea that England is the only place where proper

English English is spoken. As the world's first panguage, perhaps Globish would be a better name.

Your last words will probably be listened to with greater attention than your first, though hopefully you will have a different audience. Throughout history we have had a fascination with last words, as if they might tell us something about the experience of dying. If you become famous then people will also want your last words to distil the essence of your life and bring it to a meaningful end. We aren't at our best when we are dying. Nelson may have had one eye on posterity when he said, 'Thank God I have done my duty,' and would have been horrified that 'Kiss me, Hardy' is what has become famous. Famous last words are just that, not the *last* thing a famous person said, but the last *famous* thing he or she said. In his final moments before crossing back over the line between words and babbling incoherence and death, Nelson repeatedly murmured the instructions, 'Drink, drink, fan, fan, rub, rub,' to the people attending him. These did not become famous at the time because they aren't the sort of words on which you can build a myth. Now that puncturing myths is a popular pastime, they are likely to become more famous.

WORK

There is a good reason why work is called 'work' and that is because it *is* work. If we liked it, it would be called something else like 'pleasure' or 'holiday' or 'sex' or 'chocolate'. But it isn't. It is 'work'. Ever since the dawn of time work has been a bore. Even chasing woolly mammoths off cliffs must have got dull once you were having to do it 9–5 every day, day in, day out.

Still, work does have its compensations: the money you earn, the friends you meet, the office parties, the money, the holidays, the money, nicking stuff from the stationery cupboard, the money, the office affairs, the money and of course the money ...

The average wage is around £479 a week before tax and the idea is that rather than growing all your own food, building some kind of shelter, weaving cloth, sewing clothes, felling trees and turning them into tables, chairs and sideboards and making your own entertainment, you pay someone else to do it for you. We are surrounded by things that represent other people's work. The serrations on every knife in your cutlery drawer were once on someone's drawing board, contributing a morning's worth of work towards the local equivalent of their weekly £479. Then there are the miners, smelters, machine-tool operators, polishers, packers, shippers, customs officials, unpackers and sales staff who all played their part, just for the sake of a knife you probably never use anyway. In turn, no matter how obscure or bizarre your job is – from breeding bananas to testing different brands of dental floss – your wages are paid by the people who don't want to or can't do it themselves and you are part of the fabric of their lives.

Unfortunately work rarely feels like you are making a cosmic connection with the whole of the rest of humanity, which is a pity because it is going to consume a fair portion of your life. By the age of 22 over 50 per cent of British people are in full-time employment and will work more or less continuously until they are 63. An average working week of 44 hours (40 in the rest of Europe) means that in a lifetime you will spend ten years and eight months working round the clock. Work is second only to sleep (26.3 years) in taking up big chunks of your time and when you take off the time you spend sleeping and working, you have 42 years of life left over to spend that £479 on.

Holidays are the opposite of work. Before you start work there will have been three years, three months and one week's worth of school holidays. A childcare nightmare for your parents and a largely forgotten pleasure for you. Once you retire, in theory life becomes one long holiday of gardening, golf and bingo. In between, as a worker, you will only get an average of 28 days a year (the European average is 34). In a lifetime you will have 164 weeks, or three years and two months of holidays. Which means that by the time you have left school you will already have had more than half your lifetime's holidays.

In a lifetime's worth of holidays you will make 59 trips abroad, 48 of them by plane, nearly all in Europe, most probably France and Spain. You will spend a total of £21,774 while you are there on top of the £24,336 you will have already spent on transport and accommodation. This money – £46,110 – would take you two years, four and a half months to save up for if you spent your wages on nothing else.

Then, it will be time to go back to work. The average daily commute is 25 minutes each way. Which means that you will spend six months of your life travelling. Not wandering from village to village in the Hindu Kush or snorkelling your way along the sandy fringes and coral atolls of Bora-Bora in the wild blue South Pacific, but making the same journey every day, wearing a deep groove into the fabric of the universe.

The work–life balance would be a more valid concept if it was possible to get the tedious chore of earning that £479 down to a few painful hours a week. However, as you are more or less certain to be spending 20 per cent of your waking life at work, it isn't realistic to separate one from the other. Work is part of life. And for some people this means life is not going to be that much fun.

Enjoying your work has little to do with status. Sewage workers, refuse collectors and bicycle messengers are some of the most consistently happy workers, while GPs and dentists are the least. Most studies of workplace happiness put friendly and supportive co-workers a long way above money and status. The unhappiest workers are the ones who don't like their colleagues and can't leave.

In Britain, some children are still born into a situation where they will have little or no choice about what they will do with their lives. It is shocking that this sort of slavery is allowed to continue. The Queen, her eldest child and his eldest child do not get to choose a job. It used to be the best job in the world, but unlike the old days they cannot do whatever they like and have you beheaded if you get in the way. No, they are born to serve us, commissioning power stations, visiting shoe factories, hosting state banquets, making speeches, listening to speeches, endlessly shaking hands and accepting flowers, the small talk, the stilted politeness, the smell of paint and the rest of the time in hiding or fleeing from the media ... and they don't have any choice in the matter. They have to take up the role they have been bred for. It is surprising that the human-rights issues surrounding the monarchy aren't talked about more often.

SOURCES

The basic figures in this book are freely available to anyone from the Office for National Statistics (ONS) and have been reproduced under the terms of the Click-Use Licence.

The 2001 Census

The Office for National Statistics Family Spending Report 2007 (2008); the Time Use survey 2005 (latest available figures).

Family Food: Annual Report on Food Expenditure – Consumption and Nutrient Intakes compiled from Expenditure and Food Survey (Department for Environment, Food and Rural Affairs (DEFRA) 2006).

ADDITIONAL SOURCES

ACCIDENTS The ICD-10 codes are pretty much an alphabet of death. The accidents only start at V, which means there have already been 21 categories, each with a further 100 sub-categories of ways to die. My figures do not include assaults, medical procedures or suicide. The figures come from the ONS Mortality Statistics Series DH2 no. 32 for 2005, the most recent figures available. I have extrapolated these figures to cover Scotland as I couldn't find comparable Scottish figures. It is likely that at least some of the X59 accidents are the result of the cause of death not being recorded for reasons of overwork, incompetence or no one being able to decide which of the other codes applied. The hospital figures come from a survey carried out in 2002 by the Royal Society for the Prevention of Accidents (ROSPA).

ALCOHOL The figures come from the FAO (Food and Agriculture Organisation of the United Nations) World Drink Trends 2003. The average consumption of pure alcohol is for people aged 15+. As UK consumption is on an upward trend, this figure is likely to be higher by now. As 10.39 l a year for 64.1 years is 665.999 l a year, I have (forgive me) rounded it up to 666.

APPLES If you want to know more about the Greefa intelligent Sorter you should look at their website, www. greefa.nl/uk. Other apple facts from Sue Clifford and Angela King, *The Apple Source Book* (Hodder & Stoughton, 2007).

BACTERIA Figures from the Food Commission, www.foodcomm.org.uk. Theodor Rosebury, *Life on Man* (Martin Secker & Warburg, 1969).

BAKED BEANS Figures from Mintel quoted in the *Sunday Express*, 16 May 2008. I was unable to trace the origin of the statistic that Britain consumes 97 per cent of the world's baked-bean production. A bean without a sauce is not a baked bean and a statistic without a source is just a guess. However, I have left it in because as far as I can tell it is about right and also to make the point that this is the only figure I have used that I have been unable to pin down to a reliable source or cross-check with other sources.

BALLOONS See www.boc.com/education.
Nicola Jones, 'Under Pressure', *New Scientist*, 21–28 December 2002.

BANANAS 'Hardy Honduran banana fends off fungal infection', *New Scientist*, 17 April 1993.
Michelle Hibler and others, 'Breeding a Better Banana', IDRC Resources: Books: Reports: vol.22 no.1 (1994).
Fred Pearce, 'Going Bananas', *New Scientist*, 18 January 2003.

BATTERIES Figures from www.wrap.org.uk.

BEARDS Figures from *Marketing Week*, 19 June 2008.

BEER Stephen Mitchell, *Gilgamesh*, a new English version (Profile, 2005).

BIRTHDAYS Richard Wiseman, *Quirkology* (Macmillan, 2007).
Alison Motluk, 'Born Under a Bad Sign', *New Scientist*, 27 January 2007.

BREAD Harold McGee, *McGee on Food and Cooking* (Hodder and Stoughton, 2004).
Our Daily Bread, the Flour Advisory Bureau and the Federation of Bakers (2007).

CARBON James Lovelock, 'A Physical Basis for Life Detection Experiments', *Nature*, vol. 207, no. 4997, 7 August 1965, pp. 568–570.
James Lovelock and C. E. Giffin, 'Planetary Atmospheres: Compositional and Other Changes Associated with the Presence of Life', *Advances in Astronautical Sciences*, 25 (1969), pp. 179–193.
Though he may have felt that the search for life on Mars had already happened without going there, James Lovelock has always been a supporter of space exploration for the new perspectives and insights it gives us about life on Earth.

Both these articles are available on www.jameslovelock.org/.

CARS Car running costs from www.theaa.com. Insurance figures from Sainsbury's Car Insurance Annual Index. 'The cost of motoring has fallen in real terms ...': answer to parliamentary question 17 July 2007. Other figures from Transport Statistics Great Britain 2008, available at www.dft.gov.uk/pgr/statistics.

Reginald D. Smart and others, 'Road Rage: Are Our Patients Driving Angry?', *Psychiatric Times*, vol. XXII, issue 4, April 2005.

S. A. Ferguson and others, 'Relationship of Parent Driving Records to the Driving Records of their Children', *Accident Anaylsis and Prevention* (2001), vol. 33, issue 2, p. 229.

Orit Taubman-Ben-Ari, 'From Parents to Children – Similarities In Parents and Offspring Driving Styles', *Transportation Research* (2005), part F 8 (1): pp. 19–29.

Michael Keall and Stuart Newstead, 'Are SUVs Dangerous Vehicles?', *Accident Analysis and Prevention*, vol. 40, issue 3, May 2008.

Tom Wenzel and Marc Ross, 'The Effects of Vehicle Model and Driver Behaviour on Risk', *Accident Analysis and Prevention* (2005), vol. 37, issue 3, pp. 479–94.

CATS James Randerson, 'All in the mind', *New Scientist*, 26 October 2002.

Jaroslav Flegr, 'Effects of *Toxoplasma* on Human Behaviour', *Schizophrenia Bulletin* (2007) 33(3): 757–760.

CCTV M. McCahill and C. Norris, 'Estimating the Extent, Sophistication and Legality of CCTV in London', in *CCTV*, M. Gill (ed) (Perpetuity Press, 2003).

C. Norris and G. Armstrong, *The Maximum Surveillance Society: The Rise of Closed Circuit Television* (Berg Publishers, 1999).

CELLS There is a summary of Dr Jonas Frisen's work on determining the ages of cells in Nicholas Wade, 'Your Body is Younger Than You Think', *New York Times*, 2 August 2005.

Steven Rose, *The Making of Memory* (Bantam,1993).

CHEESE Figures from the British Cheese Board, The portal for all things British cheese-related. See www.cheeseboard.co.uk.

CHILDREN The three studies by the Centre for Longitudinal Studies – the 1958 National Child Development Study, the 1970 British Cohort Study and the Millennium Cohort Study – are all available at www.cls.ioe.ac.uk. 'Great^{100}' is great followed by 100 great-grandparents. 10^{100} is 10 followed by 100 zeros and is known as a googolplex. The most common recent ancestor is therefore your greatgoogolgrandparent.

CHIPS Figures from the Potato Council, www.potato.org.uk/.

CHOCOLATE The insect figures are from the US Food and Drug Administration Food Defect Actions Levels website, http://vm.cfsan.fda.gov/~dms/dalbook.html, but as British chocolate comes from the same tropical plantations as American chocolate I do not think it is unreasonable to use them. Sales figures stating the value of the British chocolate market as £2.23 billion from Mintel quoted in the *Daily Telegraph*, 3 July 2008. Other sources (www.foodmarketreports.com) give much higher figures, between £3.5 and £5.4 billion. Using these figures, a lifetime's consumption comes to £4,569 or £7,050.

CHRISTMAS Figures from British Retail Consortium quoted on www.politics.co.uk.

CIDER GAIN (Global Agriculture Information Network) Report UK7038, USDA Foreign Agricultural Services, (2007).
Wayne Hall, 'British Drinking: A Suitable Case for Treatment?', *British Medical Journal*, 10 September 2005, 331: 527–528.

CLOTHES The figure of £504 comes from the ONS annual Family Spending survey and, as with all these figures, has been cross-checked with what is actually spent. In this case, Datamonitor puts the total British clothing market at £31.2 billion, which, divided by the total population, gives a figure of £515 a year.
The problem of studying wildebeest comes from Daniel Dennett quoted by Steven Pinker, *How the Mind Works*, (Penguin, 1997) pp.117–118.

COLDS NHS Clinical Knowledge Summaries. See www.cks.library.nhs.uk/.

CONDOMS As they don't have sex, it might be slightly misleading directly to compare generations of bacteria and humans, but the speed at which they can make copies of themselves is why bacteria can evolve so quickly. Syphilis seems to take longer than other infections to develop a resistance to antibiotics, which is one of the reasons we have become complacent about it. The fact that resistant strains have begun to appear is a worrying development. The total number of condoms was worked out using the percentage of people using condoms (22 per cent) applied to the total number of times the average person has sex (5,037) = 1,108.
ONS, 'Contraception and Sexual Health, 2006/7', available at www.statistics.gov.uk/.
All new episodes of syphilis seen at GUM clinics 1998–2007. *United Kingdom and country-specific tables*, Health Protection Agency, July 2008, quoted by Avert, www.avert.org/stdstatisticuk.htm.

COWS The weight of living cows represented by the meat we eat was worked out using the equations in this faintly disturbing monograph: Duane M. Wulf, PhD, 'Did the Locker Plant Steal Some of My Meat?', South Dakota State University, May 1999.

CRISPS Figures from Key Note market research quoted in *The Sunday Times*, 6 March 2005.

DATA Stuart Kelly, *The Book of Lost Books* (Viking, 2005).

Steven M. Bachrach, *Scientific Journals of the Future* (American Academy of Arts & Sciences, 2001).

David P. Hamilton, 'Publishing by – and for? – the Numbers', *Science* 250:1331–2 (1990)

'The eyes have it', editorial, *New Scientist*, 6 July 1996.

DEATH The top-ten causes of death from the ONS expressed as percentages and then applied to the 1,964 people you will know from 'Friends' – see below. This leaves about 700 people unaccounted for who will die of less common causes that would fill too many pages to list.

DOCTORS The research on acupuncture was conducted by Dr Michael Haake of the University of Regensburg in the appropriately named Bad Abbach. His conclusions should raise worrying ethical issues for acupuncture but depressingly they are being edited and used to promote it. For example, 'Acupuncture Reduces Back Pain Better Than Drugs' on www.naturalnews.com/.

The length of the average visit to the doctor comes from the UK General Practice Workload survey 2006-7, Department of Health (2008). The figure of 11.7 minutes was derived by dividing the length of a surgery by the number of patients. The average time you spend face to face with the doctor is likely to be even shorter.

List of Registered Medical Practitioners – Statistics, General Medical Council (2008).

'UK Study Highlights Family Doctor's Earnings', the NHS Information Centre, October 2007.

DOGS Lyndmila Trut, 'Early Canid Domestication: The Farm Fox Experiment', *American Scientist* (1999), 87:160–169. Figures from Pet Food Manufacturers Association. Figures on the cost of owning a dog from Sainsbury's Finance.

DOMESTIC APPLIANCES The calculation of how long it would take the modern person to do the washing for the household of 1900 is a simplification as washing clothes for two is likely to take less time than twice the time for one. The fact remains that the average individual is spending the same amount of time.

Bittman and others, 'Appliances and Their Impact: The Ownership of Domestic Technology and Time Spent on Household Work', *British Journal of Sociology* vol. 55, no. 3, September 2004, pp. 401–423.

EARS Andy Coghlan, 'Dying for some peace and quiet', *New Scientist*, 25 August 2007.

S. Rosen and P. Olin, 'Hearing Loss and Coronary Heart Disease', *Archives of Otolaryngology* (1965), 82:236.

EGGS Figures from DEFRA.

The UK Egg Industry, The Farm Animal Welfare Council. See www.fawc.org.uk.

ELECTRICITY/ENERGY Digest of UK Energy Statistics 2008, BERR (Department for Business Enterprise & Regulatory Reform). The calculation for a lifetime of gas assumes 1 kg TNT releases 4.184×10^9 J. To simplify things, for the purposes of the energy calculation I have not included the conversion of fish into pellets as a step.

EXTINCTIONS Figures from the World Conservation Union, www.iucn.org/.

EYES Figures from Mintel, quoted on www.thisismoney.co.uk, 13 January 2005.

FILMS You can see some of Galton's composite photographs on www.galton.org/composite.htm. Film figures from the *Film Council Statistical Yearbook* 2008. I got the average length of a film from a project someone did to work out the average length of films in the IMDb top 500 films. This is available on www.infinitypoint0.com/60/imdb-film-length-project/.

FISH Mark Kurlansky makes a convincing case for there being a North American fishing industry before Columbus in *Cod: A Biography of the Fish that Changed the World* (Vintage,1999).

FOOD T. B. Mikkelsen and others, 'Pica in Pregnancy', *Acta obstetricia et gynecologica Scandinavica* (2006), 85 (10):1265–6.

FREEZERS Figures from British Frozen Food Federation.

FRIENDS R. I. M. Dunbar, Neocortex Size as a Constraint on Group Size in Primates, Journal of Human Evolution, (1992), vol. 20, pp. 469–493.
Robin Dunbar, *Grooming Gossip and the Evolution of Language* (Faber, 1996).
Peter D. Killworth and others, 'Comparing Two Methods for Estimating Network Size', *Human Organisation*, vol. 60, no. 1, spring 2001, pp. 28–39.
Judith Kleinfeld, 'Six Degrees of Separation: An Urban Myth?', *Psychology Today* (2001). Also, 'Could it be a big world?' on www.judithkleinfeld.com.

HAIR These figures from Boots are subject to the same biases as the inflated figures we are often given for our spending on shoes, weddings and children.

HANGOVERS Figures from Reed quoted on www.theregister.co.uk, 23 August 2004.

ICE CREAM It's no fun to eat when you are cold, but now that warm clothing is cheap and widely available you can enjoy ice cream in the parks of Moscow, Stockholm, Helsinki and the other northern capitals in ambient temperatures as low as -25 ºC.

INSURANCE Of this figure, £29,368 is car insurance. As there is less chance of crashing your house into other houses, home insurance (building and contents) is less – £13,214. Insurance figures from AA.com British Insurance Premium Index. The figure of 34 as the average age of first home ownership comes from the Future Foundation and GE Money Home Lending, quoted on www.ifaonline.co.uk/.

IRON I have been unable to find any other mention of this explanation for the King Arthur myth, which means that, in common with the other uncredited theories in this book, it may just be my own personal theory. I have taken pains to credit other people's work and ideas. If I have unknowingly reinvented your work and not credited you, I apologise.

Figures from UK Steel Key Statistics 2008, UK Steel.

JUNK MAIL Figures from DEFRA and Direct Mail Information Service 'Letter-box Fact File'.

KISSING Susan Hughes and others, 'Sex differences in romantic kissing among college students', *Evolutionary Psychology*, vol. 5 (2007), pp. 612–631.

E. Washburn Hopkins, 'The Sniff Kiss in Ancient India', *Journal of American Oriental Society*, vol. 28 (1907), pp. 120–134.

LAND FAO Global Outlook 2006.

LAUGHTER Selkirk's comment that laughter is a shared pleasure comes from a play about him I heard on the radio when I was a child and have been unable to trace or verify.

Robert R. Provine, 'Laughter', *American Scientist*, 84 (January–February, 1996), pp. 38–47.

Dr Michael Titze. He's real! Go and look at his website www.michael-titze.de.

LAWYERS The figure of £21 billion is taken from the Law Society's fact-sheet series available at www.lawsociety. org.uk. The earnings for England and Wales were £18.6 billion in 2007. I was unable to find figures for Scotland and Northern Ireland, so the additional £2.4 billion is an extrapolation based on population size.

LIES The results of Professor Richard Wiseman's National Lying Survey are on pp. 48–49 of his book *Quirkology* (Macmillan, 2007).

LOVE Bernice Kanner, *Are You Normal About Sex, Love and Relationships* (St Martin's Press, 2004).

Helen Fisher, *Why We Love: The Nature and Chemistry of Romantic Love* (Holt Rinehart and Winston, 2005).

Robert McKee, *Story* (Methuen, 1999).

MAKE-UP Figures from Datamonitor quoted in 'The rise of the metrosexual economy', http://money.uk.msn. com, June 2007, and also Euromonitor, quoted in 'A-OK in the UK', www.cosmetics business.com.

MARRIAGE Information from www.oneplusone.org.uk/ and Stonewall.

MEDICINES Figures from PAGB (Proprietry Association of Great Britain), www.pagb.co.uk/.

Geoff Watts, 'The Power of Nothing', *New Scientist*, 26 May 2001.

Daniel Moerman, *Meaning, Medicine and the 'Placebo Effect'* (Cambridge University Press, 2002).

MILK   Roxanne Khamsi, 'A Taste for Milk Shows Evolution in Action', *New Scientist*, 3 March 2007.

MONEY   Nimrod, *Memoirs of the Life of John Mytton* (Methuen and Co, 1903).
In 2006 the average gross household income was £642 with 2.4 people per household; that's £267.50 each a week or £1,100,282 in a lifetime. A survey by the Prudential Building Society suggested that we earn and spend a lot more than this – over £1.5 million.

NAILS   I have been unable to pin down a properly carried-out study of how fast nails grow. There are a lot of figures being bandied about that are no better than guesses. The commonest gives an average nail-growth rate of 3.8 cm a year which means that you would grow a terrifying 45 m of finger- and toenails in a lifetime.

NAPPIES   'Nappies and the Environment', Women's Environmental Network, March 2004.

NUCLEAR POWER   'Nuclear Industry Must Not Forget Past Lessons', *New Scientist*, 12 April 2008.

ORGASMS   Though Donald Symons originated this idea, most of the work of developing it has been done by Elizabeth Lloyd, the Arnold and Maxine Tanis Chair of History and Philosophy of Science and the Professor of Biology at Indiana University. Her book *The Case of the Female Orgasm* (a case that Dr Watson presumably tackled on his own, naked save for his moustache, without any assistance from Holmes) is published by Harvard University Press (2006).
Guillaume De Lorris and Jean De Meun, *The Romance of the Rose*, translated by Frances Horgan (Oxford World's Classics, 1999).

PEE   The theory that Kepler murdered Tycho comes from the book *Heavenly Intrigue* by Joshua Gilder and Anne-Lee Gilder (Anchor Books, 2004).
Many parts of your body are named after:
Marcello Malpighi (1628–94), Italian, also discovered capillaries.
Sir William Bowman (1816–92), awarded a Royal Medal for this discovery at the age of 25.
Friedrich Gustav Jakob Henle (1809–85), who also gave his name to the crypts of Henle, Henle's fissure, Henle's layer, Henle's ligament, Henle's membrane and Henle's sheath.
F. J. F. Barrington (1884–1956). According to his obituary in the *British Medical Journal* he really was known as 'Snorker'. As well as the zoo and yachting he liked shooting.
Bronislaw Onuf-Onufrowicz (1863–1929). Bronislaw was chief physician at Knickerbocker Hall, Amityville, Long Island, and one of the first doctors in the USA to offer psychoanalysis.
Pee figures from Terry and others, 'Intravenous Therapy: Clinical Principles and Practice', Intravenous Nurses' Society, (1995).

PERFUME Figures from Mintel quoted on www.fragrancefoundation.org.uk/.

Rehan M. Khan and others, 'Predicting Odor Pleasantness from Odorant Structure: Pleasantness as a Reflection of the Physical World', *Journal of Neuroscience*, 12 September 2007, 27(37): 10015–10023.

J. V. Kohl and others, 'Human Pheromones: Integrating Neuroendocrinology and Ethology', *Neuroendocrinology letters* (2001), 22:309–321.

M. Milinski and C. Wedekind, 'Evidence for MHC-Correlated Perfume Preferences in Humans', *Behavioural Ecology* (2001), 12:140–149.

George Preti and others, 'Male Axillary Extracts Contain Pheromones that Affect Pulsatile Secretion of Lutenizing Hormone and Mood in Women Recipients', *Biology of Reproduction* 68 (2003), pp. 2107–13.

PERIODS 'Seeing Red', Women's Environmental Network, April 2004.

PETS Brian Handwerk, 'Big Cats Kept as Pets Across U.S., Despite Risk', *National Geographic*, October 2003. Figures from Halifax Pet Insurance quoted in *Easier Finance*, 13 April 2007. See www.easier.com and Pet Food Manufacturers' Association.

PHONES Ofcom, 'The Communications Market, 2008', pp. 291–344. Available at Figures from www.ofcom.org.uk/research/cm/.

Fred Pearce, *Confessions of an Eco Sinner* (Eden Project Books, 2008).

PIGS Figures from DEFRA.

THE PILL 'NHS Contraceptive Services England 2006/7', Information Centre for Health and Social Care, www.ic.nhs.uk/.

Claus Wedekind and others, 'MHC genes, body odours, and odour preferences', *Nephrology Dialysis Transplantation* (2000), 15:1269–71.

PINEAPPLES Figures from FAO htp://faostat.fao.org.

Other pineapple facts from Fran Beauman, *The Pineapple* (Vintage, 2006).

POO The quantity of poo produced by the average dog comes from a disgustingly comprehensive study carried out by the New Forest Dog Owners' Group in response to a report in 2005 by England Marketing. See www.naturescene.co.uk.

Sewage sludge figures from DEFRA.

The figure of 9.5 l for the average toilet flush from Friends of the Earth.

The figure of 2,083 for the average flushes per person per year from www.waterwise.org.uk/.

POTATOES Harold McGee, *McGee on Food and Cooking* (Hodder & Stoughton, 2004).

Figures from the British Potato Council.

READING   David Vincent, *Literacy and Popular Culture: England 1750–1914* (Cambridge University Press, 1993).

David F. Mitch, *The Rise of Popular Literacy in Victorian England: The Influence of Private Choice and Public Policy* (University of Pennsylvania, 1992).

Figures from *The Skills for Life Survey*. Department for Education and Skills (2003).

RELIGION   Doreen M. Rosman, *The Evolution of the English Churches 1500–2000* (Cambridge University Press, 2003).

Guy Thorne (Arthur Cyril Ranger Gull), *When It Was Dark*, (Greening & Co. 1903).

Claud Cockburn, *Bestseller* (Penguin, 1975).

Peter Brierley (ed.), *Religious Trends No. 2 2000/2001* (HarperCollins 1999).

Horace Mann, *Religious Worship in England and Wales, Census of Great Britain 1851* (George Routledge & Co, 1854). The *Daily Telegraph* and *The Tablet* surveyed 1,015 people so it was a considerably smaller sample than the 2001 Census.

RUBBISH   Waste figures from DEFRA. Information on mineral resources from Armin Reller, University of Augsburg, and Tom Graedel, Yale University, quoted in David Cohen, 'Earth's Natural Wealth: An Audit', *New Scientist*, 23 May 2007.

SALT   Figures from the Food Standards Agency and www.salt.gov.uk.

SANDWICHES   Figures from the British Sandwich Association.

SEX   Prostitution figures from Diane Coyle, 'Legalising Prostitution Could Raise £250m Tax', the *Independent*, 9 April 2001; 'The Way We Love Now: Britain and Sex in 2008', *Observer*, 26 October 2008.

SHOES   Figures from Verdict quoted in 'Why the Old Shoe Retailers are on Their Uppers', the *Daily Telegraph*, 29 January 2008.

Other figures from www.recyclingconsortium.org.

SLEEP   Much of the material in this entry comes from J. M. Siegel, 'Clues to the functions of mammalian sleep', *Nature*, vol. 437, no. 7063, 27 October 2005. Also R. P. Vertes and J. M. Siegel, 'Time for the Sleep Community to Take a Critical Look at the Purported Role of Sleep in Memory Processing', *Sleep*, vol. 28, no.10 (2005) and 'Rebuttal', *Sleep*, vol. 28, no.10 (2005). However, I would never have known about them if it weren't for the excellent article by Emma Young. 'Sleep Tight', *New Scientist*, 15 March 2008.

SMOKING Sir Richard Doll, 'Mortality in Relation to Smoking: Fifty years' Observations on Male British Doctors', *British Medical Journal*, 328 (7455), pp.1519 –28.

'Prevalence of Cigarette Smoking by Sex and Age, 2005, Great Britain,' General Household Survey, www.ons.gov.uk/ghs.

The average figure used in this book (79.1) is your life expectancy at birth. The longer you live, the longer you are likely to live. Though you are less likely to reach the age of 60 if you smoke, if you do, you can expect to live another 19.1 years. A non-smoker can expect 24.

SNEEZING Bjarne Hansen and Niels Mygind. 'How Often Do Normal Persons Sneeze and Blow the Nose?', *Rhinology*, vol. 40 no. 1 (2002), 1 pp. 10–12.

STOMACH ACID Figures from the NHS and PAGB (Proprietary Association of Great Britain).

Nina Lakhani, 'Pharmageddon: The Prescription Pill Epidemic', the *Independent*, 26 August 2007.

Forgacs and Loganayagam, 'Overprescribing Proton Pump Inhibitors', *British Medical Journal* (2008) 336:2–3.

SUCKLING Figures from Taylor Nelson Sofres quoted in the *Guardian*, 12 October 2008 and also from the British Nutrition Foundation.

TALKING Figures from the *New Scientist*, 22–29 December 2007, p. 60.

TEA Figures from www.ethicalteapartnership.org and www.cafedirect.co.uk quoted in 'How Ethical is my Daily Cuppa?', the *Observer*, 3 February 2008.

Euromonitor quoted in Elliot Wilson, 'Drink of the Day Once Again', the *Observer*, 17 August 2008.

TEARS R. R. Cornelius (ed.) *Adult Crying: A Biopsychosocial Approach* (Routledge, 2001), p. 58.

TEETH Tooth-fairy statistics from the Children's Mutual quoted in the *Daily Telegraph*, 19 April 2008.

TELEVISION Neil Postman, *Amusing Ourselves to Death* (William Heinemann,1986). Though it was written a quarter of a century ago, this book is still relevant today and since it was published Postman's conclusions have been borne out by numerous pieces of research (thousands actually) that will never get on the television. These are summarised in Dr Aric Sigman, *Remotely Controlled* (Vermilion, 2005).

TIME The experiment by Craik and Hay is described by Jay Ingram, *The Velocity of Honey* (Thunder's Mouth Press, 2005).

TIME USE Figures from ONS Time Use survey 2005. I have grouped the categories 'Resting' and 'Time Spend at Home' and called them 'Lounging About the House'. These figures do not add up to an average lifetime (79.1).

They reflect what the average person over the age of 16 does through the day. Including under-16s would undoubtedly push the lounging about the house and television figures up and close this gap.

TINNED FOOD Figures from www.wrap.org.uk/. Also Business Wire Research and Markets, www.researchandmarkets.co/research/2fcec6/canned_foods_marke.

VALENTINE'S DAY Figures from British Retail Consortium, www.brc.org.uk/.

VEGETABLES Okitas and D. L. Schwartz, 'Young Children's Understanding of Animacy and Entertainment Robots', *International Journal of Humanoid Robotics*, 3, pp. 393–412.

VITAMINS 'FSIS 12/06: Survey of vitamin and mineral supplements in the UK', Food Standards Agency (2006), www.food.gov.uk.
Also the Cochrane Collaboration quoted in 'Do vitamin supplements do more harm than good?', Lois Rogers, *The Sunday Times*, 27 April 2008.

VOTING John T. Jost and Jim Sidanius (eds), *Political Psychology: Key Readings* (Psychology Press, 2004).
John R. Alford and others, 'Are Political Orientations Genetically Transmitted', *American Political Science Review* (2005), 99:2:153–167.
John T. Jost. 'The End of the End of Ideology', *American Psychologist*, vol. 61, no. 7 (2006) pp. 651–670.
Newspaper figures from the National Readership Survey available on www.nrs.co.uk/.

WATER Water footprint figures from WWF and www.waterfootprint.org/.
Other figures from Ofwat, www.ofwat.gov.uk.

WORDS Oxford English Dictionary, www.askoxfoprd.com/.

WORK Working hours from European Trade Union Confederation, www.etuc.org/a/551.
Mercer's European Employment Conditions Report, www.mercerhr.com/.
Retirement figures from Lord Turner's Pensions Commission, www.pensionscommission.org.uk.
Age of starting work from Paul Ryan, 'The School-to-Work Transition: Problems and Indicators', King's College, University of Cambridge, March 2001, http://www.econ.cam.ac.uk/faculty/ryan/marbwork.pdf
All other figures from ONS, Labour Force Survey 2008 and Travel Trends in 2006.

THANKS

My biggest debt of gratitude is to Nick Watts. None of this would have happened without him. I hope I have done justice to the book we were once going to write together.

My wonderfully supportive agent Sheila Ableman.

Rosemary Davidson for saying yes to this project and doing much to improve it along the way.

Suzanne Dean, Anna Crone, Stephen Parker, Matt Broughton, Greg Heinimann, Michael Salu and Kris Potter of the Random House design team, and Rowena Skelton-Wallace, Katherine Murphy and Tom Avery in the editorial department.

Caroline Johnson, my copy-editor, and Jane Howard, the proof reader, and

Paddy Farrington

Cathie Lloyd

Brian Farrington

Olivia Farrington

Who helped with the manuscript.

Margaret and Molly and Ben.

Who helped with everything else.